# The Lasting of the Mohicans

# The Lasting of the Mohicans

## History of an American Myth

MARTIN BARKER AND ROGER SABIN

UNIVERSITY PRESS OF MISSISSIPPI
*Jackson*

Comic book illustrations are reproduced by kind permission of the following:
*Classics Illustrated* © and ™ Classics International Entertainments, Inc., 1942, 1959, 1995
*Marvel Classics* © Marvel Entertainment Group, Inc., 1976, 1995
*Dark Horse Classics* © Dark Horse Comics, Inc., 1992
*Two-Fisted Tales* © and ™ MAD Publishing, Inc., Time-Warner, 1955, 1995

Film stills and posters are reproduced courtesy of the BFI Stills and Poster Library.

99  98  97  96    4  3  2  1

The paper in this book meets the guidelines for permanence and durability of the Committee on Production Guidelines for Book Longevity of the Council on Library Resources.

Library in Congress Cataloging-in-Publication Data

Barker, Martin.
    The lasting of the Mohicans : history of an American myth / Martin Barker and Roger Sabin.
        p.    cm. – (Studies in popular culture)
    Includes bibliographical references and index.
        ISBN 0-87805-858-3 (alk. paper). — ISBN 0-87805-859-1 (pbk. : alk. paper)
            1. Cooper, James Fenimore, 1789-1851. Last of the Mohicans.
    2. United States—History—French and Indian War, 1755–1763—Literature and the war.   3. Cooper, James Fenimore, 1789–1851—Appreciation—United States.   4. Cooper, James Fenimore, 1789–1851—Film and video adaptations.   5. Historical fiction, American—History and criticism.   6. Literature and society—United States—History.   7. Popular culture—United States—History.   8. Mohegan Indians in literature.   9. Socail values in literature.   10. Myth in literature.   11. Canon (Literature)   I. Sabin, Roger, 1961–   .
    II. Title.   III. Series: Studies in popular culture (Jackson, Miss.)
    PS1408.B37  1996
    813'.2—dc20                                                        95-29991
                                                                            CIP

British Library Cataloging-in-Publication data available

# CONTENTS

# PREFACE

It's a betting certainty that most people who pick up this book will know of, or are even fans of, Michael Mann's splendid 1992 movie *The Last of the Mohicans*. It was one of the big hits of that year, and was seen by millions of people all over the world—an unexpected success, proving that good old-fashioned adventure with a bit extra could still do well at the box office.

But for some readers the *Mohicans* story will have different associations. For some, it will conjure memories of a TV series, perhaps; or an earlier film version; or maybe one of those comic books that your parents managed not to disapprove of. In fact, *Mohicans* seems to have passed into the wider realms of culture, as this newspaper cutting nicely captured.

**Tomorrow 2**

**ARTS**

Once upon a time, The Last of the Mohicans was actually a novel, though it's been adapted so many times — remember the Classics Illustrated version in the 1950s? — it's moved entirely into the visual domain. On the movie page, Derek Malcolm and guest critic Geoff Dyer keep an eye out for Hawkeye, aka Daniel Day-Lewis, in the latest version.

For a very few, it may still connote the original novel—or an abridged, adapted, or rewritten retelling thereof.

The present book is about retellings. It has an accidental origin. One of us was teaching a course on the mass media, using comic books as its focus. A long search for materials that could illustrate the ways different renderings of a story could affect its meaning started revealing a number of versions of *Mohicans*. Then Michael Mann's film came out, and that made reference to an earlier, 1936 film version. A quick browse through film histories confirmed this and yet more film versions. Talking together, we realized we were sitting on a gold mine of fascinating materials, though we didn't yet know what exactly might be learned from studying them. What it has become is an ambitious project to try to discover why a story survives, and what it embodies of social ideas and ideals that subsequent generations are able to make use of.

Among the most difficult aspects of researching this book has been obtaining and gaining access to the array of versions of *Mohicans*, in book, film, TV, comic book, audio, and even play form. We owe a debt of thanks to many people who have helped us in doing so. Some, we suspect, did not know what service they were doing us. There are networks of collectors and distributors without whom research like this is well-nigh impossible. Puzzled salespeople across the Atlantic often couldn't understand the excitement of two Englishmen who had just learned that there were two—yes, two—cartoon versions of Cooper's book still in stock, or that there was a videotape available of a Metropolitan Pittsburgh Public Broadcasting TV version of *Mohicans* available. A book dealer would be bemused by the enthusiastic response to his call saying that a curious abridged version of Cooper's book had just come in, slimming three hundred to thirteen pages. Thanks have to go to people such as the welcoming man in the mom-and-pop video store in Los Angeles who let us buy his rental copy of the 1936 film.

Others did know what we were doing, and helped us enormously. Thanks to Rusty Witek for the inspiration supplied by his book, and for taking such trouble to help us obtain a copy of the 1909 film version—and no thanks to the Library of Congress, who made it as hard as they possibly could. Thanks to the television producer who trusted us with the only surviving copy of the last episode of a BBC series. No thanks to the BBC, who denied for over a year that they even had a copy of this episode and, when they finally acknowledged they held a copy of their entire series, denied us access. By contrast, thanks to Sky TV, who went out of their way to supply us with the pilot episode of their series which we had managed to miss.

It is incumbent on us to name a good many individuals and thank them for particular help. We do so willingly. In alphabetical order, we have appreciated the willing responses of all the following people who have gone beyond the calls of job or necessity to help us: Dick Allen and Mike Crawford, for patiently making PALs out of NTSCs, and for repeated help with the book's illustrations; Kevin Brownlow, for helping generously from your store of knowledge of early film; Tessa Chester, for allowing us to use the archive of the Bethnal Green Museum of Childhood; Gordon Harding, for generously loaning us some original materials; Herbert Kliebard, for responding so helpfully to our blind enquiries; Richard Maltby, for some photocopies that sent us running after all manner of lost versions; Dan Malan, for taking time out to provide some crucial information about the comic book versions; David Maloney, for allowing us an interview, and for letting us see his copy of the last episode of his BBC TV version; Wick Rowland, for that beautiful copy of Scribner's edition; and Alexander Saxton, for a friendly and interested response to our complicated enquiry. If we have missed anybody, our honest apologies.

Special thanks are due to partners, children, colleagues, and friends who have allowed us to try out endless ideas on them, and who have (we suspect) from time to time kept private their questions about our sanity as we insisted on the world-historical interest of yet another "lost version."

This book has been a sheer pleasure to research and write, not least because of the boundless joy we have taken in the materials we have come to study. So, how do we each feel about the story, the book, and the many retellings of it we have studied? We have personal favorites. Martin could watch the Michael Mann version many times over and still weep at the death of Uncas. He also still thrills to some parts of the Schick Sunn sentimental version. Roger also greatly admires the Michael Mann version, but in addition loves the 1920 version. But what has happened is that fascination has taken us both past liking and disliking; we simply can't avoid a rich sense of excitement at every new version that comes our way.

To our readers: a serious request. There are some versions and editions of *The Last of the Mohicans* that, despite our earnest efforts, have eluded us. We still would like to see all the following: the three 1911 versions of the film;[1] the 1924 George Seitz serial; all but the last episode of the 1971 BBC TV version; the King Classics comic book version from 1977; at least two rumored Ron Embleton versions, one in a comic annual, the other in *Comic Cuts*; a whole series of American abridgements (such ephemera—which is really what they become—simply do not cross the Atlantic). And we would like to know about all the other minor ways in which this story, its characters, or just its title have fed into American and British—and other national—popular cultures. We know of a German film version, but we suspect there are other foreign language film adaptations. And no doubt there are other national-specific uses and adaptations about which we really should have known. If there is anything you know or have or have come across that you think might interest us, write to us c/o Martin Barker, University of the West of England, Bristol BS16 2JP, England. Or if you just have specific memories of *The Last of the Mohicans* and how it entered your life. . . .

*Note*: In writing this book, we have been very aware of the difficulty of "naming" the original peoples of the North American continent. There is no wholly satisfactory solution to this problem, and therefore we decided to use two expressions, as Daniel Francis does in his excellent book *The Imaginary Indian*.[2] Wherever we are talking of actual people, we have tried to use the expression *native Americans*, to distinguish from all those occasions when we are discussing images or representations of them. In the latter case, we have chosen to use the term *Indian*.

We are also very alive to the fact that we are two white Britons writing about images of a people who still exist. They have no voice in our book. Yet our whole argument is that the image of "Indians" has had powerful consequences—one of which has been to silence the real people, the native Americans. Writing from Britain, it would be simply egregious and insulting to include a token "voice of the Mohican people." Instead, therefore, we offer this book as our acknowledgement from afar of the long and continuing struggle of native American peoples for recognition and rights.

# The Lasting of the Mohicans

CHAPTER I    **The Mohican Myth and the American Dream**

Well, reader. Mohicans. The last of. Exactly what images or ideas or memories are brought to mind when you hear these words? A book read, or a comic . . . a film or TV program seen . . . a song heard . . . a radio play . . . a game played as a child . . . where are you when you encounter it? With whom? Ask a friend, or two. If we were having a tutorial at the colleges where we work, we might suggest everyone wrote down their memories. A "Mohican"—what does that make you think of? Have you ever seen a painting, or an illustration of one? Is it something to do with a haircut, only? Where do Mohicans come from? When? Why is it the "last" of the Mohicans—what happened to them? (Why) is it a tragedy?

This project began with our discovering a mine of materials, all owing their existence to James Fenimore Cooper's *The Last of the Mohicans* (henceforth usually *Mohicans*). But though we started there, that doesn't tell what became the purpose of it all. It is worth posing at the beginning what, in the end, became our fundamental

# The Many Meanings of "Mohican"

It is not clear exactly when "Mohican" came to refer to a particular kind of hairstyle. This photograph shows American airmen in World War II wearing what was known as either a "Mohican" or a "Mohawk" cut.

Always **Open** for
*Finest quality pushchairs and nursery furniture*

**BÉBÉCAR**

This shop-door notice related to an advertisement with a garishly colored baby saying: "I used to make an exhibition of myself to get noticed."

**Scene Eleven:** Cubby titivating his hair

*Cubby:* Saturday night. Disco, yer know. Centre o' Leeds. Yer sprice up her plumage. Purron best bleach denims. An' off out. Bird 'untin'. Well, yer don't call it that no more 'cos it's sexist. But yer can't argue wi' nature, can yer? so yer get to club, right? Bloke comes up. Dickie bow an' jacket job.

*Scuffer:* All right, Geronimo, where you off to?

*Cubby:* Goin' in.

*Scuffer:* Sorry, pal. No Red Indians. Cowboy night tonight.

*Cubby:* Don't mess me abaht. Just let us in, eh?

*Scuffer:* I said. This is a civilised place. Never let Mohicans in. It's a rule.

*Cubby:* Since when?

*Scuffer:* Since they were wiped out abaht eighteen 'undred an' summat. What's it feel like to be part of an extinct tribe?

From **Gary Lyons, "Mohicans", in Rony Robinson, *They Said We Were Too Young*, London: Hodder & Stoughton 1989, 87-156.**

question: Just what is it about this story—this not-quite-frontier story of Nathaniel Bumppo, alias Hawkeye,[1] and his two friends Chingachgook and Uncas—that has given it a staying power and a pull that have made people return to it again and again? It isn't alone in this, of course. There are other classic stories that have been adapted and reused even more than *Mohicans*. But there is simply no denying that to millions of people the words "last of the Mohicans" spark an association, half-summon a memory, and set off a chain of ideas, leading . . . where?

That, for us, raised questions about "myths." *Mohicans* is a myth, in the sense that it presents symbolically rich characters in a landscape, whose adventures and eventual tragic conclusion are also rich in symbols. Myths, many people have argued, are an essential ingredient of large groups. It is physically impossible for us to know everyone else in our society, so there have to be intermediaries, shared conceptions of who we are, our common features, of what makes us a people or culture. Myths, it is said, provide that common core. And they can last. Myths also typically take story form, so that we can *feel* those common qualities; they can't be only intellectually appreciated. The story form helps them last.

Suppose *Mohicans* is a myth in this sense: what might that tell us? It would mean that we should not view Hawkeye, the central character, as an individual, but as a type, and a type who is a "founder." What exactly he is founding has to be investigated. But his ability to found anything is dependent on our recognition of him, our acceptance of him as a model—not perhaps one on which to base our actions, more one for getting a picture of our world, of what is right and wrong in it, what we can hope for, what we should fear. A myth in this sense helps us to understand and evaluate people and events around us. So, the various central elements in the story— Hawkeye's frontier spirit, his love of the wilderness, his relations with Indians, with women, with the English—all become resources for picturing our own lives. But not directly. For example, the "English" in the story won't literally represent English people. Rather it will be an *idea* of the English and what they represent: certain social attitudes, even perhaps (presaging our own later argument) a social group within America.

Myths are commonplace. We should not forget this. For British people, stories of King Arthur and the Knights of the Round Table, or of Robin Hood and his Band of Merry Men;[2] for Americans, tales of

Superman, of Captain Ahab, of Rip van Winkle: they are ordinary, fun, they can be played with, they can be laughed at. It's a rare person who invests a lot of emotion or commitment in such stories. Yet almost because they are so ordinary, they can penetrate a long way into ordinary day-to-day thinking. In Britain, Robin Hood is a good example. It is not unusual to speak nonchalantly of someone as a "Robin Hood"—enacting rescues, having a spirit of adventure. When we do so, for many people there stirs a memory of a television or film version they will have seen. For Americans, Superman is a good example. When the brother of an American president says, in casual conversation, that Superman would have been a useful person to have around at the time of the Cuban crisis, we don't look on him as a lunatic who believes that there *really* is a hyper-powerful figure in tights waiting to zap those Castroites. More likely, we hear him sharing a game, a mild joke, a repertoire of common figures with his audience. To mention a figure like Superman in the right context is to establish a link with your audience. It is a reference to a shared stock of imagination. And like all imaginary figures, they need fleshing out, making real, if they are to work as the stuff of ideas.

We should not forget, also, that culture is becoming increasingly international. Hollywood as the prime disseminator of tales to the world talks to us all, British and Norwegian, Brazilian and Nigerian; and the tales it tells are distinctively American. Even when it tells other cultures' tales, it tells them with an American accent. Yes, there is *Robin Hood: Prince of Thieves*, but Kevin Costner's English accent seems to slip quite a lot. (Mind you, we shouldn't complain, since Daniel Day-Lewis, an Irish actor, has played Hawkeye.) But the manner of telling is also distinctively a Hollywood one.[3] Give them a good story, and they will work their distinctive magic on it.

This is perhaps what Cooper offers: an outline of a character, a story sketch. One of the striking things about Cooper's legacy is the uneven interest and attention afforded to his various books. If one goes to the literary critics, there are of course studies of all Cooper's writings; but more attention has been devoted to others among the quintet of the Leatherstocking Tales—*The Prairie* and *The Deerslayer* in particular—than to *Mohicans*. Yet without question *Mohicans* has been most adapted and transformed for general social consumption. Baldly, while we know of thirteen English language film versions based on *Mohicans*, for the rest of the Leatherstocking

Tales we can find for *The Deerslayer* and *The Prairie* only two versions each, for *The Pathfinder* three versions, and for *The Pioneers* only one.[4] Perhaps *Mohicans* has specially what it takes to be a "myth."

This is partly what this study is about. It is about *Mohicans* as a survivor. Here is a tale, or at least an idea for a tale, a title, that keeps on coming back. Whatever changes people might make to it, they want to claim the "badge" of that title, and its associations. There are other ways of studying such a book, of course. It is interesting to compare our approach with, say, Brian Street's. In his study of *The Savage in Literature*, Cooper is a bit-part player alongside many other nineteenth- and early twentieth-century writers, such as A. E. W. Mason (*The Broken Reed*) and L. P. Greene (*Tabu Dick*).[5] A. E. W. and L. P. *who*? you may ask.[6] Exactly. Our point is precisely that however important *in their time* these writers may have been, their importance mostly stopped there. It is, of course, important to delve back into those lost histories. But perhaps it is more important to examine those tales that continue to resonate. And we must not assume that it is some essentially literary quality that helps the few survive when the many fade away.

A good analogy would be with the work of Jack Zipes, whose study of the traditions of telling of the tale of Red Riding Hood is so insightful.[7] Zipes shows us both the common core of the story over many generations and also the ways in which different users have reworked it for different purposes. We do not fully accept Zipes's argument, as one of us has made clear elsewhere,[8] but one point of agreement is crucial. Zipes insists that it makes sense to ask, of each instance and each version of a story like this: who owns this? On behalf of what interests is it being reworked now? Where we disagree is over Zipes's claim that the most important change was the "technological" one of writing the stories down. We argue that people can still bend such myths to a wide range of purposes, despite the loss of oral traditions. Indeed, some of the uses of *Mohicans* we have found—the punk recordings, for example[9]—are only possible because technologies of print, and film, and sound recording can be (and from time to time *are*) used by anyone.

Not that the technologies don't matter. It does matter that in this century the most important reinterpretations of *Mohicans* have been in the movies. The American film industry has become the mightiest mythmaking machine on the planet. And from the earliest days it has sought out novels that can become epics. Novels, because these have been the readiest source of narratives: it has been estimated that over 30 percent of films are derived from novels (and of course because of Hollywood's magnetic power, ever-increasing numbers of novels have been written with an eye to possible film adaptation).[10] Epics, because of the particular character of the American film industry, which has led it overall to favor what it sees as the acceptable and the safe. As one writer puts it: "The chief feature of the historical epic film is not imitation but *reinterpretation*."[11] This makes it especially appropriate to turn to novels with a "classic" feel, carrying the smell of authority and authenticity already with them.

*Mohicans* is nothing special in this respect. Although we have garnered a large number of film versions, other novels have been adapted even more often. According to the most complete source we could find, the books most often adapted for the screen have been *Our Lady of the Camellias* (Alexandre Dumas—31 versions), *Dr. Jekyll and Mr. Hyde* (R. L. Stevenson—27), *Robinson Crusoe* (R. L. Stevenson—24), *The Count of Monte Cristo* (Alexandre Dumas—22) and *Les Misérables* (Victor Hugo—22), along with a series of Shakespeare plays.[12] All these and many others deserve study in their own right. We are certainly not claiming that *Mohicans* heads any list in importance.

Except perhaps in this. Whatever else *Mohicans* may be, it is a myth of America (or we should say "America"). One of the peculiar aspects of writing this book has been writing it from Britain. Doing so has had advantages and disadvantages. The disadvantages were sometimes plainly practical. We couldn't go to the Museum of Modern Art to view their (perhaps correct) copy of the 1909 film. We had to face the problems of incompatible television formats. We weren't able to get many American abridged book versions. And so on. But distance does have its advantages. As a number of writers have shown, "America" offers a complex set of images: images of modernity and decay, of bright new technological breakthroughs, but also of crime and social breakdown.[13] We cannot claim to be immune to those images. At the same time, being abroad just does make those images more negotiable. We are not taking the risks of personal involvement or censure that American academics, doing the same, might run. But there may be other, deeper reasons why it is easier for two "Brits" to write this book, reasons which can be fully apparent only after this book has run its course.

*Mohicans*, we will argue, contributes its dime to images of America, to their history and their evolution. Not without argument—how could there not be? Its importance, we will suggest, lies exactly in the apparent freedom of interpretation it licenses. It seems to be a hollow vessel; everyone knows the title phrase, but it doesn't seem to tie you down. But whenever a conscious effort at reinterpretation is made, something seeps from the vessel into the contents, to color and flavor them.[14] To identify the results is the task of the rest of this book.

First we need to explore the general context into which the various versions of *Mohicans* were born. Here, there are two closely linked themes: the "American Dream" and the near destruction of the native American population. Each of these themes has a direct, symbiotic relationship with the *Mohicans* story. For while *Mohicans* was part of the construction of the American myth, it also played a part in molding symbolic representations of native Americans and preparing the way for their maltreatment.

What exactly is the American Dream? It is one of those amorphous concepts that is extremely difficult to pin down. It is certainly pervasive in American culture: invoked by successive presidents as something worth rallying around and by critics of the country as a concept to be scorned. It is, in short, something that Americans have that the rest of us don't. What other nation in the world prides itself on a dream and gives its name to one? But if everybody has heard the term, few seem willing to analyze it. It is almost as if to do so would destroy its mystique—and confront its contradictions.

For the "Dream" is in fact many dreams, woven together like an intricate fabric—an immensely complicated set of social and moral ideals that often conflict.[15] From the start, the Dream was designed with immigrants in mind and had little to say about the original inhabitants of the country, the native Americans. Thus it has to be seen against a background of the successive waves of European immigration to America. (Indeed, during the period 1820–1900, when the Dream was being used most effectively to justify westward expansion, the population of the country rocketed from 9.6 to 76 million.) With this in mind we can begin to simplify the Dream's abstract appeal, and to pick apart its two main threads: the notions of perfect democracy and of "new beginnings."

The tenets of American democracy were first framed in the Declaration of Independence (1776), which asserted that "all men are created equal, that they are endowed by their Creator with certain unalienable rights, that among these are Life, Liberty and the Pursuit of Happiness." This document was in the British philosophical tradition, but drew particularly on the work of radical thinkers such as Thomas Paine. It embodied a fragile balance between the freedom of what poet Walt Whitman called the "simple separate person" and welfare "en masse."

The strong element of individual rights stemmed from the tradition of religious dissension associated with the first-generation Puritan settlers. These rights were later mythologized as a vision took shape of the American "frontier"—a place that fostered self-determination, self-reliance, and a penchant for discovery. Later still, individualism came to denote a broad "free market" philosophy, encompassing freedom of choice, the survival of the fittest, and above all the freedom of the individual to make money. It became, in other words, a cornerstone of modern American capitalism.

Considerations of collective welfare were perhaps better expressed in the U.S. Constitution (drafted in 1787), which joins the Declaration of Independence as the other key document in the democratic strand to the Dream. Again, its roots were in early Puritanism, this time the ideal of a Christian commonwealth. It embodied a recognition that the new America was a coalition of minorities, any of which may become tyrannical after gaining power. Thus, power was split between legislative, executive, and judicial branches in the belief that no single faction should be able to gain control of all three branches at once. The Constitution established, in other words, a system of checks and balances, and became an essential counter to the individualistic tradition.

Beyond democracy, the Dream also held up the promise of a "new beginning," a fresh start in the New World.[16] Here, again, the Puritan ethic played a formulative role. The Pilgrims had been able to worship as they chose in their newly adopted home, and for a time the country became synonymous with spiritual regeneration—a new paradise. Later, the "fresh start" acquired more secular aspects, denoting social, political, economic, psychological, even sexual rebirth. In this way, *America* became another word for *opportunity*, a place where history could begin again, promising a Year Zero to anybody who chose to take up the challenge.

This challenge could often imply dealing with the frontier, once again a crucial factor in the mix. In his famous essay "The Significance of the Frontier in American History" (1893), Frederick Jackson Turner wrote: "American social development has been continually beginning over again on the frontier. This perennial rebirth, this fluidity of American life, this expansion westwards with its new opportunities, its continuing touch with the simplicity of primitive society, furnish the forces dominating American character." Observing that America had had a succession of westward-moving frontiers from the start, Turner argued that each one symbolized "an escape from the bondage of the past; and freshness, and confidence, and scorn of older society."[17]

Put together, these notions of democracy and a new beginning constituted a heady brew. The Dream held out enormous hope for the future. Perhaps the mistakes of the Old World could be rectified in the New; perhaps democracy was perfectible; and perhaps it was possible to start again and create a heaven on earth. No wonder potential immigrants found the idea so attractive.

But however progressive and holistic the American Dream might have appeared, it had one major blind spot: the native American. For if it meant a new beginning for anybody, it was for the white immigrant. The fact that others already inhabited the land was not taken into account, and by the Dream's very nature native Americans were marginalized, made "the other." Certainly the democratic strand argued that all men were created equal: but how long could this survive the white greed for territory? It was a short step for the Dream to become a justification for white expansion, a cover for what was in reality a ruthless and greedy policy of expropriation of the native American and conquest of the subcontinent.

Initially, European settlers held fairly ambivalent opinions about the natives they encountered. After all, they relied upon them for trade, and were not numerous enough to challenge them by force. They admired aspects of their character and society, and believed them to be primitive but capable of becoming civilized. Thus, in time, the image of the "noble savage" took hold, with its emphasis on difference and "unique gifts."[18]

By the early 1800s, things were changing. When expansion and colonization began in earnest, relationships between the two groups deteriorated. Now, native Americans became an obstacle to the Dream—in the way of expansion, of progress, of white Americans fulfilling their true potential. They would have to go, either by being destroyed or through assimilation. Moreover, the Dream implied that this was God's will: it was predestined that the natives would vanish before the onset of civilization, ordained as the natural progression of evolution.

With this as a background, a new image gradually overtook the "noble savage." Native Americans now became evil, sadistic, bloodthirsty "Redskins," warriors in war paint and feathers, ready to ravish white women and massacre white folk trying to carve homes for themselves on the frontier. Not only were native Americans uncontrollably violent, but also stupid—racially inferior to whites. This was the image that appeared increasingly in art and literature in the nineteenth century, having its ultimate expression in the rise of the Western as a genre, and the concurrent boom in "dime novels," cheaply produced pulp books intended for a working-class readership. (For more on the dime novel, see our final chapter.)

The historical consequences of this new phase in white-native American relations were drastic and resulted in a policy of native American relocation and removal, and the genocide of the so-called Indian wars. To summarize: in the early years, the government could not crush the tribes militarily, so it tried to make friends with them and to encourage westward expansion by buying lands through treaties. The Northwest Ordinance of 1789 declared that "the utmost good faith shall always be observed towards the Indians: their lands and property shall never be taken from them without their consent." These were noble words, but the fact was that the treaties were broken repeatedly. Native Americans were "removed" from occupied land and forced to migrate further and further west. The first stage was a move across the Mississippi; this was followed by expansion into the Great Plains.

In 1850 the government decided that each tribe should be confined to a reservation, "a country with well defined boundaries, within which all should be compelled to remain." Even this was not enough, however, and native Americans continued to have lands usurped by settlers. The reservations became smaller and smaller, and situated on less and less fertile land. By 1906, 60 percent of reservation lands were in white hands.

But there was resistance. A series of wars with different tribes peppered the years from the founding of the republic until 1890. The tribes were not united and sometimes fought among themselves, and this weakened their effectiveness against the government militia. One by one they were defeated, commonly with great savagery. The tribes of the Northwest were destroyed at the Battle of the Thames (1813); the Sacs and Foxes of Illinois were virtually exterminated in the Black Hawk War (1832–35); a similar fate befell the Seminoles in Florida in the Seminole War (1835–42). But it was in the west in the 1860s-80s that the government came up against its stiffest opposition. The Plains tribes, such as the Sioux, Cheyenne, Apache, and Comanche, frequently took the war to the whites but were finally defeated by a combination of superior white technology (weaponry, the railway, the telegraph) and the near extermination of the buffalo, on which they depended for food, clothing, and shelter. This phase of the war was particularly notable for its atrocities. In one incident, the Sioux killed five hundred settlers in 1862 and were subsequently hunted down: three hundred Sioux were publicly hanged. In 1864 the Sand Creek massacre took place when Cheyenne who had surrendered were shot by the Colorado militia.

The Apaches were the final tribe to hold out. It took five hundred troops fifteen years to defeat them. But with the capture in 1886 of their chief Geronimo, native American resistance effectively ended. There was one postscript in 1890, when an outbreak of religious fervor on the Sioux reservation in South Dakota caused the government to assume that an uprising was taking place. The army was sent in to the center of the disturbance, at Wounded Knee, and fired indiscriminately into the crowd, killing three hundred.

Having been conquered, the native Americans were pushed to the margins of society and largely ignored. Life on the reservations was harsh, and a lasting pattern emerged. Native Americans experienced the lowest levels of income and the highest levels of unemployment, suicide, alcoholism, and infant mortality of any minority group in the United States. Two new stereotypes emerged. On the one hand, native Americans were infantilized, re-imagined as children incapable of taking on adult responsibilities—especially governing themselves. On the other, the government tried to encourage reservation farming schemes, and the image of the warrior-turned-farmer was fostered; it did not last long.

Yet still the old image of the vicious redskin clung on, as the Western genre went from strength to strength. The dime novels were joined between the 1870s and 1900 by the phenomenon of the Wild West Show. These were touring circus extravaganzas in which "real" cowboys and Indians did battle with each other, to the delight of family audiences all over America. The most famous was undoubtedly Buffalo Bill Cody's Show, which featured an appearance by the Sioux chief Sitting Bull. Such staged confrontations inevitably influenced the way in which Western novels and later movies portrayed the past. Indeed, the Western genre added little to the Cody formula of marauding redskins versus fearless settlers, and he was followed by a string of similar cowboy heroes played by actors such as Randolph Scott, Audie Murphy, and of course John Wayne.

Only in the 1960s and '70s did a more balanced view of native American history begin to emerge. "Red Power" followed hard on the heels of the movements demanding rights for blacks and for women, and particularly the anti-Vietnam War struggles, and was accompanied by militancy. It coincided with the publication of several sympathetic histories, notably Dee Brown's *Bury My Heart at Wounded Knee*, a surprise best-seller that shocked America with its exposure of the country's "dark past,"[19] and a smattering of Hollywood Westerns telling events from a native American perspective (for example, *Little Big Man*, 1970).[20]

In the 1980s and '90s, these advances were built upon, with many more books about America's "true history."[21] Hollywood movies continued to present sympathetic portrayal of the native American. Films like *Dances with Wolves* and *Geronimo* have been labeled "politically correct" primarily because they featured tribal languages; but surely the truly PC step will come when native Americans start making movies about their own past.

But the stereotyping persists. The 1990s have seen a new stereotype gain popularity—that of the native American as a symbol of Green consciousness and New Age spiritual values. Armed with the "moral superiority" of the victim, they have become transformed into wise, mystic shamans and guardians of the environment, the token image in antipollution campaigns and Green advertising. It seems that even now native Americans cannot be dealt with on their own terms, but only as ciphers for white concerns—something we need to keep in mind when we think about *Mohicans*.

The story of white America has been that of non-natives struggling to impose their Dream, their culture, on the country and on its original inhabitants. Native Americans were always thought of as the Other, threatening to overwhelm this enterprise. They were in the way, and their only way out was to disappear. And, in one sense, this is what happened. For although today native American communities are thriving, the entire population numbers only one million, ten times fewer than the estimated population of 1800, and still small enough for governments effectively to ignore. So, if for whites the American Dream meant a new beginning, for native Americans it meant the beginning of an end.

Be that as it may, the American Dream has furnished an endlessly refreshed stimulus and shape to the collective imaginings of millions and generations of whites, and even nonwhites. Its history is the fabric within which the thread of Cooper's *Mohicans* is woven.

# CHAPTER 2    Cooper's Book

*The Last of the Mohicans* first appeared in 1826. It is best described as an adventure-romance set around events in the war between Britain and France for control of North America in the mid-eighteenth century. As the title implies, the native American population plays a major role, since different tribes sided with each colonial power. In the book, Cooper offered a picture of a "heritage," of an ideal frontier American and of his opposites—the Indian "savages" and the colonial masters. In so doing, he created not only a "classic" of modern literature, but also a uniquely American mythology.

The first thing that strikes one about the book is its size and overall serious presentation. The best-known modern British edition, in the Penguin Classics series, measures 350 pages in length and comes with a cover depicting a rather somber landscape.[1] Flipping through the text, one notices that every chapter is prefaced by snatches of poetry from Shakespeare, Gray, Bryant, and others. Everything about the book says that it has something weighty to impart and conforms to our modern notions of what a "classic" should look like. Indeed, so daunting does the book appear that it is really no surprise that most people know the story through adaptations, usually film adaptations. But this is to get ahead of ourselves.

James Fenimore Cooper (1789–1851) was born into a wealthy family in upstate New York. After having been expelled from Yale and spending five years in the U.S. navy, he suddenly turned to writing at the age of thirty. (The story goes that he was dared to do so by his wife when he complained that he could write a better novel than the English one she was reading.) He quickly became famous—most notably for his tales of an already-past "frontier"—and by the time *Mohicans* (his sixth book) appeared, he was established as a major novelist.[2]

*Mohicans* itself was the second book in a series of five: *The Pioneers* (1823), *The Last of the Mohicans* (1826), *The Prairie* (1827), *The Pathfinder* (1840), and *The Deerslayer* (1841). Though not conceived of as a series when they were written, they all starred the same central character, "the Leatherstocking," and so came to be known after him as "The Leatherstocking Tales."[3] Leatherstocking's real name in the books is Nathaniel (Natty) Bumppo, who acquired the sobriquet on account of his chosen legwear. He is also known by another nickname, "Hawkeye," because he is an excellent shot with a gun. This name is more familiar to modern aficionados of the stories and is the one most commonly used in *Mohicans*.[4]

Structurally, then, *Mohicans* is about a character—indeed characters—who were introduced in a previous book, though Cooper is careful to reintroduce them for new readers. The book was originally published in two halves, a publishing circumstance that partly accounts for the major division of the novel into two long chase sequences. (In our narrative outline below, the split comes after the massacre of the British at Fort William Henry.)

What kind of audience was Cooper aiming for? We can say with some certainty that it was intended to be middle class, educated, and monied—the same book-buying public that was interested in European authors like Walter Scott. (Publishing for the working classes did not take off in America until several years later, when *Mohicans* adaptations and cheap editions introduced Cooper to a wider audience for the first time.) Also, the readership was meant to be male: in the Preface, Cooper makes a point of warning off "the more imaginative sex" because the subject matter is too "shocking" for them.

But it is not enough to see this extraordinary book purely and simply as a macho adventure tale. To begin to understand its deeper levels, we need to look at Cooper's imaginative background, and in particular at the Romantic movement. Put briefly, Romanticism was the intellectual mainstream in Europe and America between roughly 1790 and 1870, and represented a reaction against neoclassicism (and in a broader sense against the Enlightenment). It was characterized by an emphasis on testing one's spirit; nature as an elemental force; the rise and fall of nations; the strict stratification of society (men superior to women, whites superior to Indians, Indians superior to blacks); the importance of heroes and heroic deeds; and an interest in folk culture and ethnic cultural origins.

Romanticism was more than just an influence on Cooper's work; it was a direct spur. Cooper was part of an identifiable group of writers, artists, and intellectuals, based in New York, who saw it as their mission to foster a broadly Romantic vision of America. They took poet Ralph Emerson's then-famous words, "[America has] arts to acquire, and tastes to form"[5] as a challenge, and openly discussed the creation of an "indigenous culture" at various select clubs and gatherings. Cooper's own "Bread and Cheese Club" included painters like William Dunlap, Asher Durand, John Wesley Jarvis, Samuel Morse, Henry Inman, and Robert Weir, and writers like William Bryant.

In a quite calculated fashion, therefore, the artists took inspiration from the writers, and vice versa. This is why Cooper's books were so often the subject of paintings in this period. In *Mohicans* itself, it was the landscape and sense of wilderness that was the particular attraction: the great Thomas Cole painted several scenes, which are now considered masterpieces in the history of American art, while it was Asher Durand who provided the image that now fronts the aforementioned Penguin edition of the book.[6]

So, to the book itself. The basic narrative of *The Last of the Mohicans* is as follows:

The story opens with scene-setting about the English/French wars, then takes us to an English camp to the north of Fort William Henry, introducing us to the key characters: Cora and Alice, the two daughters of Colonel

Munro, the commander of the fort; Major Heyward, who has been deputed to get them safely to their father; Magua, an Indian guide working for the English; and David Gamut, an itinerant music teacher.

Heyward and the two young women set out, guided by Magua and soon joined by Gamut. Magua proposes to lead them by a short but difficult forest route.

Now we meet three other key characters: Nathaniel Bumppo, alias Hawkeye, a lone woodsman; his friend Chingachgook, aging chief of the wiped-out Mohicans; and Chingachgook's son Uncas. They are discussing the state of the world when they hear the travelers approaching.

When Hawkeye and his companions meet up with Heyward's party, it is quickly revealed that Magua had been leading them into a Huron (or "Mingo") trap. Magua flees to join his waiting Indians, and Hawkeye agrees to try to save the travelers. They hurry to the river, get rid of their horses, and hide in an island cave.

Magua's Hurons track them, and skirmishes take place until all the defenders' powder is used up. Desperate, Hawkeye, Chingachgook, and Uncas agree to Cora's plea that they should leave to replenish their weapons, and then return to rescue the others.

Magua captures the four refugees and takes them toward his encampment. We now learn his motivation: he had been whipped for drunkenness by Colonel Munro and is now seeking revenge. Magua demands that Cora become his squaw, threatening death as the alternative. Cora rejects him, horrified, but as she and Alice face death, Hawkeye and companions arrive to rescue them. Magua escapes in the fight.

Hawkeye now leads the party toward Fort William Henry and eventually, after some dangers, they reach and enter it, although it is besieged.

During an interlude in the fort, we learn that Heyward is in love with Alice. Colonel Munro had thought he loved Cora, and accuses him of prejudice, because Cora is half-caste, being the child of a first marriage in the West Indies. Heyward successfully protests he simply loves Alice for herself.

Because help is refused by Fort Edward, Munro is forced to surrender Fort William Henry, but on good terms: they can leave with their arms and colors. But Magua has other plans, as we learn from an encounter between him and the French Marquis de Montcalm.

As the English leave, the Hurons massacre them, killing hundreds. At the height of the killing, Gamut seeks to protect the women by singing psalms, and is taken as mad by the Indians. Gamut, Alice, and Cora are spared until Magua reaches them. He again makes his demand of Cora. When she refuses, he seizes Alice, so that Cora is forced to follow him, and Gamut trails after.

Hawkeye, friends, and Colonel Munro survive the massacre and track

Magua's company into Canada. On the way they have to do battle with roving bands of Hurons. Eventually they find the Indian's village, where they encounter Gamut, now dressed as an Indian. Because he is "mad," the Indians have not interfered with him.

Hawkeye, Uncas, and Gamut devise a series of tricks to rescue Alice, and then Uncas (who himself has been captured). These involve Hawkeye dressing in a bearskin, capturing, and eventually leaving Magua tied up as an "evil spirit," and leaving Gamut behind protected by his madness. Cora, meanwhile, is being held at a neighboring village of the Delawares, and they hurry there.

Magua is freed and, gathering his warriors, heads to the Delaware village, where a council takes place in front of the ancient king Tamenund. At first he is persuaded by Magua, then half-swayed by Cora, and finally swung by the revelation of who Uncas is: the last of the rightful chiefs of the Mohicans. Thus he frees Uncas, Hawkeye, and Alice. But under Delaware law Magua is allowed to go free and to take Cora as his prize.

At dusk, when it is permitted, Hawkeye, Uncas (clearly in love with Cora), and Chingachgook lead a company to rescue her. Cora once again rejects Magua who, about to kill her, is attacked by Uncas. Another Indian stabs her fatally and is in turn killed by Uncas. Exposed by this act, he is stabbed from behind by a maddened Magua. As Magua turns to flee and jumps across a chasm, Hawkeye shoots him with his "longue carabine."

At the close of the book, the Indians bury Cora and Uncas. We learn that Heyward will now marry Alice. The grieving Chingachgook is joined by Hawkeye, while Tamenund mourns the passing of the Indians in the face of the whites, and especially Uncas, the "last of the Mohicans."

There are important episodes in the story that we have not included in this account of the basic narrative. These include, for instance, the killing of Alice's colt as they escape to the river and cave; and the execution of Reed-That-Bends and the shaming of his father at the Huron camp. Some of these other episodes are important, and we will pick them up separately. But with the intellectual background described above in mind, we can identify five main themes in *Mohicans*, all closely linked to Romanticism. They are: the image of the Indian; the image of the hero; the notion of historical truth; the image of the wilderness, and the notion of "America." For the sake of simplicity, it is appropriate to consider each of these in turn.

*The Image of the Indian*: Cooper makes it clear in the Preface that for him this was the most important aspect of the book. But he was not the first author to deal with the subject, contrary to popular belief; in fact there had been a boom in "Indian stories" in the early 1820s, and these were familiar to American audiences.[7] What set *Mohicans* apart was the seriousness of its approach and the fact that it put Indians at center stage. Key characters are Indian, and significant scenes take place within an Indian tribal setting. Cooper takes much care to ensure that they are not one-dimensional figures, and there is a great deal of description of their culture and customs. To this day, Cooper is remembered as "the Indian story writer" and even as "the Indians' friend."[8]

But what did he really think of them? His attitudes were certainly complex, but a close reading of the book tells us enough for our purpose. Superficially, he is a relativist, and in common with Romantic notions of the "volk," he appears to have believed in the purity of the races. It is made explicit repeatedly in the text that the Indians have their "gifts," while the whites have theirs. Indeed, there is a great deal on the merits and "just nature" of various tribes, and how they possess coherent belief systems and "noble traditions." Even the Hurons are not inherently evil but are corrupted by Magua, who is a skillful persuader.[9]

Also, very importantly the book concedes that the whites have behaved badly with regard to the Indians. They have broken promises, spread disease, and brutally pushed back the frontier. As a result, the noble Mohican tribe has been reduced to two people. The most graphic condemnation of this and other atrocities comes toward the end of the book, when Tamenund tells Uncas: "I have lived to see the tribes . . . driven from their council fires, and scattered. . . . I have seen the hatchets of a strange people sweep woods from the valleys that the winds of Heaven had spared!" He goes on to fantasize that Uncas may be the man to reverse the trend: "The arrow of Tamenund would not frighten the fawn; his arm is withered like the branch of a dead oak . . . yet is Uncas before him, as they went to battle against the pale-faces!"

Cooper does not like to see the Indians become extinct; indeed, the book is in many ways a requiem for them. Yet he considers it the natural way of things. At various points, he suggests that no empire lasts forever, that different races are inevitably in conflict, and that now it is time for the Indians to hand over to the whites. In this sense, the Indians are a metaphor for the rise and fall of civilizations— as we have seen, a prominent theme in Romantic thinking. This notion of "progressive history" is underscored by the climactic speech by Tamenund, when he laments: "The pale-faces are masters of the earth, and the time of the red men has not yet come again. . . ."

But is Cooper really so liberal about the relative gifts of the two peoples? There is reason to suggest not, and that he was more in tune with his intellectual background in the belief that the races are not just distinct but also stratified. Our suspicions are first raised by the very structure of the narrative, by which Cooper sets up a "good Indian/bad Indian" opposition: the Hurons are bad, the Mohicans good. Literally, by the end of the story, it might be said that the only good Indian is a dead one.[10]

There are further hints as the action progresses. Cooper refers to Indians throughout as "savages," hardly a neutral term, and contrives situations where their lack of "civilization" is contrasted with the whites. Thus, when it is explained that Magua is obsessed with revenge for being whipped by the British, it is also implied that Indians do not understand the concept of discipline. At the massacre, Cooper describes the Hurons becoming so excited that they drink the blood of those whom they murder. When our heroes are trapped behind the waterfall, the Indians among them behave in a pragmatic, utilitarian way and swim off to fetch help, whereas Heyward will not leave the women because he is "honorable." But then, that does leave us with a problem regarding Hawkeye, who also abandons the women. Is he or is he not a model of virtues?

Perhaps the strongest argument is the way Cooper deals with the issue of interracial sex. This is another major thread in the story, and is used quite deliberately both as an erotic device and to express a dread of miscegenation. It is most sensationally exploited in the episodes where Magua tries to take Cora as his squaw. Take, for example, the scene in the Delaware camp in which she gives her reaction to the idea:

[Tamenund:] "A great warrior takes thee to wife. Go—thy race will not end."

"Better, a thousand times, it should," exclaimed the horror-struck Cora, "than meet with such a degradation!"

More subtly, yet more revealingly, Cora is also attracted to Uncas. Possibly this is because her "black blood" signifies her affinity with Indians. But although Uncas is a potential lover for much of the final half of the book, we are left in no doubt as to the immorality of such a union: on appropriately germane occasions, Hawkeye comments quite pointedly that the races should never mix. In the end, the twin deaths of Cora and Uncas save this from ever happening.[11]

But before we denounce Cooper as a racist and consign him to the Politically Incorrect sin-bin, it is necessary to say a few quick words to put his treatment of Indians in historical context. He may not have been "the Indians' friend," but at least he afforded them respect, which was more than his contemporaries in the creative world were prepared to do. The conquering of native American tribes was still very much an ongoing process in Cooper's day: the policy of "Removal" was in full force in the 1820s and '30s (and the great Indian wars were not to come until the 1860s). The cultural contribution to this policy was overwhelmingly to portray Indians as subhuman and easily slaughterable. Cooper never stooped to this level, and when his books appeared, he was attacked for romanticizing them. No doubt this is one criticism that he would have taken as a compliment.[12]

*The Image of the Hero*: Hawkeye (a.k.a. Nathaniel Bumppo a.k.a. Leatherstocking) is the central character in the story, and arguably the most complex. He had a precedent in the real-life frontiersman Daniel Boone—or rather in the folklore that surrounded him. Yet Cooper's creation is more than a tough guy dressed in skins and embodies several disparate but complementary psychological qualities.

Hawkeye is an Englishman raised among Indians, a Puritan, and illiterate. But above all, despite his lack of schooling, he is honest: "his countenance was not only without guile, but at the moment at which he is introduced, it was charged with an expression of sturdy honesty." Thus he is representative of the white man reduced to his purest level, divorced from the trappings of civilization. He embodies natural moral law and believes in justice rather than any man-made decrees. For this reason, he is in the unique position of being both alienated from the British colonists (despite the fact he shares their nationality), and also being able to bond with the "pure" Indians.

But despite his affinity for the Indians, we are never left in any doubt as to which race he belongs to. It is stressed again and again that he is a "man without a cross," which is to say, without cross-breeding. This means that, if the story can be seen at least in part as an expression of the "rise and fall of nations," then he will automatically be on the side of the winners. By the same token, it can be said that he carries forward within himself (and thus symbolically within the white victors) all the good qualities of the Indians.

Inextricably linked with this quality, another facet of his character is his bravery and pioneering spirit, something that harkens back to the Boone mythology but builds upon it. He is at home in the wilderness and has become transformed by it to the point that he is both physically and mentally tough: "Every nerve and muscle appeared strung and indurated by unremitted exposure and toil." This also fits with Romantic notions of "the testing of the spirit" and "man versus nature." Yet, tough as he may be, Hawkeye could not deal so effectively with nature without his trusty gun—the final piece in the mythic jigsaw. We have seen how Hawkeye obtained that name because he is an excellent shot; but he has yet another nickname based on his gun: "La Longue Carabine." Even the gun itself has a name, "Kill-deer," and it is referred to in loving detail throughout the story. This fetishization of Hawkeye as "the loner who is good with a gun," can be seen as the model for countless imitators in the nineteenth and twentieth centuries, especially western heroes like "Shane" and "The Man with No Name." It is also a significant symbol in the context of the American citizen's constitutional "right to bear arms": it is hard not to hear the spirit of Hawkeye in the lyrics to a hit country and western song: "God, guts, and guns is what made this country strong. . . ."[13]

But if Hawkeye is an idealized figure, he is also human—and this is what makes the character work. Cooper once expressed regret that his creation was too perfect.[14] But in fact, he exhibits plenty of foibles. He is very boastful of his shooting ability, and he babbles on none too knowledgeably about religion. In fact, he is over-talkative, in stark contrast to his "strong and silent" fictional descendants. Also, he has a dark side, and sometimes his bravery crosses over into blood-lust, even sadism: he runs into battle shouting "Extarminate the varlets!" (112) and thinks nothing of stabbing his foes' corpses (" . . . the scout made a circuit of the dead, into whose senseless bosoms he thrust his long knife . . . " [114]). Hawkeye is nothing if not complicated: a legendary WASP hero who is also a recognizable man.

*The Notion of Historical Truth*: In his preface, Cooper says, "The reader who takes up these volumes in the expectation of finding an imaginary and romantic picture of things which never had an existence, will probably lay them aside, disappointed." He is keen to stress right from the start that this is the way it was, warts and all. This could be interpreted as a scam, a bit of hype to sell the book. On the other hand, *Mohicans* is certainly more careful about its facts than most novels of its era. Indeed, the level of research is often remarkable, and the prose certainly benefits from a stress on detail and description. In short, it's very convincing.[15]

But, despite Cooper's claims, the book is not historically correct, and much of the time he would have known so. The events he is describing took place in 1757, many years before the book's publication (1826), and there are bound to be errors. For instance, the Franco-British wars did happen, but the facts are deliberately altered to suit Cooper's dramatic purpose. To give the most obvious example, the massacre at Fort William Henry was based in fact, but Cooper exaggerated the role of Montcalm and the extent of the violence.[16]

More importantly, there are mistakes regarding the portrayal of Indian culture. As Cooper admits in his Preface, he borrowed much of his information from Joseph Heckewelder's *History, Manners and Customs of the Indian Nations*, itself a none-too-reliable source. The Mohicans did, and indeed do, exist; but the people Cooper describe have more in common with the Delaware tribe (or rather, Heckewelder's description of them).

We might ask why these details matter. After all, this is a work of fiction, and some measure of artistic license is to be expected. Quite so. But we have to remember that it was part of Cooper's mission to use the past to make points about "the American character" and to foster the idea of an indigenous (white) culture. The book was sold as "history," and was largely perceived as such. Inexorably, it was to be a perception that shaped America's future.

*The Image of the Wilderness:* The trees, the greenery, and nature generally play as much of a starring role in *Mohicans* as any of the main characters. The natural world is depicted as wild, magnificent, uncontrollable. From the first page we are faced with "A wide and impervious boundary of forests . . . the rapids of the streams . . . the rugged passes of the mountains. . . . "

On one level there are obvious links with Romantic thinking here. As well as being a rejection of urbanization, industrialization, and commercialism, Cooper's depiction of the wilderness also reflects a deep respect for the power of nature. Within this context, the Indian communities who populate the land are seen as an integral part of nature, while for the white man the wilderness is a testing ground, a place "full of toils and dangers," where toughness and ingenuity are required to survive—a place, in other words, where "a man can be a man."

Yet this setting is also used to pose deeper philosophical questions. For instance, who owns the land? Is it possible to "own" such an elemental force? It is made clear that, for the Indians, the individual belongs to the land, not the land to the individual; and this is something that is contrasted again and again with white ideas about colonization and settlement. True, Hawkeye is the exception—a white man who is spiritually in tune with the Indians. But almost all the other white characters in the book are caught up, either directly or indirectly, in conflict for possession of the land.[17]

Also, how far does the wilderness act as a "frontier"? What is its role in demarcating a space where two distinct and hostile forces come together? Clearly, Cooper wants us to view it in these dramatic terms: as a place where opposites meet, and where much blood will be spilled before one side wins out over the other.[18]

*The Notion of "America"*: We have seen how Cooper and his clique were anxious to establish a notion of "America." We have also seen how, in *Mohicans*, Cooper went some way toward this end by defining the country in the abstract—in terms of the wilderness, in terms of the Indian population, in terms of Hawkeye's moral goodness. But it was also important to define America as a nation-state, in the same sense as other nation-states of the nineteenth century. To do this, Cooper used the expedient of contrasting the rising nation of the United States with the declining nation of Great Britain.

Here once again we are in the Romantic realm of the rise and fall of nations, and in order for the opposition to work, Cooper needed to be very particular about his portrayal of the British, and of the (white) proto-Americans. Of course, he had history on his side: because the book was published many years after the events it describes, audiences—especially American audiences—would have been fully aware that the British were going to get ousted in the Revolution of 1776–81. Fresher still in American memories when *Mohicans* was first published was the renewal of war between Britain and the U.S. around 1812, during which parts of New York were badly damaged.[19]

Still, Cooper drives the point home: "The imbecility of her military leaders abroad, and the fatal want of energy in her councils at home, had lowered the character of Great Britain from the proud elevation on which it had been placed by the talents and enterprise of her former warriors and statesmen" (13). In short, the British are portrayed as idiots; even Heyward, honorable chap that he may be, is characterized as pompous and often foolish.

As for the "Americans," these posed a particular problem for Cooper. For, of course, there can be no Americans as such in the story. But there are settlers, and although these do not play a major role, they are symbolized to a large degree in the person of Hawkeye. There is no need here to repeat our assessment of Hawkeye. Suffice to say that he plays a unique part in the book as the quintessential proto-American. He is alienated from his (English) national background, and at the same time is adapted to the land, and thus we can see him as being symbolic of the transfer of power from one nation to the other. If, as has been argued, Hawkeye's destiny in the story is to take over the good qualities of the Indians, it is also true that he takes over the good qualities of the British.

*The Last of the Mohicans* was an instantaneous best-seller and established its author as the first significant American literary figure. However, its critical reception was not quite so enthusiastic. The main complaints were that stylistically the book was badly written, repetitive, and lacked pace and characterization, even if its historical veracity was praiseworthy. These criticisms continued to be leveled at the book through successive reprintings until the end of the century, the most famous example being a savage review by Mark Twain in *North American Review* in 1895. But there are other reasons for the criticisms, as we discuss in our next section.

The behavior of Cooper himself did not help matters. He made a point of hitting back at his critics, thereby making himself doubly unpopular. There is no question that he was hurt by the bad press: even though he was a commercial sensation and something of a national hero, he craved critical acceptance above all else. Significantly, the year *Mohicans* was published, 1826, was also the year in which Cooper left with his wife for Europe, whence he was not to return for another seven years. For his detractors, this was all the excuse they needed to suggest that the creator of the "great American novel" was behaving churlishly and turning his back on the country he had eulogized.[20]

Paradoxically, elsewhere in the world reviews were more uniformly favorable. In Europe, the book fit into an existing tradition of adventure novels and was extravagantly praised. It was translated into all the main European languages, and luminaries who were known to be fans included Balzac, Schubert, and Goethe. Intriguingly, the country where *Mohicans* had its main impact was France, where the figure of Hawkeye was interpreted as an embodiment of Rousseau's "noble savage."

After this initial reception, the book went through a number of critical reappraisals. Though still widely read, *Mohicans* was eclipsed in the latter half of the nineteenth century by the rise of the dime novel Westerns and, of course, by the rise of the Wild West shows, which were the living exemplars of those heroic stories. It was a mark of the growing separation of high and mass culture versions of the Western and has important things to tell us later on. The period 1900 to the present witnessed a predictable see-sawing of opinion in the light of prevailing literary fashion and ideology, a pattern we only need summarize here. To begin with, the first few decades of the new century were notable for essays that exactly reversed the nineteenth century critics' assessment, praising the book's style, pacing, and characterization while attacking its pretensions to "history." This trend culminated in the 1920s, when D. H. Lawrence effectively rehabilitated Cooper as a great writer: it also corresponded with the ascension of *Mohicans* to the status of a "classic," thereby placing it to some degree "above criticism." (See also our chapter 4 on this.)

From the 1930s onwards, the main thrust of critical reappraisal came from the universities, where contributors to learned journals argued over the book's merits in the light of prevailing thinking. In particular, the 1960s and '70s was the era of civil rights and the associated rise of "Red Power" (which is to say the Indian rights movement) and these movements inevitably provoked much debate about Cooper's attitudes. In the 1980s, a similar process led to the emergence of "Green" appraisals of the text (focusing on its treatment of the wilderness) and even feminist criticism (looking in particular at the behavior of the female characters).[21]

So much for the critics. There is a saying, as current in 1826 as it is today, that a book's best critic is its audience, and here there has never been much dissent. Certainly, in commercial terms, there have been periods of quick and slow sales, but always within a relatively healthy trading record.[22] The period immediately after publication saw the most dramatic boom, as *Mohicans* became the trendy book to own. (Of course, we can never be sure how many people actually read it.) In America especially it hit a nerve. Not only was it a rollicking adventure, but it also had novelty value: it spoke directly to Americans and was set in their homeland.

As the book became widely known, so it began to take on the patina of cultural significance. This was most evident in the fact that it was increasingly perceived as a "first" (the first novel to deal with Indians, the first to have an American hero, and so on), a trend that reached the point that *Mohicans* even began to be seen as "the first American novel." None of this was true, but that did not stop successive publishers from exploiting the situation and hyping the book as something that it wasn't. It was a small step to start marketing it as a "classic."[23]

*Mohicans* was not without commercial competition. Far from it. In some ways, it was a victim of its own success, and nowhere was this more apparent than in the emergence over time of other fictional heroes in the Hawkeye mold. In the 1830s, it was the turn of Davy Crockett; in the 1840s, Kit Carson; in the 1880s Billy the Kid (the first to be called a "cowboy"); in the 1880s-90s Buffalo Bill Cody, Wild Bill Hickok, Jesse James, and Wyatt Earp; and so on. One entirely unforeseen result of this competition was that *Mohicans* became inextricably tangled up with the Western genre, an association that has not disappeared to this day.

Yet *Mohicans* remained special. It became symbolic of a much wider set of values; within a very short time after publication it was clear that Americans were reading the book in order to give themselves a sense of who they were. In other words, *Mohicans* succeeded in molding a slice of a (mythical) history in such a way as to give meaning to the present. In this way, the book developed a life outside of itself and thus perpetuated its sales potential.

This brings us to the present day. To a certain degree, Cooper achieved his aim of defining America—a Romantic vision encompassing a sense of identity. And yet for all his calculation, the one thing he could not control was how future generations would interpret the book and how they would come to their own conclusions about a definition. For one of the joys of *Mohicans* is that there are a great many loose ends. It constitutes a founding myth, certainly, but a myth with ambiguities. The book is in many ways a racist book, yet it incorporates a condemnation of racism. It raises the possibility of interracial sexual relations between two of its heroic characters, yet avoids consummation. It celebrates frontier qualities, yet it mourns the passing of the frontier (though more in the other Leatherstocking books than in *Mohicans*). Hawkeye himself is a splendid and moral figure, yet he is also a loner, he is capable of real violence, he is capable of explaining and justifying scalping by the Mohicans. All in all, *Mohicans* is a truly ambivalent tale.

Perhaps we should take this ambivalence seriously. It derives, we would argue, from the specific time of its writing and from bifurcations in Cooper himself. First, remember that this was by no means the only novel of its kind. On the contrary, there was a great fascination in this period with what was being lost with the disappearance of native Americans: "Cultural historians have identified J. F. Cooper's *The Last of the Mohicans* as one of approximately 40 novels published in the United States between 1924–1834 that together suggest the existence of a virtual 'cult of the Vanishing American' in the antebellum period."[24] Of course, if the "Americans" (that is, the native Americans, the "Indians") were disappearing, then what could replace them was the new Americans. A new national identity would have to emerge. And one of the ways to establish that identity was to develop an appropriate national literature. It is therefore of real importance to note that this is the period in which a number of reviewers and critics were actually *proposing* that if there was to be such a literature, the theme of the Indian must provide its imaginative resources. As early as 1807, Theodore Dehon proposed the theme of the Indian as "the chief hope for an original literature." One reviewer of one of Cooper's pre-*Mohicans* novels, *The Spy*, even proposed the same for Cooper's next novel.[25] Meanwhile, those who disagreed with this notion tended to reject the very idea of an American literature. Granville Mellen directly dismissed Cooper's frontier romances with this comment: "The Indians as a people offer little or nothing that can reasonably be expected to excite the novelist, formed as his taste must be on a foreign standard."[26]

The Indians, if you like, were handing on their natures to the whites, as they vanished. What qualities were they seen to have? They had, of course, certain natural skills: they were fine trackers, they knew the ways of animals. But also they were famous for their powers of rhetoric. One of the things that had impressed the early white negotiators seeking land rights had been the qualities of Indians' speechmaking (a facet of their nature almost totally lost by the time the "Western" imaged Indians).[27] By the time of Cooper, this perception was beginning to change.

A wider redefinition of the position of Indians in the scale of civilization was taking place, as John Cawelti has noted: "The various seventeenth- and eighteenth-century views of the Indian with their complex dialectic between the Indian as devil and as noble savage quickly gave way in the nineteenth century to a definition of the Indian way of life as an inferior and earlier stage in the development of civilization."[28] The Puritan view of the Indian as a pestilence in paradise, the snake in Eden, managed to coexist with a Rousseau-like admiration of their naturalness. But by the beginning of the nineteenth century this was changing. Beginning in the cities, wilderness changes from being dangerous and needing to be tamed to being a source of values that the "new Americans" could inherit.[29]

A whole series of changes, then, arose together as Cooper began to write his Leatherstocking novels. Cooper wrote at the cusp of the changes. Hence *Mohicans* is inevitably ambivalent in a host of ways. On heredity, for instance, Cooper's views are perversely complicated. Late on in *Mohicans*, Uncas is captured by the Hurons. One of them, Reed-That-Bends, is arraigned before his tribe for cowardice: he had run from Uncas. The tribe condemns him to death, and he is instantly killed. His father departs the Hurons' council in shame—not for his son but for himself. Cooper's narration comments: "The Indians, who believe in the hereditary transmission of virtues and defects in the character, suffered him to depart in silence" (247). Hardly a comment suggesting agreement. Yet Hawkeye is frequently heard to confirm his own purity as being "without a taint, without a cross."

What makes the novel both curious and curiously effective is the interplay between two systems of narrative organization. In one, there is endless discussion of "essential qualities." This discussion is carried in particular by the narrator's comments on characters' motivation. On the other hand the *resolutions* in the book are founded on historically specific relations and cultural traditions. At the fort, for example, the French defy all Colonel Munro's expectations by allowing an honorable surrender, but then seem to lose that honor by not interfering (because they are scared of losing Indian support) with Magua's evident plans for the massacre. Or again, the

Delawares—"savage" as they are—are not only scrupulously governed by laws and rules of justice, but clearly have a determining history. When Uncas is revealed to be the chief of the Mohicans, the Delawares override the claims of Magua because the Mohicans represent their ur-Tribe, from which they are all descended. The Six Nations have a historical tradition that governs their loyalties. This is not just a fact within the novel. Without this second principle, the story simply could not resolve in the way it does.

We might represent this clash of narrative principles as a conflict between racial theory and determinate (albeit mythologized) history. Because the two are not and could not be resolved, the novel is inevitably incomplete. By this we mean that it *requires interpretation to produce a coherent, committed reading.*[30] Is it a racist book? Is it pro- or anti-Indian? Is Magua an evil character? What does the story suggest about interracial sexual relations? That depends on your interpretation, but now we mean something quite strong by "interpretation."

Cooper himself lived out just such a conflict of principles in his political adherence to Jacksonian democracy. Andrew Jackson became president in 1828 on a ticket that shifted the focus of attention from Europe to aggressive, buccaneering expansion to the West. Cooper supported him. Yet Cooper's own personal situation, and indeed general convictions, ought to have aligned him with the genteel and aristocratic Republicans, at their strongest in the Northeast. His association with old wealth, with a literary elite, and his fondness for all things European was not reflected in his political allegiance. He was an uneasy Jacksonian, and we will need to think how this was reflected in his romances.

In the rest of this book, we explore the fate of Cooper's *Mohicans* in many hands: some good, some awful, some faithful, some turning the story to purposes that Cooper would have hated. But for the story to survive at all, it had to have qualities working simultaneously in contradictory directions. It had to lend itself to being reworked in many opposed ways. But it had to have enough of a "presence," an inner strength, to make it worth repeatedly returning to. Yet, as we have suggested, it is not its literary qualities that have marked it out. Overall, of Cooper's Leatherstocking Tales, *Mohicans* is probably the one *least* favored by literary critics.

That is the puzzle of *The Last of the Mohicans*. It will be our argument that it is the book's very ambiguities that have made it so pliable to other people's uses. Produced on the cusp of all those changes, the story has become what we would call a "flexible template." It is incomplete, almost requiring interpretive completion, and thus lent itself to being rewritten, especially in that medium which became preeminently "American," the film. From the turn of the century, *Mohicans* became one of the resources through which each generation encountered the idea of "America," but each time in an image appropriate to its present purposes.

Is there a limit to those uses? What qualities does the template have that might restrict to what uses it can bend? In our final chapter, we will want to argue that there is such a limit. But we can only establish that after we have looked at how the novel has been used in the meantime. First, we need to explore the ways *Mohicans* established itself as a "classic," and just what that means.

# CHAPTER 3    Becoming a Classic

Consider the language used in this book introduction and in the associated endpaper:

*The Last of the Mohicans* has thrilled generations of readers by the speed and excitement of its descriptions of the thrills, dangers and romances of the frontier wars of the North American wilderness. Above all, the story has been made famous by its authenticity. No other book gives us so complete and vivid a picture of the North America of the pioneer, the uncharted forest, of the vanquished but waiting Indian.

Set against the background of the colonial war between France and England in the early eighteenth century, this story shows, as no story has shown since, what hazards the half-tamed land held for its would-be conquerors. No one understood the North American Indian better than James Fenimore Cooper, and in this work he has succeeded in portraying the Indian in all his savagery and splendour, with all his distrust of modern civilisation. In *The Last of the Mohicans* Cooper has left us a tale which is as exciting today as it was when it was written.

Abbey Classics

Some of the less colourful passages have been cunningly abridged in this modern edition of a great adventure story.[1]

Keep these in mind as we ask: what is a "classic"?

The history of "children's classics" has yet to be told. There are many good histories of books for children, histories that contain elements of the information we would need, but by no means all. In fact, when we first started thinking about this, it wasn't altogether clear what kind of a history this would be. Of all the chapters in this book, this is the most uncertain, as a result. We ask you to read it as a first attempt at writing an agenda for thinking about "children's classics."

Why is this a puzzling issue? There are a number of reasons. First, this is not a history of writing aimed at children—writing whose measure of success, perhaps, would be: Do they like it? Adapting and abridging novels for children is done to make available these "great works" so they can benefit from them. What sort of benefit? Of course, in part sheer enjoyment. A good yarn could be made accessible to children by judicious slimming of those parts where adults tend to rattle on: the descriptions of scenery, the moody bits, all the parts where the action slows down. But a lot of these books weren't chosen by children; they were given to them by adults.

Often they were given as prizes, in school or Sunday school, at scouting functions and the like, for being good at things that parents and teachers valued. They were filtered through the preconceptions of adults.

Suppose, then, the kids would rather have comics, or magazines, or records. Well, that might not be stopped, but they are unlikely prizes. They lack the aura of books. Books of literature are valued cultural commodities. They "do you good." Some books are especially good. They have come to be part of what has been dubbed the "canon" of literature, that is, a group of writings that transcends the ordinary and comes to represent "civilization." Cultural critics and even politicians have invested these works with great importance as makers and stabilizers of national life. How do books get to enter the canon? And what is this special good they are able to do?

Alongside these positive claims, there is a down side. Children's leisure time is a policed domain. There are long traditions of worrying about what populates children's imaginations. Apart from anything else, the little beasts tend to be attracted by the rude, the scatological! As Geoffrey Pearson has shown, each generation seems to worry anew about this question, but each time slightly differently, because their ideas change as to what they want children to become.[2] Reading and watching things, in this view, is all about developing the right purposes, directions, ambitions, skills, and desires. So of course "we" want children to enjoy what they read or watch. But enjoyment isn't enough; in fact, it may be downright dangerous.

There are several parts to this policing. First, there are the general culture police, who form and then operate from images of childhood. "Childhood" generally is an area of unreadiness in which some things are not nice, or right, for you to know about, because you are not ready. Kirsten Drotner nicely summarizes the paradox for the young here: childhood is a safe area, but one in which you are supposed to be learning what you will have to be and to do and to know when things aren't safe any more. So there are cultural police who watch over the young in their playpens: the bowdlerizers, the censors, the moral guardians. We should not lose the silliness of a lot of their judgments (Disney's *Bambi* was too shocking for children, British TV's *Doctor Who* was too frightening, and so on) because they expose a problem. There is a gap between the explicit criteria such moralists use, and their implicit, actually operative criteria.

For instance, take guns: the moralists often worry about children's attraction to them. Now take Westerns: for most moralists, these are fine and harmless; yet look at those guns. The point we are making is that the criteria don't sit on the surface. Here is a quotation from the British *Daily Mail*, commending a New Zealand Government report on delinquency among the young: "*Causes* of child delinquency included: Parents drinking at children's parties; high wages of adolescents; and mothers going out to work. *Remedies* should include: Tighter control or banning of sex, crime and horror publications and films, training policewomen to deal with girl offenders; and making radio serials emphasise 'Crime doesn't pay.'"[3] What is the link between causes and remedies? None, on the surface. And yet one can sense a hidden logic. There is an implication. Any useful history of the moral censors and their ideas cannot rest satisfied with the surface of their claims. Here is a further reason why our history is complicated.

Then there is another body of police. One of the side effects of the ennobling of literature has been the creation of a body of courtiers: the literary scholars and critics, the teachers, the reviewers. The teachers and curriculum designers, for example, are the ones who get the children actually to read some of the chosen texts. Their criteria will have to be met. One of their primary concerns is to preserve the essential qualities of great works: their "integrity," their "authenticity." Adaptations and abridgments therefore cause them concern. The essential qualities of these works are at risk in any abridgment—and perhaps even more so in any transformation into another medium. In their turn publishers, producers, and broadcasters know that their every move with a "classic" will be closely monitored.

There exists a third rank of the cultural police: those who particularly fear the impact of the visual on the young. Children's editions often include illustrations. That is generally acceptable, especially if good illustrators can be found. Even so, many critics have argued that the visual is too immediate. Visual images direct the imagination, so the argument goes, whereas words stimulate the imagination to work on its own. At worst, even good illustrations may short-cut the work of the words. That is a pity, but perhaps not too dangerous. But make the adaptation primarily visual, and a wider set of fears is awakened. Now we are talking about the general degradation of culture. We are talking about the loss of mental autonomy and the replacement of *good* imagination by *colonized* fantasy.[4] That there isn't a scrap of evidence that the visual operates any more directly on children (or anyone else) than the verbal is beside the point. The book and the word have cultural meanings in our society. They operate materially in shaping what is allowed in a children's classic.

We must not forget the publishers. Someone has to make and keep the classics available. Like any other commodity producer, in the end they have to have an eye to what will sell, and what will consolidate their rank among their public. The media critic Nicholas Garnham has argued that cultural producers face peculiar pressures. Because it is especially hard to predict what will succeed with the public, there is a drive to reduce risk through control over distribution.[5] Many factors thus come into play, from the operation of intellectual property law ("classics" have the great advantage of being old, hence generally out of copyright), to the need to produce books in series, to the need to get their series adopted, if at all possible, as school "readers" or at least as regular prizes. So publishers of classics have their own special interests. They know, for example, that book buyers won't usually seek out classics—unless, of course, one has just been given a film or TV treatment. Then publishers will vie furiously for the right to issue the film-related edition, using the best-known still or poster on the book's cover (even if the scene depicted does not actually occur in the book!)[6]

Because of all these pressures, children's classics have to be compromises, bending an ear to different pressures. The main ones we have identified are the pressures of images and ideologies of childhood (which have their own logic and evolution); and the pressure of current moral concerns about bad materials. Then there are the pressures of the curriculum: what is being asked of "literature" at any time? Add the pressures of "authenticity": what view of the "classics," their role, and their essential qualities is being promulgated? Finally, who are the main sponsors of these publications at any time? Who, therefore, do the publishers have to convince? Any history of children's classics will have to see its way through the interaction of all of these pressures. We cannot attempt that full account here—only enough to be able to ask what is going on in the making and shaping of children's versions of *Mohicans*.

Consider, then, the quotation and picture at the beginning of this chapter. We begin here because we have come to the conclusion that there is little worth saying about the actual process of abridging. The work of such an edition is done by its look, its market placement, and its publicity. Here, there is a clear appeal to a certain middle-class educational market. Here are two children, respectable, nicely-dressed, in a "secret garden of the soul," in the company of books that promise to people their imaginations with fine thoughts and well-constructed characters. This book, then, places itself among a body of good works. It is in a line with others that are valuable because they can fill and form young people's minds. Within the safety of this garden, then, freedom is encouraged.

The editorial text supports and adds to this effect. It guarantees thrills and excitement, but with the authenticity of history. Here is a tale of something noble that has passed. But there is no question which side the book is on: that of modern civilization, embodied indeed in books like this, with which the Indian could never come to terms. Such an appeal makes it clear that, while young readers may enjoy the savage splendor of the Indians, they will do so from the security of their literary garden. And of course, reassuringly for the adults, we can be sure that the work of abridging has been "cunningly" done.

This is a peculiarly British edition. This kind of annotation is a mark of its time—1950s Britain having seen the double concerns about bad influences from American crime and horror comics, and about the sheer shortage of books for children to fill and keep busy their imaginations.[7] Elsewhere and at other times the influences were different. For comparison, here are two other such cover introductions:

Wigwams and squaws! Scalping knives and the pipe of peace! You will find them in all books about Red Indians—but nowhere do they ring so true as in the great "Leatherstocking Tales" of James Fenimore Cooper. Here is the most famous of the five Classics—a dramatic story of action and suspense, a unique combination of realism and romance; with flesh-and-blood characters, including the immortal Hawkeye, the great white scout; and, as a superb backdrop, the swirling rapids and rugged mountain passes of the "Injun country" that the author knew so well. Countless tales have been written about the Red Indians—but this is the real thing.[8]

Fenimore Cooper's character, Leather-stocking, is said to be copied from the genuine pioneer of the American frontier Daniel Boone. But whoever he was taken from he is certainly the most famous figure in the whole of American fiction.

Leather-stocking appeared in previous books by this great author but *The Last of the Mohicans* is the best of all. In it we find two noble Indians named Uncas and Chingachgook who fought so gallantly against the white man.

In this book the reader can find the true story of Indian versus Paleface and learn exactly what happened as white men slowly and remorselessly fought their way across the great and mighty continent of America.[9]

Consider how these introductions set distinctive agendas for what these editions are supposed to be about.

The modern study of ideas of childhood really begins with Philippe Aries.[10] A French cultural historian, Aries argued that the idea of childhood was relatively recent. Using evidence from the histories of painting, of children's games, and of books about educating children, among other things, he sought to show how the idea had developed that children are "special," needing to live in a protected sphere. Aries's book had enormous influence, but it also generated waves of criticism. But amid all the criticisms, one thing remains clear: Aries was right to point to the fact that after the year 1650 there was a steady rise in *discourses* about children. Childhood increasingly became a focus of concern—and more than that, a focus through which other social concerns were considered. Childhood became one of the central symbols for modern societies. The word *child* itself reveals much. Until the eighteenth century, the word had a number of related meanings: it meant a person of noble birth (as in "Childe Roland"), it meant a servant or subordinate, of any age ("Courage, children, stand fast against the enemy!" an officer would cry in battle), it could mean a girl as opposed to a boy ("A very pretty barne—A boy, or a child, I wonder?" asked Shakespeare). What was common to all these was a notion of status: to be a "child" was to be dependent.

The late eighteenth century saw the meanings settle into a pattern. "Child" now meant innocence, and vulnerability, and a need for protection. Early on, the idea of the child (or at least the boy-child) was idealized, especially in the work of Jean-Jacques Rousseau. The child was identified with "nature" and with goodness, but this "nature" was dreadfully vulnerable. Anyone who has read the taut and severe educational regimes that Rousseau proposed will see how uneasy he was about "nature" expressing itself: "The only habit the child should be allowed is that of having no habits. . . . Prepare the way for his control of his liberty by leaving his body its natural habit, by making him capable of lasting self-control, of doing all that he wills when his will is formed. As soon as the child begins to take notice, what is shown him must be carefully chosen."[11] This is not libertarianism, but rigorous administration.

This was a period for romanticizing childhood. The child became the symbol for protesting against the dehumanizing influence of urban and industrial life: "The child could serve as a symbol of the artist's dissatisfaction with the society which was in process of such hard development about him. In a world given increasingly to utilitarian values and the Machine, the child could become a symbol of Imagination and Sensibility, a symbol of Nature set against the forces abroad in society actively de-naturing Humanity."[12] And in the work of poets, especially, this image of the child as Free Imagination, and hence as the implicit measure and critic of our society, grew and became strong. But not for long.

"We can no longer trust Nature," said J. P. Greaves, an early-nineteenth-century magistrate. Childhood therefore would not come naturally; it would have to be enforced. It was a measure of the status certain people *ought* to have. The two areas where this particularly showed was in the association of childhood with race and with class. Harriet Beecher Stowe, for example, has her character Uncle Tom say to his owner of a difficult task: "Let this chile do that." Treating black people as irresponsible children now easily reveals itself as problematic. The treatment of working class people as in need of paternalistic protection does not do this so easily.

Yet this has also often been the case: an assertion that working-class people, though they may seem self-motivated, are in fact incapable of rationality. Or as another magistrate put it in 1855: "The [delinquent] is a little stunted man already—he knows much and a great deal too much about what is called life. He is self-reliant, he has so long directed or misdirected his own actions and has so little trust in those about him, that he submits to no control and asks for no protection. He has consequently much to unlearn—he has to be turned again into a child."[13] Childhood here is a required condition, not what the (young) people actually are. It is a condition to which they must be returned, for everyone's protection. Childhood is inevitably surrounded with tensions masked by symbols. Children's literature, and perhaps especially classics for children, rode the crest of that wave, tugged by the two desires to limit and control, and to lift and educate.

The idea of the "classic" has, of course, long been in use, but it took a long time and much struggle to free it from its associations with all things Greek and Roman. Such processes are never tidy, and there are always historical anomalies. But there is no doubting the heat the arguments generated. In 1820, Lord Byron remarked: "I perceive that in Germany as well as Italy, there is a great struggle about what they call *Classical* and *Romantic*." That struggle was not long in coming to Britain. It was a struggle over what are the proper models for culture, ancient or modern writings? Even after the battle was largely won, old meanings clung on. If the Latin poet Virgil was not being directly cited, Ruskin in 1860 still associated the classic with "taste and restraint," a classical landscape as "perfectly trained and civilised"; and J. C. Fillmore in 1885 summarized "classic" as an aesthetic ideal: "clearness of thought, completeness and symmetry, harmonious proportion, simplicity and repose"—all the qualities that were perceived (erroneously) in classical literature.[14]

Yet as this was going on, the word *classic* was becoming profligate. In 1857 a book could be a "classic in astronomy"; surgeons could perform a "classic operation" (1880) and then go off to see a "classic race" (1885) such as the Oaks or the Derby. The debate about classics was making the *idea* of the classic more important generally. But the debate proceeded differently in Britain than in America. In Britain, Greek and Latin were strongly associated with the upper-class Public School tradition. But while the classics were very suitable for "training the minds" of aristocrats and businessmen, "English" was more suitable for the working classes (or "our future masters," as Robert Lowe, M.P., called them in 1867, at the height of a debate on universal education). If they could get the children of the poor to learn literature, it might "enlarge their sympathies" and so stave off the dangers of radicalism.[15] There were of course differences of degree among the proponents of literature. The extreme position, famously, was occupied by Matthew Arnold, who built an entire philosophy of education on this basis.

By the early years of the twentieth century, this class separation was being questioned, along with the formal methods of teaching. In the years after World War I especially, a series of arguments, culminating in a British Government Committee and Report, put English as the crown of the curriculum. And now it was to be experienced imaginatively, not learned by rote. But the reasons for wanting it there were perhaps not very different: "There is no class in the country that does not need a full education in English. Possibly a common basis of education might do much to mitigate the class antagonism that is dangerously keen at the moment and shows no sign of losing its edge." So wrote George Sampson, in the best known of all pre-1940 English method books, *English for the English*.[16] Sampson's hopes were embodied in the largely adopted recommendations of the 1921 Newbolt Committee, which pushed English to the fore as the basis for achieving "this much-desired spiritual unity of the nation."[17]

It is interesting to hear Newbolt himself discuss the importance of literature. Introducing a book of manly stories for boys during World War I, Newbolt offered a panegyric to the British public school system, right down to the system of "fagging."[18] At the heart of this argument was his claim that in their best period, during the early nineteenth century, these schools made no division between books and life. The future life of the boys was to "serve their country as soon as they reached the age for a commission." The training for that life was *regular contact with the right kind of literature*. But then, he wrote, "after Waterloo all this was changed; soldiering went into the background, and the old division between books and life began again. After forty years came the Crimean War and the Indian Mutiny; when they were past, the boys of England took matters into their own hands again, invented organized games, and revived the old passion for tournaments under many new forms." And they rediscovered the need for "adventure literature."[19]

Here, if we still needed it, is the decisive evidence of how seriously manly literature for boys was taken by Newbolt's social group. It is from here on, in Britain, that we see the production of series of children's classics, including *Mohicans*. Cooper's work was known there from the 1840s, but does not seem to have arrived substantially in Britain until the 1870s, when it came over as part of job lots of Western fiction.[20] It was received in the context of Empire fiction. The earliest abridgement seems to be 1890s.

If our picture is right, then it suggests that the emergence of classics series constituted the second big wave of sponsored reading for children. The first wave was produced under very different circumstances, right at the beginning of publishing specially for children. Following a brief attempt to produce "magazines of manners" for upper-middle-class children, such as *Lilliput* (1751), the big breakthrough in publications for children came with the sponsored moral tales of the Sunday School Movement. These were part of the new disciplinary movements, designed often to terrify children into goodness with tales of death and punishment. Coupled with these stories were dire accounts of the cruelty of primitive peoples.[21] If this first movement sought to scare children into right attitudes, by the 1920s it was to be done by stuffing their imaginations with the right ideas.

In America, everything about the production of classics for the young was conditioned by the long search for a "national culture." And that happened just as America began to cast off associations with the "classical period." Frank Kermode captures the moment of change in this way:

The classical quality of the Constitution was reflected in adaptations of Roman iconography, and even of Roman ceremony; Washington proceeded from Mount Vernon to New York through triumphal arches displaying, like Charles V two and a half centuries earlier, a version of the Roman Eagle. . . . The mottoes of many statues are Latin. As Howard Mumford Jones, who records these and other life facts, observes, "It is remarkable in what degree the public iconography of the nation—the statues that crown the domes of the state capitols, the figures of justice in our courthouses, the emblems of peace, or plenty, or progress or some other general ideal—are classical females in a republic that never was part of Greece or Rome." The directly classical era, imbued with the spirit of the Roman renovation, may be said to have ended only with the administration of John Quincy Adams (1825–9).[22]

Note the dates. As the classical is being shed as too "European," so *Mohicans* is being written, in response to pressure from reviewers and others for an "American literature." And the first children's books are being produced.

Even the very first native-produced children's books had this commitment to "America." Samuel Griswold Goodrich (b. 1793) began producing his *Tales of Peter Parley* in 1827. They illustrated facets of ordinary life in America, coupling that with illustrative tales of American history, and producing attempts at American folktales.[23] The subsequent development of literature for children in America took a particular path. One history of children's literature summed up its main differences from the English tradition thus:

[E]qualitarianism rather than class consciousness; a stronger family feeling; adventure, but of a different kind—adventure in the American west rather than in distant lands, adventure that made not for imperialism but as often as not for provincialism; courage and a hatred of the bully; self-reliance; work and the gospel of work, nature in the raw rather than tamed; democracy and humanitarianism; a feeling for fair play and the underdog; ingenuity and mechanical skill; humor that ran to the boisterous and the tall story, rather than to whimsy or nonsense; simplicity and morality.[24]

Though over-prettified (just how often did feelings for the underdog extend to native Americans, or black people, for example?) nonetheless, this summary does capture some of the qualities of nineteenth-century American children's fiction.

Cooper took his place easily among these stories. Children would play at "scouts and Redskins" from reading Cooper, though they might just as well do so from reading Robert Montgomery Bird's *Nick of the Woods*, or from reading about Daniel Boone, or Davy Crockett, or Mike Fink, or Kit Carson—or even play at Highlanders from reading Sir Walter Scott. Historian Martin Green has given a good account of some of the people who attested to Cooper's influence on them, from childhood, including a number who carried his stories with them as they took part in the opening of the western frontier.[25] But by and large, young people had to read the adult editions of Cooper until the latter part of the nineteenth century, or the occasional dime novel adaptation. The turning point came after 1900, when a concatenation of forces required the production of an "American literary history."

Through the nineteenth century, and especially after the end of the Civil War, a search went on for a truly "American culture." Early collectors of American literature searched for some common core that would demarcate an American tradition from its European ancestrics. Composers, painters, and sculptors visited Europe to sit at the feet of their counterparts, trying to catch a mood and a style that could be transported back and transformed into a new American idiom.[26] But the results often seemed mechanical. The painter Eugene Delacroix said of some of them: "They are taught the beautiful as one teaches algebra."[27] At the same time, European artists visiting America were greeted with extraordinary enthusiasm. And if, as with Dvorak's *New World* Symphony, they dedicated work to America, the result would be a debate on whether this work could provide the model for a new American sensibility.

Confidence seems to have arrived in the early years of the twentieth century. The ending of the Civil War produced a period of extraordinarily fast, if punctuated, growth. Railways pushed their buffers into all parts. Industry mushroomed, often overtaking European levels of efficiency because, like any late developer, American industrialists were good at going straight to the latest developments and breakthroughs. No past investments hung like albatrosses around their necks. The result, among other things, was a burst of urban development. In 1860, only 141 towns had populations over 8,000. By 1900, this figure had risen to 545. Meanwhile immigration was multiplying and diversifying America's population at a dizzying rate: 2.6 million entering in the 1870s, 5 million in the 1880s, and 4 million in the 1890s.

The turning point seems to have been 1896 when, after two terms of an increasingly unpopular Democratic administration, the Republicans were swept back into power with a formidable majority. This ushered in a period of relative calm and prosperity, a period in which American business leaders increasingly organized themselves into manufacturers associations, chambers of commerce, and the like and assumed the right to take the lead in civic direction. This wasn't new: in the last decades of the nineteenth century businessmen had invested heavily in the infrastructure of a new national culture, founding libraries, museums, universities, colleges, opera houses. The Library of Congress, completed in 1897, was seen not only as a storehouse but as a means of speeding the spread of useful information. Publishing took off in this period, with a phenomenal rise in the production of books, newspapers, magazines, manuals, portfolios, and of popular books such as Horatio Alger's rags-to-riches potboilers.

Driven by principles of efficiency, morality, and forward-looking, new systems of local control were put into place. "We are living in an age of organization," pronounced John Kirby to the National Association of Manufacturers in 1906—though he was unhappy about extending the principle of organization to trade unions. Between 1890 and 1915 a series of battles took place, mostly in the large urban areas, for control of education. The winners were local business leaders; their first target was to abolish elective superintendents. After the War of Independence, free public education for all had been a growing demand. And if local people were to pay, they wanted to have a say in what happened in education: hence the elective system. The attack on this system was done in the name of a new creed of efficiency, summed up in the words of Franklin Bobbitt: "The citizens are the stockholders; the board of education are the directors; the superintendent is the technical expert and general manager." But the battle was also over the purposes of education. Central to the new purposes of education was concern for the "Americanization of the foreign-born and their children."[28] This concern reached fever pitch before and after World War I, hurried by, among other things, the rise of syndicalist and socialist ideas among working people. There was an attempt to do away with ethnic diversity and cultural differences.

Along with this new "efficiency" came a new way of sorting the population. One of the earliest influential professors of education, Ellwood Cubberley, expressed this idea clearly in 1909: "Increasing specialization . . . has divided the people into dozens of more or less clearly defined classes, and the increasing centralization of trade and industry has concentrated business in the hands of a relatively small number." Schooling had to prepare the majority for work in subordinate roles while still being able to catch the rare individual who might progress.[29] The implement was testing. It quickly became much more than a tactic of distinguishing clever from not-so-clever. A whole science, philosophy, and ideology emerged, now usually known as Social Darwinism. Social Darwinists saw the whole world in terms of preformed racial types; these could be classified (Nordic, Alpine, Slav, etc.) and graded (with black people inevitably at the bottom—though that actually wasn't its primary concern).[30] At its worst, this ideology was spread enthusiastically by bodies such as the Eugenics Office (which was funded, inevitably, by a large business donor); in particular it promulgated laws in many states for the sterilization of those judged genetically inferior, to prevent them "breeding." It also provided ideological ammunition during the 1920s for a parallel movement abroad: the National Socialists in Germany.[31]

Most schools opted for a curriculum with a strong science and vocational skills strand, a stress on "American" traditions and history, and testing to sort people into appropriate bands for the future. This was to be the common basis of education. For a minority—the uncommon ones—higher education could give them a more liberal outlook.[32]

Within higher education, meanwhile, the literary establishment was still struggling to establish what should count as an "American literary tradition." By 1900, just about a dozen (less than ten per cent) American universities had developed graduate programs in American literature, though almost all had programs in European literature. But between 1900 and 1918 the number of colleges offering courses in American literature rose from 57 to 98 (though English literature courses were expanding at the same rate in this period). In this same period, a series of publishers started producing college textbooks of American literature: Little, Brown (1902), Houghton Mifflin (1903), Harper (1903), Scribner's (1904), Putnam (1909), and so on. Lorenzo Sears, in the Little, Brown anthology, commended to his young readers the works they would find within as "the product of our race and of our soil."[33]

A struggle took place after the First World War as academics set about trying to codify exactly what they meant by the banner of an "American tradition." This battle centered on the production of the Cambridge *History of American Literature* (1917–21). Its editors, Stuart Pratt Sherman, John Erskine, Carl van Doren (who wrote the entry on Cooper) and William Peterfield Trent (editor-in-chief) thought very much in terms of an "American literature." Opposite them stood a group of New Critics (most notably Irving Babbitt) who placed the emphasis on the formal characteristics of "great literature," never mind its source. Finally, there was a rising movement of young radical critics of both left and right, typified by Van Wyck Brooks and John Macy (from the left) and Randolph Bourne (from the right). But for all their disagreements, there was a demand in the air to identify, and thence to teach, an American tradition.

After the First World War, then, a new set of interests came together to generate a demand for a new curriculum, one mainly for the able who would go on, but for the rest inasmuch as they needed to become fully "American." In response, a series of publishers began to produce classics editions. Led by Scribner's, these years saw the release of fine editions that bore the imprint of quality. A famous painter was recruited to illustrate the Scribner's edition of *Mohicans*: N. C. Wyeth. Wyeth was already well known both as an artist and as a book illustrator. He was also a close friend of Theodore Roosevelt through their shared interest in the movement which later will provide another part of our jigsaw: the Wilderness Movement.

So what did it mean to produce a "classic"? Herbert Kliebard has depicted three strands in American educational thinking in this period.[34] The Child Development group, headed by G. Stanley Hall and aligned with Social Darwinism, sought to measure what each child had innately, and to educate just that much. The Social Efficiency group, headed by Joseph Rice (whose exposés of bad schooling had made his name) and strongly allied with local business interests, sought to teach those skills needed within the economy. The Social Meliorists, grouped around the sociologist Lester Frank Ward, sought to equip ordinary people with the means to combat the deleterious effects of urban industrial life. These three groups collided more in theory than in practice. But the curious thing to note is that for *none* of them is literature all that important. Its importance lay in that which they had in common: the need for an "American national culture." But what this meant was changing. When Harvard launched its "Five-Foot Shelf of Books" in 1909, it was clear that fine books, like fine art, were the mark of a fine mind, a gentleman's or a lady's breeding. As America moved into the 1920s, this idea became embattled.

In 1926, Harry Scherman, a New York advertising man, launched the Book-of-the-Month Club. This followed the success of a series called the Little Leather Classics, in which subscribers were sent, first, a slipcase for a book, then (if they liked the look of it) the book itself. These ventures reveal a good deal about the status of books and classics in this period. The Book-of-the-Month Club was one of many such clubs that sprang up in this period. It was by far the most successful, with over 100,000 members by 1929, and sold itself with unashamed brashness as the solution for the new rich who needed to have culture at their fingertips but did not have the time to find it for themselves. Much the same motive underlay the foundation of the *Reader's Digest* in 1922.

Scherman's success roused great antagonism from some, culminating in Dwight MacDonald's (1960) attack on what he termed "Mid-Cult." The critics particularly loathed the way Scherman promised "instant culture." Subscribe now! We'll choose for you! Don't be out of date any more! You needn't ever miss out on that important conversation again. Culture was no longer something to be developed because it set you apart, a genteel person. Now it was a means to an end, the end being acceptance and success.[35] But while classics were seen as good, at least as much emphasis was placed on the *new* in literature. The main thing was to be up to date. This is one of the ideological strands of the American Dream: the perennial renewal and commitment to change.

The results are interesting. On the one hand, the classic classics, as we might call them, have stayed in print continuously since the 1920s. Scribner's hardbound edition of *Mohicans* with the Wyeth paintings was still going strong in the late 1980s. The beauty of this no-compromise, unabridged edition lies as much in the quality of the paper and the binding as it ever could in Cooper's prose. And in 1994 Random House proudly announced yet another relaunch of the Modern Library edition, first issued in 1917. These editions seem to say: of course we should be read, but with no concessions. Simply, you will feel ennobled by the very handling of us. On the other hand we have had great trouble finding abridged American editions of *Mohicans*; we have begun to wonder whether there are many to be found!

There are exceptions, of course. Book-of-the-Month offered an abridged edition of the Leatherstocking Tales as an alternate choice in 1955; and *Reader's Digest* published a condensed edition of *Mohicans* in 1984. And for certain patriotic purposes, merciless abridgment was allowed, without pretense at care or cunning. The ultimate version of this kind has to be Keep-Worthy Books' edition. Published in 1945, this was almost certainly an edition destined for the front lines. At four by six-and-one-half inches, it would fit a soldier's breast pocket, alongside his folded *Superman* or *Captain America*. In this amazing edition, Cooper's book has shrunk to just thirteen pages![36] (see page 51.)

But this extreme abridgment is definitely unusual. In fact there seems to be a discrepancy between the ways America and Britain have gone about reproducing their classic versions of books like *Mohicans*, and thus have surrounded them with different meanings. And this, in the end, is the point.

Our argument ends up in an irony. Despite the rhetoric that surrounds them (of fine quality, the centrality of form, and so on) the most important things about classics is not their content at all. It is their name. To be a "classic" is to be assigned a place in the calendar of saints. It is to belong to a series and a social space. Frank Kermode captured this perfectly when he said that "the modern classic, and the modern way of reading the classic, are not to be separated."[37] The most important thing about classics therefore is the way they are announced, and announce themselves, to us. What most needs study is their look, their feel, their publicity, and their manner of distribution.[38] It is these, as much as anything, that make up the meaning of "reading a classic."

We have studied as many classic editions as we have been able to obtain. This was not easy. From time to time, one would emerge from a collector or a secondhand dealer. Even the British Library and the Library of Congress hold surprisingly few. One way to study them was to see what criteria governed the process of abridging the text. We could discover only two. The first of these was to eliminate those things which, for the time of publication, might prove distractions. Episodes about which publishers are nervous are the first to go. Thus, many abridged editions eliminate the killing of the colt; others severely edit the revelations of Cora's mixed race. But none change or eliminate the ending. Beyond that, the principle seems to be to reduce the descriptive load, and fit the overall length to the needs of the series.

This *is* significant. In the 1970s, boys' author Edward Blishen became a series editor of classics adaptations for the Piccolo Adventure Library. In a discussion of this work, he makes an interesting point about what is involved in rewriting a text and making it accessible:

To take an example from the Piccolo list: 20,000 *Leagues under the Sea* could obviously be translated into an urgent, laconic, modern narrative. But part of the experience of reading Jules Verne lies in the rounded, now and then mildly pompous, Victorian quality of Verne's story-telling. His aeronauts, off to the moon in *From the Earth to the Moon*, do not snap: "All systems go," they talk, like leisurely clubmen, about the opposed advantages of lying down and sitting up. A major sign of stress in the party engaged in *A Journey to the Centre of the Earth* is that, finding the bowels of the planet uncomfortably hot, they remove their waistcoats. It would not be Jules Verne a young reader was receiving, in any form, if these nineteenth century elements of style were altogether removed.[39]

Sad to say, the other functions of being a "classic" threaten to overwhelm its meaning as story and as myth. One abridged edition we came across took these other functions very seriously. It posed its readers proper teacherly questions, such as: "10. Women often show great and unexpected courage in times of danger. Give an incident to illustrate this in the case of Cora."[40] If any child managed to find pleasure, let alone classic meanings, in so pompous an edition, he or she deserves a very special school prize!

Turning *Mohicans* into a "classic" was an achievement. Certainly the novel has qualities that helped in the task, but more than that it depended on the investment of social and cultural energies. And this process did not happen automatically. We can demonstrate this fact by looking back *before* the achievement to the very first adaptation, an 1842 British dramatization. We have not managed to discover anything about the history of this version, which was published in Sheffield.[41] We do not know how often, if ever, it was performed. It is certainly British in origin—not just because the publisher was British but because of the form of the overall drama, which is a classic pastiche of Shakespeare. Written for the most part in blank verse, it borrows heavily on Shakespearian conventions. A "fool" called Triptolemus is introduced, who plays the role of comic foil to the heroic Heyward. Triptolemus is in love with another character, Kate, servant to Cora and Alice. She too acts as a foil, to the story's class differences. In mid-play, Kate discourses on her dependency on the two women: "Ay, there they go! Well, high folks can take a license of their gentility to do as they like; but if we poor ones would speak with other, we must e'en seek out opportunity, as Gammer Gurton sought her needle." And she goes to pursue her romance with "Trip."

Aside from the introduction of new characters, the broad sweep of the story remains. The two women journey with Heyward and Magua, who deceives them to get his revenge for past injuries from Munro. Hawkeye and the Mohicans rescue them and take them to the cave. The English are captured, and Cora refuses Magua's explicit demand that she become his bride, or face, regardless, being "the plaything of his passions." The play, however, elides everything from their rescue to the final scenes, by having Magua escape with Cora. But it holds back nothing on the deaths of Cora and Uncas, nor on the evident love between them (though it had introduced the curious note earlier of having Cora secretly also in love with Heyward).

The meanings the play attaches to all this, however, are vastly changed. For a start, the mock-Shakespearianism is a message in itself. It isn't easy to picture Hawkeye as some untutored frontiersman in an exchange like this:

*Heyward:* Our danger but begun! 'Tis strange methinks,
If we're discovered, that these Hurons come not.
*Hawkeye:* They wait the glent o'morn. An hour hence,
Will prove it my feelosophy be true;
I never larn'd to read, save in the book
Which natur shows me; but of Indian ways
I'll face the 'cutest scholar; ay, and tell
The habit of each beast that haunts the prairies.
Is't not enough? bring your deep scholars here,

(They that would scorn a simple man like me,
Which never knew a stroke that made a letter.)
Bring 'em with figures, rules, and compasses,
And set 'em i'the woods, that they may try,
By making longitudes, to free themselves.
Let them catch beavers with their lines o'latin . . .

To which Heyward's reply ("'Tis true indeed; each fits best in his place; / The woods,—the woodman' and his books—the scholar. / Elsewhere each is as ignorant as the other") sustains the sense that Hawkeye is not a mythic figure at all. He is just different, and belongs in another world.

This sense of the separation of worlds is there again when Chingackgook [sic] learns of Uncas's attraction to Cora: "I fear my son / Has look'd, when he forgot the white chief's child / Could never be an Indian's bride. Ah! youth, / Roving in wishes maketh worthless things / Desir'd because forbidden." Here are different worlds and peoples, best kept separate. But it is not to be divided by crude prejudices. Uncas, dying, speaks Lear-like of Cora: "The white chief's daughter! / Is she not dead?—Ah! Uncas will attend, / To clear her path from briars. Death—is—sweet.—[dies.]" Hawkeye then reveals to Munro Uncas's love for Cora and asks that they be buried together. Munro, who has not known of this love before and who has said nothing through the play about his attitudes to Indians, seems nonetheless to undergo a "change of heart": "Let it be so. An idle prejudice / Would ill beseem me, in this sorrowing hour. / Let one sod cover them." Since this is not a change in his character, it has to be a commentary on an assumed audience reaction.

The 1830s-40s in Britain saw the rise of a movement in solidarity with black slaves in America. Interestingly, this movement was especially strong in Sheffield. This may be entirely coincidental, since we do not know who wrote the play or where, if at all, it was performed. But certainly in its picture of race relations, this 1842 version is a mishmash of unresolved tensions. But, all in all, it is a confusion between past and future. On the one hand, in its dramatic form and in its use of an older language of race, it is "antique" and devotedly continues past modes. But threaded through these modes, on the other hand, are confused strands of newer discourses. But there are two things it most definitely is not. It is not a mythic version of *Mohicans*. Hawkeye is simply one good guy, but one best kept in his own place; he does not specially signify. And it is not by any definition a "classic." The story has not yet passed into that domain, and that is significant in itself.

CHAPTER 4    Movie Mohicans,

1909–1936

It should come as no surprise that the foremost medium through
which people know the *Mohicans* story is film. In large part this is
because *Mohicans* is a quintessentially American story, while film
is a quintessentially American medium. One might even say they
were made for each other.

It was realized early on in America, the "land of immigrants," that
film could reach parts of the population that books could not. For
print assumes literacy; film does not. (Cooper's book was initially
hampered in this respect.) It is significant, therefore, that in the
early history of American film the urban working classes were the
first commercial audience, often of foreign stock, illiterate, and
poor. For a nickel, a world of breathtaking movie entertainment was
made available to them. The middle class followed later, but not
after much complaining that the new medium was gauche and culturally debasing.

The period leading up to the First World War saw cinema established in a permanent fashion, as nickelodeons overtook theaters as the main leisure venues. By 1914 it is estimated that there were 14,000 nickelodeons, selling upwards of 30 million tickets a week. For the production companies, vertical integration was the next logical step, and they opened chains of cinemas that they owned directly. Another theme was the exportation of American movies overseas: in Europe especially, there was a ready market among those countries whose economies had been crippled by war.

Yet, although America came to dominate the world market in the postwar years, cinema remained essentially a medium through which Americans could talk to themselves. Hollywood became known as the "dream factory," in one sense a place where celluloid dreams were manufactured, in another a reflection of the American Dream itself. Indeed, the ever-expanding number of movies did not just echo the Dream, but added their own modifications. Consciously or unconsciously, they returned again and again to the themes of new beginnings, democracy, individualism, and the frontier.

So, too, they inevitably dealt with the native American, the Other in the Dream, in a genre that was to become a staple of the industry—the Western. It is ironic that, at a time when native Americans were fast becoming a forgotten people, they were remembered here as bloodthirsty savages in war paint, the enduring stereotype of the dime novels. Film could also lie as convincingly as any medium. But with Cooper's *Mohicans*, we hope to show that film became the medium par excellence for America to reflect on its secret self: "America."

## "The Indian, as an Indian, is rapidly disappearing"[1]

The 1909 movie *Leatherstocking*, a black-and-white "silent," is interesting primarily for two reasons. First, it was the earliest film adaptation of *The Last of the Mohicans*; despite its title, it took its cue from this particular Leatherstocking tale rather than any of the others. Second, it was directed by D. W. Griffith, one of the most influential film directors of all time, who, despite his politically controversial output, is still considered the founding father of American cinema.

Made by Biograph, one of the most important and most prolific early film production companies, the movie is essentially a "one-reeler," lasting fifteen minutes. The cast includes about twenty people, and of those identified, only one name would be recognizable to a modern audience, that of Mack Sennett, who went on to become the director of classic comedy movies. The film was shot on three consecutive days in August 1909 in New York state and was released the very next month.

Before we discuss the content of the movie itself, we need to look at the context of the rapidly changing market for film in the 1900s. Like the vast majority of movies, *Leatherstocking* was made to make money. But beyond that it was designed to fulfill a demand for a particular kind of narrative production. For it appeared at a time when the nature of cinema itself was changing, both artistically and commercially.

The medium was still very much in an embryonic form in the first decade of the century. The first movies had appeared as recently as the 1890s, and until 1907 cinema had played very much second fiddle to theater. Unsurprisingly, the two forms had a close, symbiotic relationship: initially, there were no cinema chains as such, and films were used as openers at vaudeville shows, to settle the audience down before the main performance (vaudeville being the American equivalent of the British music hall—populist theater entertainment mainly for the working and lower middle classes). Indeed, there was a history of visual novelties used in this way. Precursors to the movies included sing-along illustrated slides and Edison's Projecting Kinetoscope tours.

Very early movies designed for this market tended to be documentaries or news reports lasting only a few minutes. Their initial impact was startling: there are newspaper stories of audiences ducking under their seats during a film of an approaching train. But gradually, as the 1900s progressed, comedies and dramas become more numerous. They were generally easier and cheaper to make, and for these reasons they often lasted longer than the traditional fact-based material.

As these narrative films took off, the first cinemas designed solely for movie presentation became established. Because they charged a nickel (five cents) admission, they were dubbed "nickelodeons"—a derogatory term indicating the fact that the audience was primarily working class (the same constituency as for vaudeville). The usual bill in such early cinemas would include about an hour of mixed shorts, each lasting between eight and fifteen minutes, with screening times varying wildly depending on projector speeds. But it wasn't until 1907 that this trend really began to take off. Historians have ascertained that in that year there was a dramatic rise in the number of nickelodeons, with over five thousand in operation throughout the country by 1908.[2] Cinema had finally come into its own and had begun to eclipse theater as the primary medium of entertainment. The shift to cinema brought with it a greater demand for films, and this in turn led to many more dramas and comedies being made. 1907 was thus also the year in which comedies and dramas eclipsed documentaries as a proportion of film output.

Biograph was very much part of this new wave of moviemaking. Although companies sprang up all over the country to feed the new demand, New York played host to the "big three": Biograph, Vitagraph, and Edison. They pumped out films at an astonishing rate, using the same production teams and the same casts, which were interchangeable and moved from one film to the next. They also made large sums of money, and became models for the big studios of the 1930s onwards.

But not everybody was enthusiastic about what they were doing, and there was certainly a lot of prejudice surrounding the cinema boom. Most strikingly, there was a class-based antipathy. Middle-class commentators scorned the new medium: if vaudeville was "cheap" and gauche, movies were doubly so. Paternalists argued that movies would be detrimental to the spiritual well-being of the working class, because they would distract from more "improving" pastimes such as reading. One critic condemned the crossover for making audiences who would love film for its own aesthetic pleasures "endure the stupidity, the inanities, the crudities, sometimes the indecencies of cheap low vaudeville."[3] Less overtly, there were also fears that the new medium might not be controllable, and that it might be capable of transmitting subversive messages. On top of this, there was a lingering unease about the psychological effects on an audience of watching movies. There were scare stories in the press that, on the one hand, film acted as an opiate and caused lethargy and, on the other, that it led to "copycat" behavior; there were even tales that cinema-going could damage one's eyesight. Unsurprisingly, none of these claims was backed up with evidence, and all could be used to legitimate more political objections.

David Wark Griffith joined Biograph in 1908, just as the new wave was hitting its peak and the criticisms were gathering momentum. He began as an actor, screenwriter, and director, and ended up taking on the entire responsibility for Biograph's output. During his five years with the company, he made over 450 films and established himself as a major player in the world of film.[4] *Leatherstocking* was made early in his Biograph career and was part of a whirlwind production schedule. For this reason, not very much is known about it—and indeed many histories of early cinema (and Griffith biographies) do not list the film at all. Most of what we can say about it can be inferred from what we know of Griffith's career within Biograph generally, and, to an extent, from his post-Biograph output.

During his time making shorts at Biograph, and then later on much lengthier projects such as *Birth of a Nation* (1915) and *Intolerance* (1916), Griffith experimented with the creative use of the frame and rhythmic editing to push forward the boundaries of what could be achieved in a movie. He also employed young actors who were open to direction for movie performance, rather than established names who were more bound to the style of stage acting. He did not invent these techniques, but developed them to the point that they became an accepted syntax. In so doing, he almost single-handedly raised the status of the job of director from a "nothing job" to that of auteur.

But recent evaluations of his career have focused on the content of his films, and especially *Birth of a Nation*, rather than just on his contribution to the development of a "film language." *Birth of a Nation* was an epic story set during the Civil War that portrayed black people in an openly racist manner and featured the Ku Klux Klan as the saviors of the nation. Of course, the politics of the tale are obviously unacceptable by today's standards, but we should also know that the film caused a storm at the time and was banned in a number of states for inciting racial hatred. *Birth* was some seven years in the future when Griffith started at Biograph, but it was here that we can see him starting to develop many of the traits that would later make him famous—and infamous. Historians have established that he was a supremely ambitious man and saw Biograph as a place where he could experiment and make a name for himself.

In terms of the craft of filmmaking itself, he investigated the possibilities of framing and editing from the earliest shorts and gained confidence over time.

Part of this process involved developing a day-to-day working method that could withstand the rigors of the schedule, to which end he went about making working partnerships with actors and crew members that could survive film after film. Perhaps the most important of these relationships was with cameraman Billy Bitzer, who worked on *Leatherstocking* and stayed with Griffith on *Birth of a Nation*. There is no question that many of these partnerships turned into genuine friendships, and Griffith often asked cast and crew for suggestions, which he would use. Nobody was in any doubt, however, about who ruled the set. As far as the content of the films was concerned, Griffith never hid his southern, noble background or his political views, and this influenced the kind of films he made from the start. He liked action pictures and argued that silent films lent themselves naturally to dramatic chases and fight scenes. Interestingly, there is evidence that part of his interest in action stories stemmed from a love of the work of Fenimore Cooper—especially the emphasis on chases, and the idea of "families in peril." The two men certainly shared a belief in the dramatic possibilities of placing white protagonists at the mercy of "savages," be they black or Indian.

But more than this, Griffith believed that cinema had the potential to be, if not art, then something better than eyewash for the masses. Although it was inevitable that most of his Biograph films were cranked out by the week and only lasted for a few minutes, he liked the idea that they should contain a message. Some were simple morality plays; others were overtly political. Later, he would argue that film could be an agent of change in a more proactive sense, and *Birth of a Nation* was the ultimate expression of this belief.

This desire to raise the status of the medium led Griffith to adopt the idea of adapting great works of literature. In short, they were great source material for the kind of morality plays he enjoyed. In addition, adapting them for the screen would fulfill two financial objectives. First, it would attract people to the cinemas because the stories already had a "product awareness" factor in the market. Second, it would counter middle-class prejudices against the film medium and possibly even open up a new bourgeois audience.[5] *Leatherstocking* was thus an obvious choice for a Biograph film.

THE LEATHERSTOCKING
Director: D. W. Griffith (1909)[6]

The film opens outside a house (intended to be a barracks?) with two soldiers and two women. One of the women picks up and hugs a little girl who is with them. A surly Indian (Magua) enters and speaks to one of the soldiers. In response, the two women go into the building, to get ready to leave.

The party leaves on horseback, led by Magua. The remaining soldier waves goodbye as they depart.

Magua leads them down a track past some trees, with one soldier in the rear, walking. We see an Indian behind, stalking them. Then again, further down the track, with dust flying up, we see the Indian shadowing them.

By a river, another Indian (different clothing and icons) is watching. A frontiersman enters and greets him joyfully. (They are Chingachgook and Hawkeye.) They talk, then hear sounds, and hide behind a bush: enter Magua leading the white party. Magua senses their presence, and leads the horses quickly away, followed by the soldier.

On the track again, Magua leaps aside, turns on the soldier, knocks him unconscious, and makes off with the horses. Meanwhile Hawkeye and Chingachgook come out of hiding to greet Heyward and the women. The soldier on the track recovers and runs back to warn the others. The party exits hurriedly.

An open stretch of scrubland. Magua emerges cautiously from cover, followed by more Indians. The white party is advancing nervously along a road. Suddenly Magua appears in front of them, leading an attack on them. The little girl is seized and dangled upside down, but the Indian is shot just in time to save her. The Indians retreat. Then more appear, there is more gunfire, one soldier falls. Retreat. The Indians advance, capture the fallen man, and scalp him.

The white party is running over an open field, closely pursued by the Indians. They enter an old Fort, and slam the gate shut just in time. The Indians try to scale the palisade walls but are driven off.

A siege. In the fort, the women pray and clutch the little girl. Outside, the Indians continue to fire at the fort. Inside again, in a sustained shot Hawkeye reveals a plan to Heyward, takes off his coat and puts on a bearskin headcover. The camera pans to him being helped out a small opening near the river. He enters the lake, managing to avoid the eyes of watching Indians. Eventually they see him, but think him a bear.

In the fort, the little girl is being hugged tenderly. Chingachgook is leading the defense. Outside, the Indians are again beaten away.

On the lake, the Indians spot Hawkeye and give chase. He goes down the rapids, with Indians pursuing in canoe. (Intercut, the Indians backing away from the fort under fire.) Hawkeye overturns the canoe; one Indian drowns, the other is killed.

Inside the fort, Chingachgook discovers he has run out of powder. The Indians attack again and force open the gate. After a fight inside, they are all captured, and led out of the fort. Hawkeye arrives back at the barracks, delivers his request for help, then collapses. A guard rushes off to gather help. The soldiers, led by Hawkeye, rush towards the fort to try to rescue their party.

The prisoners are put to the test. Neither Heyward nor Chingachgook will flinch when threatened with a knife or a tomahawk. Chingachgook is tied to a tree, to be burned alive. The troops arrive at the fort to find it already empty. Chingachgook is surrounded by wood, and the Indians begin to dance around him. We see the troops setting off in pursuit. Fire is set to the wood around Chingachgook, but as it catches the troops arrive, drive off the Indians, and free all the prisoners.

A pull to focus on a parting: all the whites are leaving together. Hawkeye says an affectionate farewell to Chingachgook. Chingachgook, alone, does a slow farewell dance, arms raised, and the film ends with his head slumped.

END

Technically speaking, this film is not exceptional. Some innovative editing is in evidence, and this is especially true of the scenes in which Hawkeye and the soldiers race to rescue Magua's prisoners before they are harmed (with Chingachgook about to be burned at the stake). Here, there is some effective intercutting between the parallel storylines, used to generate tension and drive the plot forward. It works well, and indeed many historians are agreed that this particular technique was the invention of Griffith himself. Elsewhere, however, the editing is not so interesting and demonstrates few of the flourishes of Griffith's later films. Most of the other cuts are very simple, and all the shots are fixed-angle, except a couple that incorporate pans. Similarly, the performances are not nuanced in the way that later Griffith films would demonstrate. Henry Walthall (who stayed with Griffith on *Birth*) does his best as Hawkeye, but the other roles are desperately hammy—and it is difficult to imagine that 1909 audiences would not have thought so, too. Perhaps this is an indication that for all Griffith's editing skill and his desire to use fresh actors, his dramatic sensibility remained rooted in the nineteenth century (he was born in 1875).

In the same way, the women's roles are hardly notable. This is unusual for a Griffith film because the director was well known for nurturing female talent (most famously, the Gish sisters). The statuesque Linda Arvidson, who plays Cora,[8] was one of Griffith's early favorites, but she does not have the opportunity to shine, and in this version of *Mohicans* the women are little but simpering fools, there to be rescued.

The portrayal of the Indians similarly shows little flair. It sticks pretty much to the stereotype favored by the dime novels of the period: the "bad" Indians are essentially bloodthirsty sadists, while the good ones are faithful followers of the whites. All the Indians are played by white actors, and at the time there was considered nothing wrong with this. White actors in "redface" had already been on stage for over fifty years; Indians were considered incapable of playing themselves—or rather, of portraying the white image of themselves, which more polished white actors could do much better. Who indeed could bring to life the stereotyped white conception of the Indian more accurately than a white actor in redface?[9]

But for all the shortcomings of the editing and performances, the plotting of Griffith's film is truly remarkable. In this respect, the film's main strength is also its chief weakness. The way in which the *Mohicans* story has been edited and abridged to suit the aesthetics of a fifteen-minute silent movie is a triumph of action screenwriting. Everything has been pared back to the most exciting parts of the story: the initial chase, Hawkeye's daring escape, the massacre at the fort, and the final rescue. Each dramatic incident follows the other without a breather, like a boxing combination.

The punches seem doubly hard because of the violence of some scenes. In particular, there are various tomahawk attacks, a child is shaken in the air by its leg, and there is a scalping that is edited at the last moment. (The scene at the fort is especially highly charged—as well as being quite spectacular—and forms one of the highlights of the film.) This violence is arguably the aspect of the film that is most striking to a modern audience because, viewed from a perspective in which movies are assumed to have become more violent over time, it is unexpected. In fact, many examples of early cinema contained graphic violence, as well as scenes of drug-taking and nudity, and this was not censored until the Hays Code of 1930. Thereafter, American film became bowdlerized, and sex and violence did not reappear to any degree until the 1960s and '70s.

But, even if *The Leatherstocking* works on its own terms in this regard, too much of the story has been cut for it fairly to reflect the

The closing shot of Griffith's film—Chingachgook performs his "dance of death" and goes the way of all "vanishing Americans."

original book. In short, there is no room for subtlety or depth. There's no wilderness, no love interest, no notion of "the rise and fall of nations," and, above all, *almost* no sense of a "dying tribe"— in other words, none of the things that made Cooper's tale special and raised it above the level of a simple adventure story. Of course, to have tried to include these themes in a fifteen-minute film would have led to disaster. Yet, if one of Griffith's intentions was to show that film was capable of the task of adapting literature, his success was severely limited in this instance.[10]

Ultimately, this is why the film as a whole disappoints. It is constrained by the limitations of the medium and thus by the horizons of its makers. Griffith was less interested in mobilizing the *Mohicans* story to make a point than in fulfilling a commercial demand. If anything, he was making a statement about film itself (that it was capable of being taken seriously) rather than about society in general. For these reasons it is a film overdetermined by the circumstances of its production, and thus more important for what it represents than what it says.

Movie Mohicans, 1909–1936     65

But there is one moment that deserves our attention—the final shot. It is remarkable, first, for its abandoning of Cooper's original story. Cooper had had no doubt but that Hawkeye would stay with Chingachgook, not abandon him. Griffith has the Indian left alone, as the white party returns to civilization. It is unusual as an early attempt by Griffith to use the camera to attach an emotional tone to the shot. The pull-to-focus which he uses marks the shot out as having significance, revealed in the slow dance of death that Chingachgook performs. Alone in the wilderness, he is, literally, the last of the Mohicans. There was at this time a veritable cult of the Vanishing Native. Photographers and filmmakers from the East regularly headed West to capture the "dying tribes." Expeditions were funded to gain knowledge of them before they all disappeared. It was as if, with the end of the Indian Wars, whites could only remove Indian peoples from their minds by telling themselves that they were literally passing away.[11] Griffith, in the one moment of real emotional intensity in his film, fully participates in this deletion. It is a sad irony that he should be creating one of his filmic techniques precisely in order to tell a lie about native Americans.

## ". . . so widely separated by the mystery of birth . . ."

*"Everything unnecessary is kept out of the picture. It is what Mr. Tourneur excludes that makes his individual scenes complete."[12]*

After Griffith's 1909 version, Griffith himself went on to make a number of other "Indian" films, among them *The Indian Runner's Romance* (1912). Two other early filmmakers, Powers and Thanhouser, also made single-reel versions. Of these films, we can find no surviving copies or detailed information. But in 1920 a new version was made, the first in fact to turn Cooper's novel into a major film.

*Last of the Mohicans* was filmed on location at Big Bear Lake and the Yosemite Valley, the latter a very popular site with filmmakers and already a national park (one of the earliest successes of the American wilderness movement). Though this film is credited to Maurice Tourneur and Clarence Brown, in fact the latter was largely responsible for its shape. Two weeks into the production, Tourneur had an accident that confined him to bed for a long period. Brown took over responsibility for all the filming, and Tourneur only saw the resultant rushes. Toward the end of its production, the film went way over budget, and Brown had to persuade the directors of Associated Producers to go out to Universal Studios (where the film was edited) to view the half-completed film. The directors were persuaded to put up an additional $25,000, and lived to be glad, if Brown is to believed: "It proved to be the only financial success Associated Producers ever had."[13]

Brown brought all his cinematographic skills to fruition in the film. He filmed early and late rather than at midday in order to get a depth of light into the scenes. According to Brownlow, one of the cameramen subsequently recalled that they pioneered the use of panchromatic stock for this film. Among the special effects the film developed was the use of smokepots in order to generate an effect of sunlight through mist, the use of a fire engine to simulate a forest rainstorm, and, for one shot, mounting a camera on a perambulator in order to track Cora and Alice's escape from the massacre.

The resultant film was splendidly received. But it had done curious things to the narrative and meanings of *Mohicans* in the course of its transformations.

THE LAST OF THE MOHICANS (1920)
Directors: Maurice Tourneur & Clarence Brown
Starring: Harry Lorraine (Hawkeye), Barbara Bedford (Cora), Lillian Hall (Alice), Wallace Beery (Magua), Albert Roscoe (Uncas), Henry Woodward (Heyward)
[Note: For ease of understanding, captions are shown in italics.]

Opening scenes: *A summer afternoon in the Year of Grace 1757, on a hilltop overlooking the valley of the Hudson river.* There is a long shot over a hill. *Two tragic figures, remnants of a once huge Indian tribe—Chief Great Serpent and his son Uncas.* A shot of them against the hills. *"The palefaces are our friends. Go to the Fort yonder and tell them of the danger that threatens."* Uncas nods and runs off down the hill.

*Fort Edward . . . , one of the few outposts not yet attacked.* The yard inside the fort, soldiers exercising. *Even in a wilderness, gently-bred women somehow maintain the grace and quality of life.* We see a room with dancing women, soldiers, and children. *Cora Munro, on a visit* plays the harp; *Alice— her lighthearted sister* is teaching two little girls to dance. Next *Captain Randolf—more interested in women than warfare.* Cross shots of him and Cora. *Major Heyward—in love with capricious Alice* sees Alice dancing and almost leaves. He is recalled, and joins her. *The eternal spirit of youth, joying while it may—heedless of the gathering storm.* The dance comes to an end.

"*Do tell us a story, General Webb.*" This older man stands in storytelling position, but stops when Uncas enters. Cora looks concerned. "*The Hurons are on the warpath. They have drunk the firewater of the French and have listened to their lying tongues.*" Cora looks at Uncas: *Her girlish fancy investing the young Chief with a halo of romance.* Webb and Uncas exit after a brief conversation. Cora turns to Randolf: "*Surely among his own people he is a prince.*" Randolf looks shocked, angry: "*You! The daughter of Colonel Munro! Admiring a filthy savage!*"

Fort William Henry. A caption tells us about Colonel Munro's defenses against the French. Enter an exhausted soldier, warning that Montcalm has managed to cross the lake. Magua arrives carrying a message. Colonel Munro, picking up a "haloed" picture of his daughters: "*God grant my messenger has reached Fort Edward—else I may never see my daughters again!*"

Magua delivers his message to General Webb and his officers. We see it, handwritten. Webb dictates a response. He tells the girls they can go, with Magua, to meet their father.

Bedtime, Cora and Alice in virginal white nightdresses. Cora comforts Alice: "*Nothing to fear, we'll soon be with father.*" But Alice, *haunted by fears*, has a premonition of trouble: "*Promise me you'll never desert me!*" Cora cuddles her.

*Dawn.* Marshaling the troops and marching out. As the women enter, we see Magua playing with a knife and a scalp. Alice is fearful of him. Randolf walks towards him: "*Are you the guide?*" Magua nods, coldly. Webb to Randolf: "*Perhaps Captain Randolf will aid Major Heyward in protecting the ladies.*" Randolf declines, saying his "*duty lies with his troops.*"

Riding out together, until the parting of the ways. *A secret path, which only Indian eyes can find.* Magua cuts a way through the dense forest. Here they're joined by the grotesque-looking David Gamut, who sings a psalm to them. An Indian watches them from the bushes. *Hours later, drenched and discouraged in a blinding rainstorm.* Hawkeye and the Mohicans are sheltering under a tree. In back, Magua and his party enter. Heyward approaches Hawkeye and asks for help—they're lost. "*Impossible . . . !*" When Hawkeye goes to look at Magua, he's gone. "*I suspect the varmint covets your scalps! Come—the woods are no longer safe!*" Again, a rear-view shot of them being watched.

They go to a *hiding place known only to Hawkeye*, in a series of caves. They settle down to sleep. "*Uncas watches,*" says Chingachgook. Cora looks at him meaningfully: *The bond of a common danger—drawing together these two, so widely separated by the mystery of birth.* There are repeated cross shots of Cora looking at Uncas silhouetted in the cave entrance. He joins her, and they watch the moon rise. He speaks to her *simple words of a savage—yet revealing depth and imagination.* Hawkeye and Chingachgook smoke.

Cora begins to contemplate her attraction to Uncas, who is out of shot standing on guard. Hawkeye stands at the back, symbolically diminished here as he actually was in the whole film.

Gamut gets out his flute, but Chingachgook stops him brusquely; they must have silence.

Canoes land; the Hurons are hunting for them. They all wait, nervously. Uncas to Cora: *"Will you not be afraid?"* Cora shakes her head. Outside, the men wait and the Hurons get nearer. There are exchanges of fire (with brilliantly simple photography capturing the materiality of the fighting). Cora and Alice are loading the rifles for the men. Now, there is hand-to-hand fighting, including one struggle on the edge of the cliff. Eventually the Hurons are driven off. Cora discovers they've run out of powder. At the front of the cave, they all look out, worried. A sniper fires from a hiding place in a tree. Hawkeye shoots and wounds him, and he dangles in agony. Hawkeye wastes his last shot in *A deed of mercy*. They retreat into the caves.

Hawkeye and Chingachgook ride off on the horses, to make it seem they've all fled. Uncas is stopped by Cora, and meaningful looks pass between them: *"What the Great Spirit wills, shall happen."* A long smoldering look, then Uncas runs. The Hurons come hunting and eventually find them.

Enter Magua: *"Magua does not kill his prisoners, he tortures them."* They are taken away. *Keen eyes have watched the failure of the ruse.* The three captives are hauled away by the Indians as far as an abandoned blockhouse. From a distance we see Hawkeye and the Mohicans watching. Magua throws Alice to the side and turns to Cora: *"If you would save the Yellow Hair, consent to be my squaw!"* Cora, horrified, nonetheless seems ready to agree, to save Alice. *"No! No! Rather let us die together!"* cries Alice.

We see Heyward tied up, and a hand coming round the corner and cutting his bonds. A fight ensues. Alice is rescued just before she is raped by one of the Indians. Magua and Chingachgook battle with knives, and Magua falls apparently killed—but then jumps up and escapes.

Now to Fort William Henry, without further ado. At the fort Randolf makes an approach to Cora, touching her hand; she pulls back. *Smarting with the rebuff, Randolf determines to have it out with her.* We see Cora and Randolf together, her rejecting him, and his offer of a cloak: *Meekness first, then a burst of pride and anger*, and Randolf storms out. Uncas arrives, and in a long slow scene offers her a cloak. She smiles, opens to him and accepts it. Randolf, walking outside in a huff, has disturbed something. He calls some soldiers. Cora hides Uncas. Enter Randolf, suspicious, who exits angrily in the face of her denials.

Munro's HQ, discussing the crisis. Enter Randolf to listen. Munro explains that if Montcalm's Indians knew how weak they were, they could have their scalps by the next day. At end of conference, Randolf remains to ask: *"Is our condition really so bad, sir?"* Munro nods. Exit Randolf: *The fear that grows in the heart of the coward.* The next thing we see is *Within the enemy lines, the traitor.* Randolf is being received by Montcalm. Fade out and up on *Under a flag of truce, Montcalm summons Munro to a conference.* Montcalm speaks to Munro: *"Colonel, the fall is inevitable . . . I know the guns on your left rampart are useless. You will never be able to resist my attack."* Munro is horrified: *The very words which he himself had spoken.* Munro looks at his officers, only Randolf can't meet his eyes. *"What about the women and children?"* Montcalm looks at the Indians behind him, they nod: *The honor of Montcalm.*

*That night—to the everlasting shame of our civilization—covetous white men sold firewater to the Hurons, debauching the red men with drunken orgies . . . The war-dance of the flaming arrows—overture to the chant of Death.* We see curiously unclear shots of Indians riding and firing burning arrows against the backdrop of the lake.

*Morning, under a leaden sky.* The English march out, flanked by the French. We see the Hurons drinking. Magua leers at Cora. There is much taunting, then . . . the attack.

The massacre scene is long, mostly in dense longshot, cut in with occasional scenes of an Indian drinking then attacking a mother with a baby in a cart. He kills the baby, though the mother clubs him down. In the midst we see Gamut leading Cora and Alice away. Magua searches for the women and finds them: *"The day of Magua has come! Follow to my wigwam, Dark Hair!"* When Cora refuses, he grabs the fainting Alice and runs. Cora has to follow him. This is intercut with a shot of Gamut running away absurdly into the forest. The massacre continues, with scenes of drunken Indians reveling and killing wounded soldiers. We see Randolf, trying to hide from the battle in the powder magazine. But Indians find it and drop torches in, blowing him up. The massacre winds on, with more shots of Indians chasing and killing. The scene closes with a shot of a live horse licking the nose of a dead one and a wide-angle shot of the fort, with fires and bodies.

*Amid the smoldering ruins*: Chingachgook, Uncas, Munro, and Hawkeye. Uncas finds a scrap of the cloak he gave to Cora, and shows it to Munro. They head out in pursuit. Cut to *Magua—seeking hospitality in the camp of the peaceful Delawares*, who drags in Cora and Alice, both terrified. Hawkeye and the Mohicans are close behind.

Inside the main Delaware tent: *Indian justice—the ancient tribal laws of the Delawares, impartially administered by a council of three wise men.* Magua and Uncas eye each other, while the women look on distressed. The oldest judge delivers their verdict: *"According to the laws of Manitou, Uncas will take the Dark Hair."* There is delight among Uncas, Hawkeye, and his friends. *"But Yellow Hair is Magua's lawful captive."* Horror strikes them; but when they try to intervene, they are hauled off by the Delawares. Magua curses them. The Chief to Magua: *"Magua, the law of sanctuary protects you until sundown."* Magua seizes Alice, who faints. Cora pleads, first with the Chief who rejects her plea, then with Magua: *"I will go with you, Magua—in place of my sister."* Hawkeye pleads with her not to do this, but she is resolute. The parting scene. Magua imperiously summons her to follow; she strokes and kisses the head of her sister. A desperate Uncas cries after Magua: *"When the sun goes down, I will be on your trail!"* Magua curses him.

*Afar in the wilderness—a camp in the night.* Cora seizes a chance to run away. Magua gives chase: *Ever behind her—the leering face of Magua.* They come out on a high promontory, seen from far below then in close-up. Cora is trapped at the edge, with Magua behind her; *"One step nearer, and I'll jump!"* Magua slowly sits, facing her. *Through the weary hours of the night . . . Waiting with the Indian's inexorable patience, for the outcome of her struggle against the overpowering desire to sleep.* We watch as she is nearly nodding off, with Magua watching, apparently off-guard.[14]

*Across the trackless waste—the cry of heart to heart*: Uncas is tracking her. Finally Cora's eyes droop, and she sleeps. Magua creeps up on her, his shadow envelopes her, he grabs her wrist, there is a frozen tableau, then she throws herself backwards. Uncas arrives to find her hanging from Magua's hand, dangling over the cliff. Uncas can do nothing, but Magua takes his knife and hacks at Cora's hand. We see her fall, a dot plunging through the sky. Now Magua and Uncas fight on the promontory. They roll back off the promontory, down the cliff side. At the bottom, Magua rises and in slow motion plunges his knife into Uncas. Too late, Chingachgook and Hawkeye arrive to see Magua limping away. Hawkeye shoots him from a great distance, and there is a dramatic shot of him falling and tumbling over the waterfall. They find Cora dead next to Uncas, who is dying. Before he dies, we see his hand reach and take Cora's.

*In a beautiful sunlit valley.* Indian girls carry flowers and a body: Cora's. *And on a lonely crag*, a funeral pyre has been erected for Uncas. Down below, Gamut sings quietly as we see Cora's body being strewn with flowers. Above, a dove is released for Uncas. Hawkeye looks at Munro, telling him to take horse and leave with Alice. Munro nods. Alice throws herself on her sister's grave, but is led away. Hawkeye stands beside Chingachgook, who utters the words of mourning: *"Woe for the race of red men! In the morning of my life I saw the sons of my forefathers happy and strong—and before nightfall I have seen the passing of the last of the Mohicans."* Hawkeye offers his hand to Chingachgook and it is taken. A final silhouette shot shows the funeral pyre against the sky.

END

This epic version of the story is beautiful to watch, even to many who have lost the skills of watching silent films, and has passed into an undeserved oblivion. What is remarkable about it is not so much that it introduces an important additional character (Randolf, the coward and traitor) but the way it marginalizes Hawkeye and Chingachgook. Though present at the beginning and the end, their role is minimal in the crucial parts. The focus is on the triad of Cora, Magua, and Uncas. This is not an accidental outcome. As film historian Jan-Christopher Horak has shown, other scenes that would have placed Hawkeye more centrally were in fact shot, but were left out of the finished film.[15] Horak in fact reads the film in a very literary way, as a visual debate about "culture" versus "nature," and Cora's fatal transition to the latter. This seems to us to be not so much wrong, as too abstract to make sense of the film's strength and appeal. We can understand the film better if we place it more firmly in its time.

By 1920 the film industry had achieved a stable position in American culture. The number of cinemas was rising, investment in film was growing, and cinema audiences were socially mixed and acceptable in a way that they had not been before 1915. The latter date is highly significant: it is the year of *Birth of a Nation*. Griffith's racist masterpiece, with its paean to the Ku Klux Klan, had contradictory effects on the place of cinema. On the one hand, it made cinemagoing thoroughly respectable. Here was an epic and a wonderful piece of filmmaking. Now middle-class audiences could feel culturally safe in going to the movies. On the other hand, the film had been greeted with great protests from black communities, and with riots in a number of cities.[16]

Birth of a Nation is centrally a story of the American Civil War and of the divisive horrors of the war between North and South. It is in effect a plea for reconciliation between whites. But its central villain is the Negro, personified by a black politician who is not only corrupt but lusts after "white flesh." The female he most desires is Little Sister. One of the turning points in the film is his attempt to capture and rape her, which results in her committing suicide by throwing herself from a high rock, in a scene not only reminiscent of Cora's death scene in Mohicans, but which (according to Kevin Brownlow) was almost certainly directly borrowed from it.[17] Griffith was famous for his love of such classic American tales. In short, then, the climactic moment in Birth of a Nation is probably directly lifted from Cooper's tale, visualized in a way that exceeds the skills Griffith displays in the 1909 film (in which Cora does not even die).

Griffith's 1915 film immediately came to symbolize racial division in America: One had to be for or against it. The film seemed to make an explicit argument for the irreconcilability of racial differences. The black, the nonwhite, was the enemy. Though we cannot be sure, we suspect that part of the appeal of Mohicans to Tourneur and Brown was the ability of that story to offer an answer to Birth of a Nation. Certainly, at this time, Tourneur was regarded as Griffith's main competitor as a director. And as Griffith's career went into steep decline after 1915, so Tourneur's rose. What better way to seize the ascendancy than to make a riposte to the other master's film?[18]

For that is what the 1920 version of Mohicans surely is. If, as our opening review quotation suggests, the film's completeness is in what it leaves out, then the biggest change is in its placing center stage the sexual attractions of Cora and Uncas, and Magua. The film opens with as stark a contrast as you could conceive between the world of the Mohicans (lonely, misty mountaintops) and that of the English (pleasantries and dance within the fort). From the moment Cora sets eyes on Uncas, she is fascinated, to the open disgust of

Cora and Uncas, symbolically united in death as they could not be in life.

Randolf who also desires her. At the scene in the cave, again she is drawn to Uncas; and the narration tells us of "the bond of a common danger—drawing these two together, so widely separated by the mystery of birth." Then when Uncas speaks to her, the captions tells us they were "simple words of a savage—yet revealing depth and imagination."[19]

The end of the film, in this interpretation, is of great significance. After the high drama and wonderful photography of the confrontation between Cora and Magua, after the fall of Cora, Magua and Uncas fight to the death. Uncas falls, and Magua runs, to be belatedly shot by the arriving Hawkeye. Dying, and with his friends kneeling beside him, Uncas reaches out slowly and takes the hand of the dead Cora. It is a moment of sad reconciliation. Having sought to protect what he could never have in life, nonetheless, dying he can touch and hold his loved one. What had been irreconcilable in *Birth of a Nation* has become symbolically resolved, albeit in death.[20]

The context of the film, of course, was much more than a conflict between two leading personalities in the film industry. In American society, generally, a great conflict was brewing over the "mystery of race." This was the rising influence of social Darwinist ideas, the myths of IQ and of innate intelligence and, in its extreme forms, the rise of deeply racist ideologies that did not stop in the U.S. but crossed the Atlantic to Germany and provided part of the intellectual justification of National Socialism.[21] There were many strands to this new fascination with "race" and heredity in America. There was a driving wish on the part of American businesses to see an "American" character formed. There was a vicious assault on poor whites, after the threat their 1880s populist movement had posed. This expressed itself particularly in the eugenicist statutes passed in twenty-seven states, permitting the enforced sterilization of women deemed to be genetically disordered. The evidence for such disorder? This ranged from "feeble-mindedness" through alcoholism and masturbation to the simple offence of having too many children.

A national Eugenics Record Office was established in 1917, funded by the widow of a railway magnate. Its intent was to press into law in all states such eugenically inspired legislation. At the same time, an increasingly vigorous and successful racial ideology preached the impending doom of America because of immigration. Perhaps the low point of this campaign was Madison Grant's *The Passing of the Great Race* in 1918. Immigrants were denied entry to America on the basis of spurious tests, often carried out in a language they hardly spoke, but deemed to prove their inherited deficiencies. Easily remediable diseases, such as pellagra (a condition resulting from malnutrition) were blamed on racial failings. In short, American society in this period was riven with distress lines, all centered on supposed "mysteries of birth." In the face of this division, it is hard not to see Tourneur and Brown's film as a weak but genuine attempt to reassert a liberal belief in the possibility of "races" living together.[22]

But for all that, the film is a work of genuine beauty and power. Visually, some of its shots have never been bettered in any other version. The whole scene leading to the death of Cora contains some of the most stunning use of scenery it has ever been our pleasure to see. This film undoubtedly is due a revival—preferably in one of the tinted editions in which it was first shown.

**"The Last of the Mohee-cans is a great book, but when do we eat?"**

Two other *Mohicans* films were made in the 1920s. The first, a *Leatherstocking* compilation made in 1924 by George B. Seitz, sadly has disappeared. The second is a real oddity and worth a digression, if only because it shows the ready availability of the *idea* of Cooper's story for quite contrary purposes. Made in 1926, *The Last of the Mohee-cans* is more than a spoof on the original. It is a loving acknowledgment of what at the same time it debunks.

THE LAST OF THE MOHEE-CANS (1926)

*One Punch McTeague . . . The life of a prize-fighter is like a woman's skirt— getting shorter every day.* Two men are sitting on the steps of a hospital. One is being unbandaged by the other. *One Punch McTeague—so dumb he thinks an aspirin tablet is something to write on.* The attention shifts to the man doing the unbandaging. *The wise-cracking manager who ate dog biscuits so he could growl louder at the referee.* We learn that McTeague has lost, yet again . . . *and he's still stuck on that dame who's got him readin' highbrow books.*

They go hunting for food, and after some Chaplinesque gags and pratfalls they seek out McTeague's girl. She is being persuaded by McTeague's rival to come to his upper-class party. He lends her a good book to read—the kind the party will be celebrating. It is, guess what? As he leaves, they arrive. McTeague to the girl: *"The Last of the Mohee-cans is a great book, but when do we eat?"* After more visual gags, they arrive at the party, but quickly display how out of their place they are. At the meal, McTeague doesn't know what to do with the artichokes. But at the same time, the "literati" partygoers appear effete and silly.

It is time for an after-dinner story from McTeague. As he begins, the scene dissolves into the fiction: *"In the days of Columbus all good Indians were dead except one who was entitled Mohee-can. He was saving the heroine like in the movies but got caught."* Indians are war-whooping round a couple who are being burnt at the stake. Enter the hero, blacked up like a minstrel: *"The hero calls for help on a primitive radio."* The radio looks as though it is weaved out of twigs. *"So Paul Revere and his 'Iron Horse' go to the rescue."* Revere rides in and effects the rescue but runs out of bullets. So he stuffs a book down his trousers, and waves his buttocks in the sky so all the arrows are embedded harmlessly.

Revere to Mohee-can: *"Fly with the girl, I'll meet you at the Corner House!"* There follows a hilarious scene, in which Mohee-can and the girl run, while Revere bashes the pursuing Indians on the head with a frying pan. As they are congratulating each other on the rescue, up jumps the last, stunned

Indian to kill our blacked-up hero. Revere is left to say: *"That was the last of the Mohee-cans."*

Back to the party, and the literati have been fooled. They loved the story! But then, McTeague is recognized by his rival. Shift to the boxing ring, and a challenge from the rival. There follows a long slapstick fight scene involving a violin accompaniment, a pin stuck through the canvas to rouse McTeague when he is knocked out, and two homosexuals who are cheering on the boxing excitedly. In the end, the heroine, seeing McTeague losing, tells him he must win for the sake of their future. Aroused like a demon, he finally wins. And there the film abruptly stops, with the heroine offering a kiss to McTeague and the manager.

END

This curious film, about whose origins we know nothing, is revealing in a number of ways—first, for its intense class-consciousness, in which Cooper's book is evidently redolent of a middle-class, literati view of the world. But the literati are the object of great mockery. *Mohicans* may be a topic for middle-class dinner parties, but almost certainly all they know is the title. McTeague, the working class interloper, readily fools them with his spoof tale.[23] There is also a happy blurring of characters and episodes, with the real Paul Revere contentedly cohabiting with Cooper's fictional character. And of course, above all, there is the self-conscious play with the ways the cinema uses and confuses histories, so concisely captured in those wonderful sentences: "In the days of Columbus all good Indians were dead except one who was entitled Mohee-can. He was saving the heroine like in the movies but got caught." Above all, though, this film made us both laugh!

## Serial Murder . . .

By 1932, film was not only established, but had become the dominant form of entertainment. The arrival of sound after 1927 brought a seismic shock. Stars famous for their looks could not survive the test of being heard. Some companies resisted the transition too long. But this period also saw the consolidation of cinema as a children's medium. One of the effects of this consolidation was the evolution of the serial—extended (often dragged out) stories produced at high speed, often by small companies, to keep a young audience returning for more.[24] Such a thing was the 1932 version of *Mohicans* released by Mascot Films. Mascot was a relatively new company, having released their first film (*King of the Kongo*) in 1929. Virtually all of Mascot's output was serials, a mixture of various adventure genres. Mascot ceased production in 1937. Out of kindness to readers, and to the world supply of paper, we have tried hard to truncate the retelling of this twelve-chapter "stretch."

THE LAST OF THE MOHICANS (1932)
Twelve-chapter serial from Mascot Films
Directors: B. Reeves Eason and Ford Beebe
Starring: Harry Carey (Hawkeye), Hobart Bosworth (Chingachgook), Junior Coghlan (Uncas), Edwina Booth (Cora), Lucille Brown (Alice), Bob Kurtman (Magua)

Chapter 1: Magua is trying to persuade the Mohican tribe to side with the French against the English. He reminds them that their land has been stolen and shows them the scars from his beating. Hawkeye arrives to tell the full story of the beating, that Magua had got drunk and boasted of being a French spy and had been lucky to be let off so lightly. Magua departs, threatening vengeance.[25] When Hawkeye leaves, the Sagamore and Uncas follow to make sure he is safe from Magua. While they are away, Magua leads his Hurons in an assault on the Mohican village. Discovering the massacre, the Sagamore calls on Uncas, a boy of no more than 14, to take up the battle-ax and seek vengeance.

The boasting Hurons arrive at the French camp. Montcalm, though shocked, merely asks for news of the English. If he can get that, "Magua's medals shall be of silver, his pouch shall be filled with gold, he shall be the highest chief at my council table." A captured British officer, Major Heyward, is brought in, who tells them he was on his way to escort the daughters of Colonel Munro. Magua sees his chance, and later pretending to be a British spy among the French, helps Heyward to escape.

The two surviving Mohicans meet Hawkeye again, who is on English business. As they are talking, they hear a party approaching. It is Heyward, Magua, Gamut, and the two women. Magua makes a run for it. Hawkeye tells the party that he was "leading you straight to the scalping knives of the Hurons" (a much-repeated phrase). The party flees towards the river, closely pursued. Hawkeye is wounded. He and the Mohicans put the rest into boats, then follow along the river bank. Nearly captured, the canoes go over a waterfall. Then Hawkeye and the Mohicans appear to be shot, and tumble into the river.

Chapter 2: The Hurons think they are gone, probably dead. Magua is angry: "Even in death they escape our scalping knives." We now see the three hiding under a rock overhang. Enter a new character, wearing what looks like French Resistance costume. This is Dulac, a Frenchman who, having rescued Cora and the others from the canoes, hands them over to Magua, who tells Cora of his plans for revenge through her. Gamut, declared mad for his singing, is left behind. Dulac, left alone, encounters Hawkeye and steals his dispatches.

The two Mohicans overhear the Hurons planning an ambush for Hawkeye. Hawkeye and Gamut are pursued, trapped in a cave, and saved at the last moment by the Mohicans after hand-to-hand fighting. Now the four plan their rescue of the women.

To the Huron camp. Magua is preparing to send Heyward to the fort, to offer a deal: surrender, or the women die. Cora orders Heyward not to go: "No, a thousand times, no. We are but two lives. To save us and surrender the fort might mean the loss of an Empire to our country." She leads Alice to the stake, seeming ready to die. Outside the camp, Hawkeye, seeing the women at the stake, fires at the Hurons. Soon Hawkeye and the Sagamore are apparently shot, Uncas is fighting a Huron twice his size, and the flames are licking around the stake.

Chapter 3: recapitulates the rescue attempt. This time the rescue succeeds, and Hawkeye recovers his stolen dispatches. The group escapes toward the fort but encounters another ambush. Hawkeye sends the rest to a cave while he takes his vital dispatches to the fort. But a bogus Major Heyward (Dulac in disguise) manages to get in with "news" that all the party are dead. He steals the dispatches again and disappears. Colonel Munro is desperate; the information in the dispatches could sink the Empire. Hawkeye swears he'll recover them or die in the attempt. In the meantime a relief party is sent to rescue the party in the cave. There, Uncas is battling with the Hurons, watched by Alice's large eyes as a Huron creeps up on her.

Chapter 4 recaps the fight scenes and the recapture of the women by Magua. Taken to the French camp, the two women are graciously received by Montcalm, to Magua's irritation. Hawkeye, after so often losing his dispatches, burns them to ensure their safety. Then we overhear talk about a relief powder train. Back at the French camp, the four English meet up again, another rescue attempt is set in motion, more derring-do, and Magua (scorning his French allies) goes hunting for them again.

Now there appears on the road a French wagonload of weapons. Heyward (in a stolen French uniform) and the others manage to steal the wagons. Realizing the trick, the French, now with Dulac and Magua, give chase. The wagons are set on fire, causing explosions.

Chapter 5: We see that the English have managed to jump to safety from the exploding wagons. Dulac and Magua fall out over whether the English can be presumed dead. The English/Mohican party leaves a false trail for Magua, then escapes on horseback toward the fort. Magua decides to cut them off at the fort.

At the fort, a wounded soldier arrives to warn of the impending French attack. Battle scenes are followed by a surrender. Magua and Montcalm fall out again. Magua still wants revenge, but he signs (unwillingly) the guarantee of English safety. The English leaving the Fort: the massacre. Magua captures Alice. Cora, trying to follow, has her horse shot from under her and falls.

Chapter 6 recapitulates the "red swirl of the massacre" with its "wave of yelling savages." Montcalm belatedly tries to stop the slaughter. A messenger arrives (overheard by Dulac and two associates) to say that a bullion wagon—payment for the Indians—is on its way. Montcalm swears the Hurons will not be paid. Dulac lays an ambush for the wagon, but it gets away; we see the driver tipping the gold into the river, to hide it. Fleeing on, the wounded wagonmaster collapses, close by Cora who is recovering from her fall. She is soon recaptured by Dulac, and Magua gets her, for now. Dulac, wanting the information about the bullion, is furious but helpless.

Back at the fort, Dulac watches Montcalm "groveling" to Munro over the massacre. They learn that Magua has the women: "Magua! I'd rather they were dead than in the hands of that fiend!" says Munro. Dulac cunningly offers to lead a search party. Hawkeye and the Mohicans meanwhile attempt a rescue, but wake the sleeping Hurons. In the ensuing fight, the good guys seem to be going under.

Chapter 7: Dulac's party intervenes and saves them. Dulac wants Hawkeye shot as an English spy. In the end, he and the Mohicans are stripped of their arms and left. They follow, separately. The Mohicans overhear Magua planning yet another ambush, of Dulac's party, and of Hawkeye. There follow long travel and chasing scenes. Now we see Dulac, separated from the rest, play his hand for Cora. A melee ensues in which Cora breaks loose and runs, Alice is captured by the Hurons, and Hawkeye and Heyward seem to be shot.

Chapter 8 elongates the fight scenes, during which we learn that Hawkeye and Heyward had played dead to trick the Hurons. A confused situation is clarified when we see Cora, Gamut, and the French renegades besieged in a hut by Magua, who uses threats to Alice as a ploy to get Cora. Dulac, wanting Cora for his own purposes, bars her going. Hawkeye sends Heyward to rescue Alice, who has been tied to a stake. Meantime, Magua sets fire to the hut.

Chapter 9: Hawkeye finds a tunnel to the hut. But Gamut and Cora have been recaptured. Hawkeye sends Alice and Heyward back to the settlement for safety. Cora seizes a knife and threatens to kill herself if not given proof of Alice's safety (which Magua had promised, if she gave herself up to him). Magua calls off the pursuit canoes he had sent after Alice.

Dulac searches for the gold where Cora had told them it was, but finds no sign of it. Seeing Alice and Heyward in a canoe, he decides to capture them as barter for Cora, to get more information. Hawkeye and the Mohicans also take to the river in pursuit. Magua realizes he's being followed and sets yet another ambush. This is followed by further chase and shooting scenes.

Chapter 10: After recapitulatory battles, all arrive at the Huron village, but separately. Dulac sends Heyward in to get the information he wants from Cora, on pain of Alice's life. Magua tells the old chief that Cora has come to serve in his wigwam. This upsets an Indian maiden, Redwing, who was betrothed to him. She helps Cora by giving her a knife. Enter Uncas in a bear costume just in time to stop Cora killing herself. Captured together, Uncas offers to die in Cora's place, as "the last of the Mohicans." At that moment Heyward walks into the village bearing Dulac's threats. Cora reminds Magua of his promise of Alice's safety, and Magua has to send a party to free her. In an interlude, Gamut tries to teach Huron women and children to sing hymns.

Outside the village, Hawkeye has a plan. The Sagamore walks in, offering himself in place of Uncas, but warning that from outside the village is "the long rifle" aimed right at Magua's heart. But "the plan" falls apart when Dulac captures Hawkeye and takes his gun from him.

Chapter 11: In the recap, we learn that Colonel Munro has sent troops in pursuit of them all. At the village, Magua makes Dulac stay to celebrate Magua's wedding to Cora. Outside, Magua's party closes in on Alice and Dulac's companions, who are saved just in time by Munro's troops. Hawkeye, Chingachgook, and Uncas are about to be burned when Gamut does a "David" act with a sling, and the terrified Indians can't understand what's happening. Gamut now dons the bear skin and tries to cut them free. Spotted, he is knocked out by Magua, who drops a torch into the brushwood around the stakes. Heyward and Cora run to safety in the confusion and meet Munro's party. Munro leaves Alice and Cora guarded by two soldiers while he leads an attack on the village to rescue Hawkeye and the Mohicans. Outside, Magua, on the run now, sneaks up on the two guards, kills them and recaptures the women. Inside, Hawkeye and the Mohicans are surrounded by fire.

Chapter 12: A long recapitulation, ending with the troops saving Hawkeye and the others in the nick of time. The three hunters go hunting again. Dulac, also hunting Magua, manages only to shoot his horse, forcing Magua and Cora to walk into a high rocky area. Heyward, driven by desperation, catches up with Hawkeye and companions. Says Hawkeye: "I was wrong to say you couldn't keep up with us, Major. You travel a higher road and a nobler occasion than I ever tried." Now the final chase scenes in the rocks. The Sagamore is wounded by Magua. In the gathering gloom, Cora refuses to go any further, tries to throw herself off the rocks, is grabbed and dangles by one arm. Hawkeye, arriving, bargains for her: he will let Magua go if he saves Cora. But Dulac shoots Hawkeye, and Magua pulls Cora up for himself, at which point Dulac shoots Magua and grabs Cora for himself. Hawkeye, recovering, shoots Dulac at the pinnacle of the rock—a slow motion fall. Finally Uncas arrives to find his father dead; now he is the "last of the Mohicans." The series closes with the ceremony of mourning.

END

This appalling nonsense has to be seen to be believed. Yet in its own way, it is quite revealing. Its awfulness is a product not only of the story being stretched beyond all endurance (Cora and Alice undergo at least twelve captures and rescues, the dispatches do only marginally better, and we could not keep count of the number of "plans" and ambushes). It is also a function of the way every possible motif has been drawn in: hidden gold, French spies, tricks and counter-tricks, biblical references—all are worked in, yet all within a just-recognizable framework. These endless addenda are surely a function of the pressure to produce cheap children's serials for Saturday morning entertainment, an attempt to assimilate *Mohicans* to the Western tradition, at this time steadily gathering pace.[26]

What is also interesting, however, is the running tension between the filmic qualities of this version and its spoken rhetoric. Magua, who behaves (and acts!) no better or worse than most other charac-

A portly Hawkeye gets ready to sweat it out at the stake of the Hurons, watched by the turncoat Dulac . . . who??

ters, is *described* repeatedly as a "bloodthirsty savage." Amid endless scenes of standard conflict, there is a recurrent talk of the "nobility" of some characters, especially Heyward. Cora, about to die at the stake, discourses about the importance of "saving the Empire." And amid scenery that reminds one of any bit of managed woodland, the talk on the lips of Hawkeye is of the "savage wilderness." It is dull lip service to a set of ideals, which the makers could use as "saving grace" justifications to set a stamp of correctness on four hours of filmic waffle. In this respect, it might be said that the 1926 film parodies the unctuousness of what would be produced six years later!

### "I wonder if you can imagine what it feels like to be the first."

The 1936 movie was a major Hollywood production, with a big budget, a big star (Randolph Scott as Hawkeye), and big pretensions. It was the most lavish film version of *Mohicans* thus far and would remain so until 1992, when the Michael Mann film (which used the 1936 script as its basis) appeared. "The Randy Scott movie," as it became fondly remembered, was such a success that for an entire generation it became the definitive reading of Cooper's story.

In fact, it was a radical reworking of the *Mohicans* narrative and, as far as our analysis is concerned, it's one of most interesting versions for this reason. Here, the fate of Indian tribes is incidental, and the wilderness nonexistent. Instead, the film has three main points of interest: the way it co-opts some of the conventions of the western; the way in which it places U.S.-British relations at the center of the story; and the not-so-subtle manner in which capitalism is eulogized.

The responsibility for these changes is invariably attributed to the screenwriter, Philip Dunne. His name appears on the credits, and every review and reference book entry since has identified him as the chief architect of the adaptation. Dunne was to become a major figure in Hollywood as a screenwriter, director, and producer, and was twice nominated for an Academy Award. His films included *How Green Was My Valley*, *Pinky*, and *The Ghost and Mrs. Muir*. Due to his openly liberal politics, he was subject to witch hunts and blacklists in the 1940s and '50s, and partly as a consequence, moved increasingly into politics. A passionate defender of the First Amendment, he became a speechwriter for John F. Kennedy.[27]

Randolph Scott gets the full "romantic
hero" treatment in this Foyer Card.

In fact, however, Dunne was only partially responsible for the
film. The original script was co-written by Dunne and a noted anglophile, John Balderston, once the London correspondent for *The
New York World*. But due to studio politics, the script was taken out
of their hands at the last moment and given to an anonymous new
team for "modifications." Dunne was horrified at the result. In his
autobiography, published in 1980, he recalled: "[*Mohicans*] was a
only a pallid ghost of what John and I originally wrote. Our script . . .
painted an authentic picture of colonial America in the eighteenth
century. . . . [But] the film was appalling. . . . The characters even
spoke to each other in twentieth-century colloquialisms, and each
had been rendered banal beyond belief."[28]

If the script was made banal, the rest of the film is not particularly
good either. George Seitz's direction is adequate enough, but suffers
from the studio-bound nature of many of the scenes: the film is
remarkable for having no sense of "outdoors" whatsoever. Seitz tries

to make up for this with elaborate crowd scenes and the imaginative use of musical scores, but the tone remains oddly flat.

Similarly, the acting is workmanlike but never particularly inspiring. Randolph Scott gives his standard square-jawed, self-righteous performance, but looks like he's having trouble with some of the lengthier monologues. This is a supremely wordy film, and the overall impression is one of a history lesson as well as of a piece of entertainment. (Indeed, the introductory subheading, "Cooper's Classic of Early America," lets us know that we are supposed to take things relatively seriously.)

But if the film had faults, it was certainly the product of its time, and we should remember that the historical context for movies had changed drastically since the last feature version of *Mohicans* in 1920. Most obviously, in 1936 America was still suffering from the effects of the Great Depression. Unemployment was rife and soup kitchens continued to be a feature of many big cities. The prospect of the country veering toward political extremes—communism on the one hand and fascism on the other—seemed like a real possibility. If this was the "crisis of capitalism" that Marx had predicted, then the capitalists had better come up with some answers, and quickly.[29]

The film industry, too, had changed. Since Tourneur's *Mohicans*, Hollywood had become the center of the world film, a dream factory in an era when dreams were a desperate hedge against reality. The introduction of sound had led to the emergence of new acting celebrities, and by the 1930s the "star system" was a major economic factor in the industry. The first step in a film's production was to secure the star. Then the rest could be built around him or her. (It was a system that has endured, more or less, until today.)

Similarly, the demands of marketing Hollywood films led increasingly to their categorization by genre. A movie was no longer just a movie—it was a comedy, a thriller, a Western, a romance, or whatever, and certain actors (and directors) became associated with certain genres. Getting the formula right became a preoccupation of all the major studios; the right names on the poster could mean the difference between success and failure.[30]

But perhaps the most important influences to note were those relating to censorship. During the 1920s the Hays Office had increased in importance and power. Its role was not simply to control matters of decency. More and more, it played a political role. In the

1930s, this meant two things more than anything else. It meant the exclusion of anything that might offend overseas governments. The German embassy was able to use the Hays Office to prevent virtually all films critical of National Socialism until 1939, and even then, the film companies largely fought shy of offending. They had their reasons: foreign income constituted a large part of all film companies' income. The second factor, increasingly important as Europe moved inexorably towards war, was the overwhelming instinct for isolationism in American politics. Nothing was to be shown on film that could be judged propaganda for American intervention.

By and large the film companies played along with these restrictions without much trouble. Warner Brothers broke ranks after their Berlin agent was murdered by Fascists in 1937. And United Artists, among whose ranks Hollywood's anti-Nazi league was particularly strong, was also prepared to take on the Hays Office. Besides, by 1935 United Artists had seen its European earnings collapse. Therefore UA felt it could defy the censors in 1938 over Walter Wanger's *Blockade*, a film that openly sympathized with the republicans in Spain.[31]

The relevance of this wrangling is that Europe was more than a place; it was a symbol. The isolationists, whose core support was significantly from the Midwest, wanted no dealings with Europe. The interventionists, egged on by Roosevelt more and more as the 1930s progressed, had to challenge that Western image of "America." We should not be surprised to find resonances of this battle in the United Artists' version of *Mohicans*.

THE LAST OF THE MOHICANS (1936)
Director: George B. Seitz Screenplay: Philip Dunne
Starring: Randolph Scott (Hawkeye), Binnie Barnes (Alice), Harry Wilcoxson (Heyward), Heather Angel (Cora), Bruce Cabot (Magua)
Edward Small Production (United Artists)

After the title sequence, a narrator speaks: "1757. The Seven Years' War storms Europe. France and England fight on three continents. With North America at stake George II, 'German George' has called to his side the great commoner William Pitt." In St. James Palace the king meets with an aristocratic adviser (counseling that they abandon North America) and Pitt, who advises reinforcing Colonel Munro at Fort William Henry. The king (pictured as a glutton and impetuous) sides with Pitt. The aristocrat warns that Pitt is mad. Major Heyward is dispatched.

The scene changes to a map of New York, moving to a close-up on Albany. Dissolve to a coach arriving with Heyward, being greeted by surly colonials who make fun of his subaltern. Inside to a dance scene. Cora (here, a blonde) is dancing, and General Webb is heard commenting that she is the happiest he's seen her since she lost her loved one at sea. Heyward arrives with dispatches, and is sent to find Alice (the brunette). Alice welcomes him warmly, but makes clear she doesn't respond to his evident love for her. They have very "British" exchanges.

General Webb appeals to the colonials to fight with the British. They respond that it is "not our war." Webb declares he will fight, regardless. Then Magua arrives, and Webb learns that Montcalm is about to surround Fort William Henry. Now his appeal to the colonials succeeds, provided they can leave to defend their homes if the French/Indians break through to threaten them. Webb agrees. We meet Hawkeye (with his friends Chingachgook and Uncas) for the first time, as a doubting colonial.

Cut to inside. Alice to General Webb of Hawkeye: "I thought we hanged traitors." Webb, more pragmatic, says you can't stop people speaking their minds.

Magua is given a message to deliver. As he leaves, Webb remarks to Heyward that he is the best scout they have, though he once had to "give him a touch of the cat." Magua destroys the message but is spotted and recognized by Hawkeye. Hawkeye is prevented by Alice from warning Munro.

Next day, setting out, Magua offers to guide the women by a shortcut. Heyward volunteers to go with them. As they march out, the British troops strike up "The Grenadiers"; the colonials respond with "Yankee Doodle." Magua leads them astray, watched from a distance by Hawkeye, Chingachgook, and Uncas. When they stop to eat, Magua leaves them to send a fire signal to his tribe (after a curt "pack these things up" from Heyward). Further on, Magua is joined by other Hurons and announces his intentions for Alice and Cora. He will also kill Heyward. Just in time, Hawkeye and company rescue them. (Heyward at first tries to shoot Chingachgook, on the principle that no Indian can be trusted. Hawkeye strikes him to stop him.) Alice, Cora, and Heyward watch horrified as Chingachgook and Uncas scalp the dead Hurons. "It's just the same as getting medals with you, Major," says Hawkeye.

Hearing Hurons hunting them, they flee. There are chase scenes, with unsuccessful attempts at deception. Cora faints, and Alice starts to believe in Hawkeye, despite Heyward. Heyward: "I wonder if he can be trusted. After all, he's little more than a white savage." Cora and Uncas, meanwhile, are beginning to fall in love.

Now a boat chase.[32] The fugitives split up to escape the Hurons, with Alice and Hawkeye going on alone. Going inland to a cabin to find refuge, they find it burned, and its occupants all killed. Alice accuses Hawkeye of being unfeeling when he comments that they've had a "Huron haircut." He tells her they were his friends, that his parents died the same way. She apologizes, beginning to understand him.

Alice proves herself tough in Hawkeye's eyes, as they flee and hide. Now Hawkeye talks about his past. Brought up by the Mohicans, he tells Alice, he is at peace in the wilds. Elsewhere Cora and Uncas talk, and we learn about the killing of all the Mohicans in the Huron wars. "You're all alone, and so am I," says Cora. But when Uncas gives her food, Chingachgook rebukes him: "Mohican chief no wait on squaw!"

Now they join up and flee towards Fort William Henry. Montcalm is preparing for the siege. Hawkeye's party arrives, to Munro's relief. Hawkeye rejects Heyward's thanks (because of his attitude), while Heyward tries to stop Cora from thanking Uncas for saving her.

Hawkeye, Chingachgook, and Uncas prepare to leave the fort at night. There is a tender scene between Uncas and Cora (with Chingachgook angry because it makes Uncas's heart "weak like water"), then Alice tries to persuade Hawkeye not to leave. The start of the French attack persuades him. There follow war scenes. Forward to ten days later, and supplies are running out. Munro comments bitterly on "the War Office." Uncas is sent with a message to General Webb, is injured and nearly caught by the French. Heyward rescues him—but only for the message. Cora visits Uncas at the fort's infirmary.

Hawkeye and Chingachgook decide to check out the Ottawa camp (having identified an arrow that wounded Uncas as Ottawan). They find them readying for an assault on the colonials' homes. They try to persuade Munro to let the colonials return home as promised. Munro refuses, wanting "more evidence." When Heyward denounces Hawkeye as a traitor, Hawkeye replies: "Major, some day you and I are going to have a serious disagreement."

The colonials prepare to escape at night. Hawkeye, Chingachgook, and Uncas stop the guards shooting at them, are arraigned, and are put in prison to await hanging. Alice pleads with her father for Hawkeye's life, but is refused. Angrily she rounds on him: "Justice? If that's your idea of justice, then the sooner the French guns drive the English out of America, the better!"

We see now messengers from Webb to the fort ambushed and killed, and Magua delivering their message to Montcalm. Munro agrees to a parley with Montcalm. The message says that the relief column has been delayed at sea, and General Webb recommends they surrender. Reluctantly, Munro agrees.

The surrender. Munro prepares to leave quietly, sadly. Cut to Magua rousing his Hurons, who attack the fort. Long fight scenes ensue, during which we see Hawkeye in prison, Cora and Alice being trapped, Munro being shot, and many scalpings. Hawkeye, Uncas, and Chingachgook manage to break out. Montcalm learns of the massacre and, appalled, sends a column to quell it, enabling Hawkeye and friends to set out in pursuit of Magua and the kidnapped women. There are "worthy" exchanges between Montcalm and the wounded Munro, who dies as his sword is returned to him.

The forest chase: Hawkeye, Chingachgook, and Uncas meet up with Heyward. They have to split up to find the trail. Uncas and Heyward arrive at the Delaware camp (which looks like a large wooden hut) ahead of the others. Here we see Magua again demand that Cora become his wife. The old Indian chief says she must accept. When Alice berates him for lack of any justice among Indians, he angrily offers her the choice between squaw-dom or the fire. Uncas goes in to rescue the women, and manages to get Cora out, but is spotted and pursued up a high cliff. On the cliff face, Uncas refuses ever to leave the exhausted Cora as Magua closes in behind them. They come to the precipice edge. Uncas falls at Magua's hand and plunges over the cliff. Cora hurls herself after him rather than be captured. Uncas manages to lay his hand over hers before he dies. Chingachgook challenges Magua to combat, and there is a long fight sequence until eventually Chingachgook drowns Magua in the river. The scene ends with Cora being buried, and Uncas's body raised up on a funeral pyre, Indian-style.

Cut back to Alice, still held by the Delawares, ready to be burned. Hawkeye and Heyward try to think of a way to rescue her. Hawkeye says he will offer himself as exchange. Heyward knocks Hawkeye out, takes his clothes, and goes in his stead. The chief eventually accepts the exchange, and Heyward is seized to be burnt. In comes Hawkeye, recovered. Alice refuses to identify the real Hawkeye. They have a shooting contest. Hawkeye of course wins, and is chosen to die by fire. Heyward and Alice are allowed to depart. We see Hawkeye being prepared for torture by Indian women. Heyward and Alice, leaving, meet a column of British and colonial troops who attack the Indian village just as Hawkeye is set in the fire. The film cuts direct from our seeing his face of pain in the fire and the realization of his rescue, to reading a letter of arrest for treason.

A court scene: Hawkeye is on trial, Heyward is his accuser, who still seems to blame him, even after the near self-sacrifice. Then Heyward's speech turns into a defense, telling the whole truth on Hawkeye's behalf. Hawkeye is excused, if he will become a British scout. "Well, I guess after all we are fighting for the same thing, general," he says.

The troops prepare to march out for Canada, Hawkeye going with them. There is a tender scene of farewell from Alice, who now declares she is staying in America, for she has nothing to go back to England for: "You know it takes more than rifles to build a new civilization. It takes spinning wheels, too." She'll wait for him to return. They clasp each other and he leaves with the soldiers.

END

The 1936 *Last of the Mohicans* was very much a reflection of the new order. There is a definite attempt to mold the story to the conventions of the Western. These conventions had evolved over the previous fifty years in response to the Wild Bill Hickok "Wild West Shows" of the 1880s, the dime novels of the early twentieth century, and early movies such as *The Covered Wagon* (1923) and *The Virginian* (1929). Although the great age of Western films was yet to come, by the 1930s they had a recognized marketing niche.

In this respect, the casting of Randolph Scott was very significant. According to one source, "no name was so closely associated with the Western genre than Scott's."[33] His career had taken off as a result of a number of hit cowboy dramas in which he played noble heroes (for example, in *Wagon Wheels* and *The Last Roundup*, both 1934, both based on Zane Grey stories). Indeed, his performance as Hawkeye in *Mohicans* is essentially that of an honest sheriff rather than a rugged colonialist. For this reason, it could be argued that he was not the ideal choice for the role. But he *was* chosen, of course, and that affected the kind of film that resulted.

There are other tell-tale signs. The Indians, for example, are quintessentially "western" Indians, with their war cries and feather headgear, while the music is dominated by a jagged "Wild West" Indian theme and tribal drumming, interspersed with a romantic string section. Well might Philip Dunne complain: "They had succeeded in turning our authentic eighteenth-century piece into a third-rate Western."[34]

But if the script was being bent in certain directions to make it more commercial, it also had deeper levels. One of these was the way in which British-American relations were brought to the fore. Politically speaking, the growth of American power had been a challenge to Britain's hegemony in the world since the First World War. The growth of fascism in Europe in the 1930s merely brought their relative strengths and weaknesses into focus. The "special relationship" was undergoing a period of strain, and was being redefined in the face of this unprecedented threat. With the likelihood of another European war, Americans were asking themselves whether they should be involved.

Colonel Heyward, jealous of Hawkeye, imprisons him on a charge of treason. The Indian tribes get out of hand, and Alice and Cora are again captured. In saving them both Chingachgook and his son, Uncas, die.

Heyward's testimony vindicates Hawkeye at the court-martial.

Film magazines became an important factor in promoting new movies. *Picture Show* specialized in single page visual plot summaries. Their preview of the 1936 film (13 March 1937) has a revealing error. In fact Chingachgook does not die in the film, he simply disappears. As a representative of "wilderness," he has no place in the brave New Deal world that Hawkeye envisages early on and joins at the end.

The film, too, asks this question and provides its own idiosyncratic answers. The differences between the British and the (proto-) American settlers are very strikingly drawn. The tension between them is signaled early on when both parties march out from the fort together: the tune they sing changes from "The British Grenadier" to "Yankee Doodle Dandy" (another anachronism that is surely deliberate). Similarly, the British are portrayed as dullards, imperialists who do not understand the land they have conquered. To give two instances: Hawkeye, symbol of the new colonial populace, states with some contempt that he has "more sense than to wear a red coat in a wood"; and when Cora suggests to Heyward that Chingachgook and Uncas are different from other Indians, he can only reply that "I don't trust any of them." There are numerous other examples.

Yet the British are not all bad. They may be stupid, but they are honorable, and that makes a concluding rapprochement possible.[35] The two sides wind up earning each other's respect and recognizing that they have a mutual interest in ridding the land of Indians—who by the end of the film seem simply to represent injustice. In the final reel, Hawkeye ends up shaking Heyward's hand and enlisting in the British army. "After all," he says, "we are fighting for the same thing."

But what is it, exactly, for which they are both fighting? In an obvious sense it is to make America safe for God-fearing white folk. In the context of the world political situation in the mid-1930s, the subliminal message is clear. Whether the threat is communism or National Socialism, the two leading capitalist nations must stand together.

But perhaps the most striking new meaning this version of *Mohicans* offers is of the wilderness, and urban and industrial development. If the Tourneur/Brown version starkly contrasts the world of the Indians and the English (and in the process reduces the role of Hawkeye to that of onlooker), this version puts Hawkeye at the center of a new vision: a vision of the future in which, in truth, there is little place for wilderness. Its value is only in what it can become. All that we see of wild forest looks tamed, like parkland. And at a critical moment in the plot, Cora comes to understand and be attracted to the scout when he enunciates his philosophy: "A man could spend his life walking this country and never walk the same trail twice." He tells her that he imagines cities being built at the end of every new trail he blazes. "I wonder if you can imagine what it feels like to be the first." This is a New Deal version of the frontier. In dream and imagination we can be the "first," but the point in doing so is to take us forward, away from wilderness to the making of cities, a developed future. To hide in the past, in a vision of primitive "America," is futile and dangerous.

CHAPTER 5    Movie Mohicans,
1947–1992

The American film industry emerged from the Second World War
in remarkably healthy shape.[1] The bad times would come later,
with the anti-trust actions of 1948, the rise of the anti-Communist
witch-hunts, and the emergence of television. But for now profits
were at an all time high. The Hays Office controls had been largely
replaced by the more approachable Office of War Information, which
had positively encouraged the big companies into association. True,
there had been awkward moments over whether actors, directors,
and the like should enlist, and over filming at night during the 1941
blackouts against feared Japanese bombing raids. As in many sectors
of the American economy, women had come to play a larger role,
right up to quite senior levels. But for all the disturbances, the industry came out of the war full of confidence and money.

The end of the war also saw some of the independent producers
collapse back into the laps of the major companies. After a touch of
nerves as to whether profits would fall when peace came (in fact they

rose to $125 million for the eight biggest companies in 1946) the only new threat immediately came from the British businessman J. Arthur Rank, who set out to challenge American domination. Scorned and reviled, but nonetheless watched with caution, Rank even bought an American cinema chain. His bid failed, largely perhaps because of the weakness of the British economy and the sheer scale of the Hollywood companies. But it introduced a sour anti-British note into Hollywood.

Riding its confidence did not mean the production of unthinking patriotic entertainment. In fact, along with the obvious standard fare of Westerns, domestic dramas, and the like, those early years produced two sorts of films in particular. First, there were the reappraisals of the war, best exemplified by William Wyler's brilliant *The Best Years of Our Lives*, which explored largely without sentimentality the problems facing returning servicemen. The second sort was film noir. Noir has been the topic of extensive argument and analysis (not least by feminist film critics because of the way films such as *Double Indemnity*, *The Postman Always Rings Twice*, and *Mildred Pierce* center on female characters who are deceitful, dangerous, and sexually provocative). There can be little doubt that these films were an angular comment on the changed position of women in the American economy. And certainly, a drive began almost immediately to return women to the home. In this context Columbia decided to make what all critics have seen as the poorest feature version of *Mohicans* so far: *The Last of the Redmen*.

## "Hawkeye, you were right—there isn't room in America for weepers"

The first *Mohicans* adaptation since the Second World War is a dreary affair. (Despite its title, the credits state specifically that it is "adapted from *The Last of the Mohicans* by James Fenimore Cooper.") A B-movie in every sense, the acting is poor, the sound quality appalling, the cinematography uninspired, and the direction heavy handed. The limitations of the budget are perhaps best illustrated by the fact that the biggest star in the film is Buster Crabbe (as Magua), a has-been best remembered for his role as Flash Gordon in the classic 1930s serial.

The timing of the movie was curious. Coming only eleven years after the 1936 *Mohicans*, there can be little doubt that this was, at least in part, a cash-in. The "Randy Scott version" had been such a success that it had redefined notions of what the story was about. Thus any film made so soon afterwards would necessarily have to be a response to that new interpretation, rather than to the original book (despite the claims of the credits). No wonder, then, that many film histories cite the 1947 film as a remake. But this is clearly not the case.

THE LAST OF THE REDMEN (1947)
Director: George Sherman   Screenplay: Herbert Dalmas and George Plympton
Starring: Michael O'Shea (Hawkeye), Rick Vallin (Uncas), Buster Crabbe (Magua), Evelyn Ankers (Alice), Julie Bishop (Cora), Buzz Henry (Davy), John Hall (Heyward)

Narration over the titles: "In August 1757 the French and English war was at its height. General Montcalm, the French commander, with a large of force of French troops and Indian allies was moving down from Canada to attack British-held territory at Lake George." Magua enters the fort and tells General Webb and another officer that the French are approaching from the South. The officers, very "English" in manner, declare their amazement. This reverses their strategy, including what to do about Colonel Munro's daughters.

Open countryside: a road, and a carriage with passengers. To jaunty music, two women, Major Heyward, and a young boy discuss the countryside. Heyward calls it "beautiful and dangerous." "Like a beautiful woman," retorts Alice, the blonde. "Hey, I bet I just saw an Indian," says the boy. "Davy, will you please stop using those Yankee expressions." "Aw gosh, sis." Ahead, a party of Indians lies in ambush. Just in time, an escort sent to meet them arrives.

The party arrives at the fort. Davy scoffs at the local militiamen. "Such amusing costumes," says Alice, to Cora's irritation. Greeted by the general, they exchange pleasantries. "The country between here and Boston has become quite civilized," says Heyward. They hear that a dance is due to take place in the women's honor. Outside, two new arrivals (Hawkeye and Uncas) are greeted by the local men. They hear Magua's news. "So the renegade Magua's here again," says Hawkeye, who tries to warn a disbelieving Webb. Hawkeye and Uncas are reduced to watching the dance, a mannered, flirtatious affair. Webb interrupts it to announce a preemptive strike against Montcalm.

Next day, the troops set out, while Heyward waits to lead the "charming" women. Enter Davy stripped to the waist after a race with the local yokel for some feathers. "I've decided I'm going to ride like this," he tells Cora. "You're not going to let your father see you looking like a savage," she insists. As they prepare to leave, Webb and Heyward discuss the relations between love and war: both are "campaigning." Exit to more jaunty music.

An Indian runner in the woods is shot and searched by other Indians; a letter is taken. It tells General Montcalm's real position, to the north.

The traveling party sets out. Alice can only think about the men they may get to meet. Cora is different: "One might travel for days in this forest without coming to an end. And who knows what's beyond it to the west— or to the north and south. All that wilderness waiting for men to come and tame it." Alice: "What a dreary thought." The camera pans away to Hawkeye finding the dead scout and identifying the fatal arrow. Now Magua leads the party off the path. Heyward does not tell Cora and Alice he suspects trouble, but he does tell Davy, who leaves the path to follow a noise. An Indian with a tomahawk creeps up behind him. Just in time the Indian is shot. Enter Hawkeye.

Hawkeye negotiates for the right to lead them. Alice is "offended" by his gracelessness, but Hawkeye is chatty and very "Irish," properly charming to the "most beautiful young ladies." "Not a bad speech for a backwards Irishman, eh?" he says when his leadership is finally accepted. He makes them get rid of the horses and all unnecessary clothing, and leads them to the river, closely pursued by the Indians (Iroquois). There are long chase scenes on the river. The first group reaches the island. Uncas sends Heyward, Cora, and Davy up to a cave. There is no sign yet of Hawkeye and Alice. Uncas reassures them that Hawkeye will not be lost: "Hawkeye too wise. You, follow me. Hide in cave." Hawkeye finally reappears at the end of a long digression in which Heyward confronts Magua and is nearly killed for his pains.

In the cave, there is byplay about eating "wild food," making Hawkeye seem deprived by living in the wilderness. That night, while the women sleep, Hawkeye and Uncas discuss them. Hawkeye: "Tell me, son, how do you think you'd go about handling the fair one. D'you think she'd make a good squaw?" Uncas: "Maybe . . . after much . . . hard work." Hawkeye: "And the weight of her husband's hand now and then." Uncas: "It is good way."

Dawn. In the cave, Alice panics and proposes to give herself up. Davy calls the men. Outside, fighting begins. Cora, Alice, and Davy watch from above. When Heyward is shot and wounded, Cora rushes to help and bind the wound. Hawkeye and Uncas decide they must take "the last chance." Showing the English where to hide, they will leave to get help. Hawkeye tells Davy to leave a trail if they are captured. Alice looks thoroughly discombobulated.

The Iroquois land and hunt. Eventually they catch the English. Alice tells an unconvinced Magua that Hawkeye ran away because he was scared of him.

Magua likes the idea, but knows better. As they are taken away, Davy manages to drop buttons, but the trail behind is obliterated. When Heyward tries to bargain with Magua, Magua tells of his desire for revenge for his beating: "Each stroke of the lash will be year of suffer for Munro." But he won't kill the women; he will take Cora as his squaw. Davy attacks the Indians to protect his sister, and Magua has to stop one Indian, Little Bear, from killing Davy for the "offense" of attacking an adult. That night we see Little Bear about to kill Davy when a shot rings out. Rescue—but the women have gone. Hawkeye and Uncas realize they have been taken to the Iroquois camp.

The Iroquois camp, and Hawkeye's rescue stratagem. Uncas is to walk into the camp. He pretends to have killed Hawkeye. But then a series of explosions begin, and the horses are scared off. Davy repeats a trick from earlier in the film, mimicking trumpets sounding an attack. The women are rescued. The Indians give chase. The English hide in a ruined cabin. Alice, still pursuing her romancing, proposes that she get Heyward transferred back to Britain. He isn't attracted: "There's something about this country I like." Alice: "Wilderness . . . full of savages." Heyward: "It'll change. There's real opportunity here for a man. Besides, England's so dull and civilized." A frustrated Alice gives up.

When they are found asleep in the morning, Alice is deeply offended at Hawkeye hauling her to her feet: "I've never been treated like this in my whole life. In England ladies are looked up to, honored, even adored." Hawkeye: "The people in this country are respected for what they do." He calls her the "worst weeper" he's ever met. As they approach Fort William Henry, they see a column of soldiers, all battered and defeated, and with them the girls' father. The fort has had to surrender. What about the Indians? "They've departed to their villages. Montcalm assures me there'll be no trouble with them." Hawkeye: "Oh did he now? That's mighty handsome of him."

Now the Iroquois attack. This is done in classic low-budget Western style, Indians war-whooping towards them down a track on horseback, the column forming a defensive circle. Munro is shot. Uncas goes for help, pursued by Magua. Running out of bullets, the defenders fire blanks to fool the Indians. The film intercuts between the Uncas/Magua chase and the besieged wagons. Uncas kills Magua but is wounded. At the encampment, Davy keeps tripping Indians so they can be killed. Alice suddenly screams and runs into the open, and is immediately stabbed. Uncas meets the cavalry, and directs them to the scene. Alice, dying, admits: "Hawkeye, you were right—there isn't room in America for weepers." The troops arrive. Uncas, behind them, falls dying from his horse. The Iroquois run. There is a military salute over the graves of the dead, then the troops head out to military music, leaving Hawkeye standing alone by the grave of Uncas.

END

There are certainly similarities with the 1936 movie. First, we are once again in the realm of the Western. Hawkeye, despite his Irish accent, conforms to the stereotype of tough-talking masculinity so familiar in the genre. He exhibits none of the psychological complexity of Cooper's original model (this is the sort of movie where Hawkeye, in mortal combat with a foe, can utter lines like "why you dirty, thievin' . . ."), while the physique of the man hardly accords with Cooper's vision of taut muscles honed by the elements; this Hawkeye is rather portly.

Similarly, the Iroquois are wild West Indians, one-dimensional in the dime novel tradition. Even Uncas is relegated to a kind of Tonto role, while Chingachgook, the most articulate Indian in Cooper's original, is omitted altogether. When Uncas died, therefore, it really was the "last" of the Mohicans—though the film makes nothing of the point. The theme music is a kind of Indian war-dance interspersed with romantic melodies, much in the fashion of the 1936 film. Also, the film's outdoor locations are invariably in rather sedate countryside; as in the 1936 film, there is no notion of wild nature "full of toils and dangers."

Finally, like the 1936 film, British-American relations are a major theme. The British are portrayed as "civilized" in the sense that they are overly-mannered, arrogant, and supercilious. Alice is forever making snide remarks about the New World settlers, while Hawkeye is distanced from the British by dint of his Irish origins. Like the 1936 film, there is an eventual rapprochement between the British and the settlers, but this now takes the form of the British learning to acknowledge the attractions and superiority of the "American way"!

But ultimately it is the differences from the 1936 movie that are more striking than the similarities. *Redmen* makes no real attempt at being a commentary on its times in the same way as its predecessor. The script could have been used as a symbolic representation of issues but consistently avoids this path. For instance, in terms of America's place in the world, much could have been made of the fact that the country had emerged from the war in a far stronger position than Britain, and that a new Cold War was beginning. Similarly, in terms of the representation of Indians, there is no attempt to reflect post-Nazi Holocaust attitudes to ethnic minorities.[2]

Instead, *Redmen* is content to rework *Mohicans* as a family-

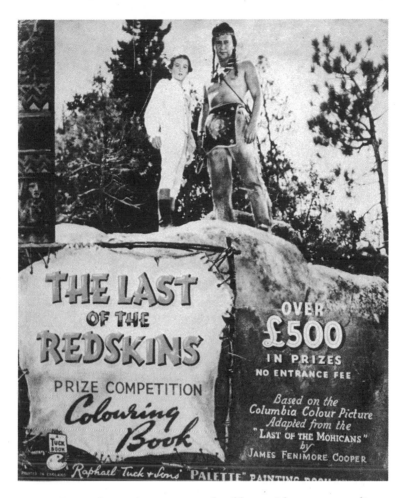

By 1947 it was becoming common for films with younger audiences to generate accompanying merchandise: in this case a coloring book, with a competition you could enter. (Above, the British title for the film.)

oriented adventure-romance. The deeper political levels of the 1936 movie are largely eschewed in favor of an old-fashioned tale that builds up the roles of Cora and Alice, and adds a new character (Davy, their kid brother) to appeal to a juvenile audience.

To be more specific, here the two sisters are glamorous in a very 1940s Hollywood fashion: one fussy blonde, one cool brunette, both with immaculate makeup and coiffed hair. They have a lot more to say than in previous adaptations, but it is strictly within the parameters of a similarly stereotyped image of femininity. Alice does not so much talk as twitter, and both women perform the function of being the object of rescues and romantic overtures.

Davy is also a stereotype familiar to cinema audiences, the juvenile sidekick. It is Hawkeye who assumes the role of father figure, dispensing wise words about how to survive in the wilderness. The two have a lighthearted relationship, with the energetic, mouthy Davy frequently becoming the focus of some heavy-handed humor. He is also portrayed as an innocent who naturally takes the side of the settlers—even if, at first at least, we are treated to images of them as rather dimwitted "peasants."

But ultimately, it is these fresh twists to the story that deprive it of any profundity or significance. It is as if the movie is being pulled in too many directions at once, and cannot decide what it wants to be: an adventure or a romance, a kids' or an adult film. In this sense, far from rehashing the "big themes" of the 1936 movie, it is a reaction to them: banal, unfocused, and finally very forgettable.

Perhaps the film is interesting in only two ways. Comparison with the other films shows how much the image of "England" has changed. If in 1936 England and Europe were arrogant and unjust, here they represent foolishness. In the characters of Cora and Alice, especially, Englishness is vanity. It is helpless silliness that in the end must change or die. America is to be learned from. It may be demotic, but it knows what matters. It is possible to sniff the tendrils of smoke from the 1947 Marshall Plan and rescue of Europe (at a price) that were being put in place just as the film came out.

If Alice half-represents the Europe that must now decline in the face of the new American empire, she also always remains a woman. And just as in all those films noirs, she is punished for trying to use her wiles. If noir explored a "dark side" of femininity, we should not forget that Hollywood was capable of much more conventional revenge on women. As Heyward feels the magnetic pull of America, its manliness and new opportunities, the cast-aside Alice may as well die. There is no place for weepers, as much as there was no place for women workers. Alice must die, too weak a figure to have any future in "America." And "America" is where the future is and lies. As the United States, then, geared up for the Cold War, the Korean War, and (soon) for McCarthyism, so it girded its filmic loins, and began to preach the necessity of toughness to its denizens.[3]

**"The meanin' of 'savage' depends on who's speakin' it."**

By the mid-1970s, America's film industry had undergone a series of transformations, many of them resulting from the rise of television. Initially fearful of the new medium, in the end a number of film companies had adapted to its challenge, some of them turning over production in a big way to producing TV series. Among these, perhaps most important were the production of police series[4] and Western series. Among those launched into later successful film careers from these inauspicious beginnings was of course Clint Eastwood.

A more specific change was the growing movement in the 1960s among native American peoples to challenge their continued marginalization within American society and the many forms of discrimination they encountered and, as part of those efforts, to challenge their continuing characterization as "savages." One effect of this challenge was Hollywood's production of a number of "revisionist" Westerns, beginning to tell the story of the frontier in a way sympathetic to native Americans. Perhaps most notable among these films were *Little Big Man* and *Soldier Blue*[5] (both 1970), two films that brought to the screen the indiscriminate violence and sheer viciousness of white suppression of native societies. Following the campaigns by native Americans and the impact of these films, it was hard for any Western or frontier film not to think about the real historical record of treachery, rape, murder, theft of land, and destruction of environments—and the concomitant deceitful representations of Indian peoples. It was at this time, also, that the book appeared that most popularized the reevaluation of treatment of native Americans appeared: *Bury My Heart at Wounded Knee*.[6]

Another important effect of the rising importance of television was the growth of small film companies, often devoted to making TV movies for one or another of the major networks. In 1977, one of these marginal companies was to produce a version of *The Last of the Mohicans*. Schick Sunn followed *Mohicans* with Cooper's *The Deerslayer* and H. G. Wells' *The Time Machine* in 1978, Washington Irving's *The Legend of Sleepy Hollow* (1980), and Mark Twain's *Huckleberry Finn* (1981). Schick Sunn was the property of Patrick Frawley, who had bought all rights to the Classics Illustrated series in 1967 (see chapter 7 for the story of Classics Illustrated). Frawley was a successful but restless businessman who had, in his time, owned Papermate (the pen company), a film company (Technicolor), and a Catholic publishing house. Having folded Gilberton's operations in 1971 (because of falling sales), he nonetheless was keen to retain the rights—including suing another company, Regent Classics, in 1986 for breach of copyright. Successful in this action, Frawley in fact allowed Regent to continue their use of CI materials (including reprinting CI's 1969 version of *Mohicans*) on payment of royalties.

Several things may have prompted the 1977 film version and its sequels. It was important to Frawley to retain his intellectual property rights to the CI titles; and each film displayed the logo at beginning and end (although they are missing from the 1990s British video release, distributed in association with W. H. Smith). But perhaps more importantly, 1976 was the bicentennial year. The founding of America was to be remembered, and inevitably a vast amount of material was produced to remind people just what constituted "America," most of it of an uncritical, celebratory nature.[7]

Schick Sunn's version, made in association with NBC, is a pleasing low-budget movie. Lacking dramatic scenery and large-action scenes, it nonetheless is a memorable retelling. It is clearly directed at children, in its use of actors, settings, and styles with strong childhood appeal. (Major Heyward, for example, is remarkably young looking for a senior officer!) The disappearance of all scenes involving the fort (the negotiations, surrender, and also the massacre) readily serves both purposes. It saved the expense of the set and the large crowd scenes, and of course avoided the problem of how to film the massacre in a way that parents and teachers would accept. There are no big-name stars in this version, although Steve Forrest and Ned Romero in particular would be known to some viewers from television roles. It has a homely feel that becomes, at important points, part of the very meaning of the film. Hawkeye, as we will see, is given to cracker-barrel homilies, delivered in a slightly avuncular but earthy way. His buckskins stay tidy, looking like adult versions of a child's birthday present set. Even so, the film has its fair share of drama and emotion—and also its fair share of alterations to the story, in order to become the first "politically correct" rendition of the story.[8]

THE LAST OF THE MOHICANS (1977)
TV Movie from NBC/Schick Sunn Classics
Director: James Conway
Starring: Steve Forrest (Hawkeye), Ned Romero (Chingachgook), Don Shanks
(Uncas), Andrew Prine (Munro), Michele Marsh (Cora), Jane Acunan (Alice),
Robert Tessier (Magua).

The film opens with soft music, as titles rise over a pleasant shot of a
mountain, then a deer, a wandering bear, a hawk on a branch, a wooden
shack. All seems peaceful. Then we see Indians creeping up in war paint. The
Indians attack with burning arrows. The fire catches. The woman prays and
hugs the wakened child to her. Two figures appear over the hilltop: "Looks
like those folks need some help." They fire and the Indians flee, shouting "La
Longue Carabine!" The family escapes the burning house.

The family approaches the rescuers, who introduce themselves as Hawkeye and Chingachgook. The boy asks his father what "La Longue Carabine"
means, and why the Indians ran away from him. "Because Hawkeye and
Chingachgook live here in the wilderness protecting people like you and I
from danger. They've been together since they were boys. The story goes
the Indian had a son and the three of them lived in the forest together.
When the French. . . . " (As this dialogue proceeds, the camera goes into
flashback to Fort Edward.) [The father remains the narrator through the rest
of the film, coming in from time to time in voice-over.]

At the fort another officer talks to Heyward: "That's the Huron world out
there. He's clever, devious, and deadly." Cut, to somber music, and pan up
the legs of an Indian who's looking in on two women (Cora and Alice). Alice is
blushing and laughing over her attraction to Heyward. Back to the officers,
discussing getting troops through to Colonel Munro. But Heyward has another commission, to get the girls to their father. Magua, the Indian, is
summoned; again somber music as he enters. Gamut also introduces himself to Heyward and asks to accompany him. Heyward refuses coldly.

A mountainscape, with soothing music. Hawkeye and Chingachgook are
resting, the latter suddenly becoming aware of being watched. "Those Mohican ears of yours!" laughs Hawkeye. Chingachgook relaxes, grins, and
spears a fish for them. Cut back to the creeping Indian who comes up and
jumps for Hawkeye, who rolls aside laughing. Uncas, for it is he, reports
"strange moccasins": Hurons. They go to see what is happening.

We see the traveling party approaching. Magua hears horses, and they
hide. It is only Gamut coming after them, who asks to accompany them.
Alice pleads for him, gigglingly, and Heyward grudgingly agrees. Gamut
bursts into a hymn, and is coldly silenced by Heyward. They move on, while
we see an Indian face peering from a bush.

Dissolve to a river. *Narrator:* "As the day wore on, Major Heyward grew suspicious of his Indian guide." Heyward rides ahead to look and walks into Hawkeye, Chingachgook, and Uncas. "An Indian lost?" says Hawkeye. "You must be the one they tell so many stories about, La Longue Carabine," says Heyward. "Hawkeye . . . just Hawkeye, Major." As they return to the others, Magua sees them and runs off. "That Indian's name is Magua. He's the leader of many Huron war parties," announces Hawkeye. Uncas chases Magua. Heyward wants to pursue Magua, but Hawkeye dissuades him: "When you're fooled by an Indian, you've been fooled by the best." They escape by boat. To pretty shots of a waterfall, the narrator says: "Sometimes the forest can be deceptively peaceful, offering only an illusion of safety."

Nighttime. In the cave, they are eating . . . racoon. Gamut chokes when he learns what it is. Cora looks intently at Uncas: "I find it quite difficult to imagine that a man with such sensitive eyes could be a savage." Hawkeye: "Miss Munro, I've met more savages in lace collars and velvet pants than in war paint." Cora: "But all the stories I've heard about the Indians, the way they torture . . . scalp. . . . " Hawkeye: "Ah, most tribes don't practice those ghastly habits. Them that do learned it from the Dutch and the British. Like scalping: white men taught that to the Indian so the Indian could be paid a bounty every time he brought in a scalp from a white man's enemy—proof of the kill." Cora: "The British never resorted to such barbarous acts!" Hawkeye: "You'd better bone up on your history, ma'am. Scalping started in Europe long before the white man brought his poison here and taught it to the Indians."

They settle down to sleep. Uncas lays branches for the women. Hawkeye tells them he's "paying you a most uncommon honor" because warriors don't cater to women. Cora thanks him, then asks about his pouch and reaches to touch it. Uncas backs off fast. Cora is confused. Hawkeye explains the sacred significance of the "pouch of life." Uncas stands guard. The narrator takes us to the next morning and "new dangers," over shots of wild animals looking nervous. Magua is closing in. There is gunfire over the river. Too late, they see the Indians making off with the supply canoe.

Hawkeye proposes that he and Chingachgook try to cut off the canoe, since it is going upstream. Uncas stays with the women, Heyward, and Gamut. All are quickly captured, to be "traded for guns," except Gamut, who is useless for trade. About to be killed, he sings a psalm, and Magua declares him mad and untouchable. Led away, they are tied to trees, except Cora, to whom Magua offers food. She rejects it. Magua: "Pride, always pride. You people have nothing to be proud of. When the British first came, they ask only to move wagons through our land. Soon they ask no more. They took, and when we refused, they tricked us into slavery. Whipped like dogs. Are you proud of this?" (he shows his scarred back). Cora is shocked silent. Magua tells her she will soon learn from the "whips of the French." Cora says she will rather kill herself. Magua threatens to kill Alice as well. Uncas sidetracks him: "Does Magua wear a skirt? Does he fight only women?" Magua walks to him, sneering, threatens him, then takes his pouch of life, and empties it on the ground, Uncas straining in anguish to stop him. As Magua menaces Alice, Hawkeye arrives. In the ensuing melee, Magua throws gunpowder onto the fire, and the Hurons escape.

Freed, the travelers move on together, joined again by Gamut. They camp in an Indian graveyard. Hawkeye tells them its story. It is the site of a massacre over many days of whites and Mohicans, when the Mohawks were "prodded into war" by white land speculators. Only six survived the massacre: three others plus Hawkeye, Chingachgook, and Uncas. "All the rest are nestled here in the bosom of this green mountain, red and white alike and little Jenny Rose of the bright brown eyes." The camera rests on his face, sad but resolute, and on Cora's, astonished but learning.

They find they are trapped between two Huron war parties. There are long flight/chase scenes. Eventually Magua recaptures the women and Heyward and takes them north. Hawkeye, Chingachgook, and Uncas follow. The three followers capture a canoe, then are chased on a lake. There is a fight scene in the water, at the end of which Uncas doesn't come up: worried music takes us into what must have been a commercial break. When he reappears after a dissolve, his father joyously clasps him.

The narrator tells us of Magua's trick, splitting up his party and the captives, taking some to Tamenund's Delaware village. We see Cora and Alice separated, crying. Heyward is tied up to a pole while Alice is dragged away. Hawkeye and friends rescue Heyward before the war party returns. Gamut dies here, saving Heyward as Uncas is fighting another Huron. Finding Alice, they set out to get Cora as well, at the Delaware village.

At the village, Tamenund sees the sign of the turtle on Chingachgook and Uncas, and emotionally summons a council to discuss what to do. But Indian law requires Tamenund to hand over Cora to Magua. Heyward is infuriated, calls it "barbarous." Hawkeye counters by again making comparisons with barbarous European traditions. "The meaning of 'savage' depends on who's speakin' it."

Magua arrives to claim Cora. As soon as he leaves with her, the Mohicans and Delawares set out in pursuit. Cora, hands tied, is led out onto a promontory, and left with a guard as Magua sets up an ambush. The pursuers close in, and stalk the Hurons. Fighting breaks out, first with guns, then with knives. Cora's guard is killed, and she flees into the rocks. Uncas runs after, and kills a Huron who was about to stab her. Magua raises his rifle to shoot Cora, Uncas throws himself between and is killed. Hawkeye and Chingachgook arrive too late, to find him dead. Chingachgook races after Magua. They fight and fall into a pool where they grapple, watched by Hawkeye and the Delawares. Magua is finally killed by his own knife and is washed away down river. Chingachgook goes to Uncas over whose body Cora is weeping. There is a dramatic shot from below as he lifts Uncas and howls his grief.

The burial. We hear Chingachgook's thoughts in valediction to Uncas. English troops arrive and meet Heyward. They've been searching for them following the surrender of Fort William Henry and the massacre of most of the people as they left. Colonel Munro is alive, though, and they will take the three to him. First, they ask what will Hawkeye and Chingachgook do now? Chingachgook, says Hawkeye, will "go alone into the hills until he's ready to come down. Then we'll go together into the forest to find what we've lost." Heyward: "What is there?" Hawkeye: "Peace. Peace, Major. The most precious thing a man can have. Chingachgook and I will help those who want to see peace grow." He walks away, following behind Chingachgook.

The credit sequence comes up over a shot of a library of books.

END

There are obvious and important changes to the events within the story. Cora does not die, and Uncas's death is a simple self-sacrifice, as he threw himself between Cora and Magua's bullet. Gamut also dies, although this seems more extraneous to the flow of the film. Although there are hints of possible romance in the relationship between Cora and Uncas, they are very marginal. Indeed, one of the most striking things we would point to about this film, is its paradoxical mixture of very "right-on" attitudes towards native Americans, coupled with a strangely nostalgic, chivalric attitude to women.

The heart of this version, though, has to be the continual hard work it embodies at correcting any sense of Indian wrongness. Magua may be bad, but he is bad because he is not a proper Indian. After we have learned the mystical significance to Uncas of his pouch of life, it is Magua who despoils it. He is also and importantly ugly, by straight comparison with Uncas's flowing locks and bold young face—the essence of simple nobility. Magua therefore is an Indian gone bad, though we never quite know why, except perhaps through an "understandable" hatred of whites. But Hawkeye makes sure the other characters (and we) understand very clearly the balance of right and wrong in the wider picture. Here is a typical exchange between Hawkeye and Heyward. They are within the Delaware camp, as Magua is about to claim Cora as his lawful prisoner:

*Hawkeye*: Don't be blasphemin' what you don't understand.

*Heyward*: What civilized people would return a prisoner to her kidnappers?

*Hawkeye*: Well, it appears to me that I've heard tell of some dukes and princes that are snatched from one country and dragged into another against their will, and they use some fancy word like "asylum" instead of "kidnap" . . . .

*Heyward*: These are savages!

*Hawkeye*: By whose reckonin'? The British, who chop off a red man's hand for stealin'? Or the French, who taught him the finer points of torture? The meanin' of the word "savage" depends on who's speakin' it.

*Heyward*: I'm sorry. . . .

*Hawkeye*: So am I. . . . So are the Delawares, the Kiowas, the Senecas, and every red man who's seen his land taken away from him day by day, piece by piece, till he's pushed into a corner, with nary a place to grow his corn or hunt his deer, by your "civilized people."

In every such exchange, Hawkeye challenges the orthodoxies of "savage Indians," and turns the tables on white behavior. In every such exchange he also wins, filmically.

This is a Disneyesque version, garnished with political correctness dressed in the vernacular. It is Disney in its use of narration, to guide and lead us, and in its use of the homely opening to give us a child's eye view of Hawkeye. Thereafter his attitudes are offered as just the right ones. It is also Disneyesque in its use of animals to warm the countryside for us. There is no wilderness in this version. There is, instead, tamed Nature, with deer, bears, and birds waiting to become our friends. Fish rise to be caught by Chingachgook. The scenery is never so much wild as empty; but waiting, gently, for our arrival in it.

The curious part of this, as we have already hinted, is the old-fashioned attitudes to women that permeate this film. Gently admonishing in his attitudes to the sisters all through, Hawkeye reproves Alice mildly at the Delaware camp: "Women aren't allowed in the Delaware council tent." She falls back obediently. Uncas dies rather than see a hair of Cora's head hurt. The function of Cora and Alice seems to be to "bring out the best in the men," through their need for protection. But what exactly are they being defended from? Being such a childlike version, now all threat of rape by Magua is gone. Repeatedly, almost obsessively, the film tells us that the only danger is ransom—bad, but not disastrous, one would think. Yet lurking at the back is something more, something unspoken, unspeakable.

This is *Last of the Mohicans* for boy scouts, a camp fire version. Well done, and at points quite moving, it has to work too hard to make sure its "message" is right: the story may be exciting, but remember your real history, boys. Native Americans are to be pitied for what we did to them long ago; and don't forget, in the middle of all the excitement, to look after your sisters.[9]

## "The whole world's on fire, isn't it?"

And so to Michael Mann's 1992 adaptation, inevitably the one most people today will first call to mind. This beautiful film won an Oscar for its sound and great praise for the performances of (among others) Daniel Day-Lewis as Hawkeye, Madeleine Stowe as Cora, and Wes Studi as Magua. The film acknowledges Philip Dunne's 1936 screenplay, to which Mann bought the rights in 1989. It keeps many of the changes that Dunne and the other 1936 scriptwriters made to the original: the fates of Cora and Alice are reversed, and it is Hawkeye who gets the woman at the end, but this time after a very unpleasant end for Heyward, his competitor for Cora's heart. The film was sumptuously set and shot in the North Carolina mountains, whose vistas put an unforgettable visual stamp on the film.

Michael Mann is in many ways an outsider in Hollywood, a director who sets his own agendas and who therefore has to take his chance whenever his reputation earns him the possibility of financial backing. There is a suggestion that he got his way with Twentieth Century Fox over *Mohicans* precisely because this was an American classic. The issue of his treatment came later. Mann came to film by studying literature at the University of Wisconsin, then attending the London International Film School. From there, as a radical, he got access to the Paris "May Events" of 1968. Selling unusual footage to the American networks earned him a name, through which he eventually got work writing for the early episodes of *Starsky and Hutch*, and later *Miami Vice* and *Crime Story*. In among these jobs he had his first opportunities as a film director, notably with *Violent Streets* (1981) and the superb *Manhunter* (1986).

Having obtained the rights to *Mohicans*, Mann worked hard to get his cast. At this stage, Day-Lewis was not an obvious choice, especially for a classic American tale, and indeed turned Mann down at first. Many members of the cast were relative unknowns, and there was certainly no individual big star around whom the film could be sold. Shooting the film was grueling. The bad conditions led to a strike by crews and part-players. For a while the film company had refused to negotiate a union deal, but was forced to do so by a solid picket line slapped on a very expensive night location shot. The film was a box-office hit, though (as we shall see) it was not so clearly a critical success. It was received, of course, in the context of other new revisionist picturings of native Americans, most notably Kevin Costner's *Dances With Wolves* (1990).

There is a problem in retelling the Michael Mann version in words, since it is more filmic than any other account of *Mohicans*. Moving at times very slowly, Mann engenders a powerful mix of moods. It is as though all his characters have trouble expressing themselves. They are very inward and self-contained most of the time, not showing their feelings and desires through words or actions. Instead the camera in many scenes dwells long on faces as people reveal by their very physicality what they are feeling. Scenes of violence are very bloody and convey the materialness of war and pain and death, but they also study the reactions of those caught up in them. There seems to be a continual shifting between bewilderment and determination in the faces of characters. And in many scenes, we get to see people changing, learning and understanding things about the world and about themselves that have evaded them until now. It is a world gone mad, out of control, and people are digging into their inner resources to survive it, or to die in dignity if necessary. This is important to keep in mind as one follows the bare narrative.

THE LAST OF THE MOHICANS (1992)
Director: Michael Mann
Starring: Daniel Day-Lewis (Hawkeye), Madeleine Stowe (Cora), Jodhi May (Alice), Wes Studi (Magua), Russell Means (Chingachgook), Eric Schweig (Uncas), Steven Waddington (Heyward)

The film opens with a running drumbeat, as captions tell us: *1757. . . . The American colonies. It is the third year of the war. . . . Three men, the last of a vanishing people, are on a frontier west of the Hudson river.* As the resonant theme music bursts through, the title sequence follows, followed by panoramic scenes over mist-shrouded mountains and forests. Then, through the forest, we see three men in turn, running fast, leaping over gorges and rivers, finally closing on a deer and shooting it. Stillness falls as they approach it. One, Chingachgook, speaking in a native tongue (with subtitles for us): *We are sorry to kill you, brother. We do honor to your courage and speed, your strength.*

A new scene: a log cabin at night. The three hunters, Hawkeye and his compatriots, approach carrying the deer. They are warmly greeted by the family and soon sit down to a meal with them, playing also with the children. There is talk of the troubles on the frontier, and the news that the French are sweeping south. A militia is being formed by the English. The following morning, an uptight English officer calls on them to enlist. What if our houses are attacked, ask the colonials? The officer demands that they fight "for king and country." Hawkeye responds with irony: "You do what you want with your own scalp." As the scene closes, we see the men playing a game like lacrosse together—with white and Indian men indistinguishable in the laughing melee.

Albany. The colonials are told by Webb that if they join the militia they will be allowed to return to defend their homes, if necessary. "You've got your colonial militia, General," says John Winthrop, their spokesman.[10] Major Heyward, just arrived with dispatches, is shocked at an English officer negotiating with his troops. He is treated acidly by Webb. The rebuffed Heyward asks after the women he has to take to their father and is introduced to Magua, who is to guide him.

Heyward meets with Cora, whom he wishes to marry. When she declines him, he puts pressure on her: "Why not let those whom you trust—your father—help settle what's best for you? In view of your indecision, you *should* rely on their judgment, and mine." Cora delays her decision, and Alice—shown very much as a young, coltish girl—arrives to greet Heyward.

The next day, the party of four sets out with some accompanying troops. As the two women tire, Heyward arrogantly demands of Magua that they stop. Magua curses the English as dogs (in his own tongue) then appears to concur. We cut to seeing the three Mohicans (for that is how Hawkeye appears) finding marks in the forest and following them. Magua now suddenly turns his tomahawk on one of the soldiers to signal an attack by a large band of Indians. At the height of this bloody massacre, Hawkeye and the other Mohicans arrive, moving coolly and fatally among the attackers, driving them off. Magua vanishes. Heyward, now and later, continues to display an English officer's arrogance, even towards his rescuers.

Crossing a river, the rescued group is set against the background of a vast, untamed Nature. The people are small and weak by comparison. Uncas is drawn to the almost helpless Alice, who appears like a stunned child.

Hawkeye and Heyward argue about duty. Coming to a clearing, they approach a burned-out log cabin. The family with whom the Mohicans had eaten the previous day lie murdered. The Mohicans read this fact as a sign of a war party moving fast down-country. When they leave the bodies untouched, Cora protests in anguish and accuses Hawkeye of "indifference." Coolly, he looks her down and tells her he will not bury his friends. That night, they talk at last. Cora tells of her bewilderment at what she is seeing. Hawkeye retorts: "My father Chingachgook told me, do not try to understand them [the white people]. And do not try to make them understand you. That is because they are a breed apart, and make no sense."

As they talk, Hurons are heard approaching. All including Cora take rifles. But the Hurons will not approach their hiding place, a burial ground. Indeed, it is the burial ground of Hawkeye's parents who were murdered when he was a baby. He was raised by the Mohicans, who sent him to Mission school to learn English later. Cora asks why the murdered family chose to live in such a lonely place. Hawkeye: "After seven years indentured service in Virginia, they headed out, because the frontier is the only land available to poor people, and here they're beholden to none, not living by another's leave." Cora is learning. Rejecting his apology for the harshness of it all, she says: "On the contrary. It is more stirring to my blood than any imagining could possibly have been."

They move on at night. As they approach the fort, we see it in the distance under attack, a beautiful, horrible scene of lights and explosions. At last the women are with their father: exhausted, dirty, and scared. Munro realizes that none of his messages have gotten through. But when told of the war party, he brusquely refuses to hear the pleas for the colonials to be released. Alone with Heyward, he orders: "Those considerations are subordinate to the interests of the Crown. A terrible feature of wars here in the Americas, Major Heyward. Best keep your eye fixed on your duty—to defeat the French."

Cut between the French and English camps. Magua, talking with Montcalm, reveals his deep hatred for "the Grey Hair" Munro; we don't yet know why. Meanwhile, looks and talk between Hawkeye and Cora reveal their growing attraction to each other. Once again, Munro refuses to release the colonials, on pain of death. Heyward lies, in front of Cora, about what they saw at the log cabin. Winthrop denounces Munro: "Does the rule of English law no longer govern? Has it been replaced by absolutism?" Hawkeye suggests that perhaps they would be better off negotiating with the French. When Heyward threatens this "treasonous" remark with hanging, Hawkeye turns coolly to him and says (in words taken directly from the 1936 film): "Major, some day you and I are going to have a serious disagreement." Outside, Cora decisively rejects Heyward's suit.

That night, some colonials plan an escape. They will not live under a "yoke of tyranny." In the quiet of the night Hawkeye and Cora meet and in the urgency of war consummate their love. As day breaks, the escape is discovered, and Hawkeye is seized to be hanged. Cora's pleas for him are dismissed, and she also now condemns the English as tyrants. Going to the stockade, she and Hawkeye cling together, to await the day. "The whole world's on fire, isn't it?" she cries in his arms.

In the night, a further deadly bombardment. The next day, a parley. Montcalm shows Munro the captured messages from Webb and pleads with Munro not to sacrifice his men. There can be surrender with honor. Munro, turning to his officers, remarks that he sees too late that death and honor might be separate things. The parley over, we see Montcalm and Magua meet. Now we learn why Magua so hates "the Grey Hair": his children and whole village were wiped out by the English. "The Grey Hair was the father of all that." For that, and to prove himself a leader, there must be blood. Montcalm gives tacit approval because he knows Webb will not keep to their bargain of returning the troops to England.

The departure from the fort, with the women riding together near the head of the company. At the back, among ragged camp followers, Hawkeye, in chains, tries to keep his eye on the women. Magua watches as they enter a forest path. The attack begins. In the bloody mayhem that follows, Magua fells Munro. Telling him he will soon have his children under his knife, he plunges his knife into Munro and literally cuts his heart out. Hawkeye breaks free of his chains, and he and the Mohicans battle through to the two women. Desperately, they break away with them to the lakeshore, where they take canoes: the three Mohicans, the two women, and also Heyward. Pursued, they hide behind the great curtain of a waterfall and wait. Here Uncas takes and holds the broken Alice. They see torches reflecting in the water; Magua has found them. The three Mohicans will have to leave if a fight is to be avoided. Urgently, Hawkeye holds and speaks to Cora: "No matter what happens, stay alive. I *will* find you." Then the three Mohicans hurl themselves into the water. The others are quickly and brutally taken prisoner, and dragged away.

Downstream, the three struggle from the river and set off in pursuit of the prisoners, accompanied by the film's theme song (Clannad's "I Will Find You"). Now the prisoners are brought into the Huron's village in front of their elderly Sachem. Magua asks for honor as a great Huron chief for his exploits. He has killed many whites and brought prisoners: the white officer to ransom, the two women to be burned in their fires. We read the words in subtitles. As Magua boasts of his deeds, Hawkeye walks into the village through a gauntlet of angry Hurons who repeatedly knock him down, but can't stop him.

In front of the Sachem, he and Magua finally confront each other and argue. Hawkeye claims that Magua broke the peace against French wishes. But Magua seems to be winning the argument: "When the Hurons are stronger from their fear, we will make new terms of trade with the French. We will become traders as the whites. Take land from the Abenaki, furs from the Osage, and the Fox. Trade for gold. No less than the whites, as strong as the whites."

In the stillness that follows this declaration, Hawkeye turns to him: "Would Magua use the ways of les Français and the Yengees? . . . Would you?" Yes, the confident Magua responds. "Would the Hurons make their Algonquin brothers foolish with brandy and steal their lands to sell them for gold to the white men? Would Hurons have greed for more land than a man can use? Would Hurons fool Seneca into taking all the furs of all the animals in the forest for beads and strong whiskey? Those are the ways of the Yengees and the Français traders, their masters in Europe infected with the sickness of greed. Magua's heart is twisted. He would make himself into what has twisted him."

At this climactic moment, the Sachem delivers a terrible judgment. He talks of the coming of the whites as the night of his people. What are they to do, they have asked themselves? But Magua's way is not the Huron way. Let him take, therefore, the younger daughter of Munro as his wife, so that his seed shall not die out. Let the white officer be returned, to placate the anger of the English. Let the older daughter die in their fires, as a memorial to Magua's dead children. And let the Long Rifle go in peace.

In the awful moments that follow this, both Hawkeye and Heyward offer themselves to die in Cora's place, and Heyward is seized. Meanwhile Magua storms out of the village with Alice to seek out his Huron cousins who are not dogs, cowards. As the fires begin to burn the screaming Heyward, from outside the village Hawkeye takes his rifle and puts him out of his agony. Then he, Cora, Chingachgook, and Uncas turn in pursuit of Magua.

In the wilds now, Uncas running ahead intercepts the Huron party, and finally confronts Magua, who kills the Mohican with near contempt. Chingachgook sees him fall and runs on in despair. Alice stands at the edge of a great precipice and, ignoring the hand that Magua finally offers in place of his knife, leans away, and falls a thousand feet to her death. Now Chingachgook, arriving too late, confronts Magua. In a slow-motion fight, he slaughters him and pours out his anguish in his blows. All emotion spent, Hawkeye leads Cora away—to a final scene, as Chingachgook says farewell and calls on the gods to receive his son. Standing on top of the very mountains we had seen at the start of the film, Chingachgook—the last of the Mohicans—Hawkeye, and Cora are left standing as the sun touches the misty horizon.

END

There is a great deal to be said about this film, which we admire enormously. Some transformations are very evident. Hawkeye has become a Mohican. Rescued by the tribe after his parents were killed in a massacre, he is, for all intents and purposes, an Indian. He thinks and speaks like them; he identifies with them. The scene at the village, however, suggests something more: that the distinction between Indians and whites hardly matters. A more important difference is that between ordinary folks struggling to survive and the overcivilized English and French.

Mann did extensive ethnographic research in preparing for the film, using evidence from the neighboring Mohawks and Iroquois when he could not find information on the Mohicans. In the film's depiction of Indian life, there is an evident quest for authenticity. It is there in the use of Indian language with subtitles at many points in the film. It is there when Hawkeye refuses to bury his murdered friends. Even the viewer does not know for a while why Hawkeye does this (although we know more than Cora, for we have already seen that these were his good friends). Whatever his motives, we know he is not indifferent. In a way, therefore, we both share but stand above the misunderstanding between them. Mann's research is grained into the film not just in details of costume and lifestyle but in, for example, the continuous stress on this gap between Cora and Hawkeye. She cannot understand him, nor he her. Only when, in the night scene as they hide from the Hurons, she makes a breakthrough toward understanding can love between them grow. Cora begins to move away from her father's "civilization" towards the values of the new land—whatever exactly they may be. She feels the pull of something but cannot yet say what it is.[11]

But if we know things that she does not, we are not allowed any detachment. The film *wills* our participation in its emotions through its extensive use of close-ups. Importantly, the close-ups are not simply of the heroic characters. We are invited to see and be involved in the feelings even of those with whom the film find fault or whom it condemns. This manner of filming gave pause to a number of reviewers. In fact, there is an interesting division among them. One group sees the film as an action-adventure and romance "amid the chaos and visual splendor of a crashing war."[12] This was typical of the popular reviews, implying a separation of the action and the manner of filming. The scenery and the concentrated close-ups were an add-on, to be enjoyed separately.

But those who sought to locate the film more within the classic, mythmaking tradition had trouble. Reviewer Henry Sheehan, for instance, damning with faint praise, said that it "strives for the picturesque and fails to achieve it," finding a "self-defeating combination of widescreen compositions and long, shallow-focus lenses." Significantly, he goes on to suggest that Mann is more "racist" than Cooper in that he shifts the romance to Cora and Hawkeye, leaving Uncas only sidelong glances at the young Alice.[13] Exactly the same thing happens in Derek Malcolm's review in the British *Guardian*: "Admittedly Uncas, the actual last of the Mohicans, is allowed a putative romance with the younger sister. But that's not quite the same thing, racially speaking. Nor does it effectively illustrate Cooper's now naive-seeming thesis that the 'new America' would be built across racial divides. What remains is a splendid-looking action-adventure and romance."[14] Something instructive is going on here. Mann is being judged against a view of Cooper that, curiously, corresponds quite closely with the one that lies behind the 1977 version of the film. This is Cooper rehabilitated as an anti-racist. Cooper certainly did *not* see a new America being built across racial divides. But certainly, too, the ambiguities in his book permit the temper of readings of him in the 1970 and '80s that preferred to see him in just that way.

Both ends of Malcolm's judgment are important. Failing as a myth, Mann's version of *Mohicans* can still be an adventure film. That matters in itself. A "classic" has been brought back to life, once again becoming pleasurable, comprehensible, meaningful for a new generation. But for those who need the myth to be more coherent than that, there is a problem. Mann's film tends to fall apart. And on close examination, it does indeed have three different aspects, signified and carried by different modes of filming:

(a) There are "environmental" shots. These are not simply the panoramic opening and closing scenes, though they are important, but also the scenes in which Hawkeye and the Mohicans are shown in harmony with their world. They kill a deer and bless it, Indian-wise, for giving its strength to them. They tumble and frolic, white and Indian indistinguishable, in a natural game of physical skills. They have a natural quiet and grace, like wild creatures in wild places. So when Hawkeye denounces Magua to his chief, he speaks with the voice and authority of a natural man. Magua would be a trader, an exploiter. He would kill all the beavers *and* get the Indians drunk for the sake of gold. It matters not whether Hawkeye is white or Indian, the point is he has a proper respect for and harmony with his environment. And the entire "feel" of the environment is enriched by the musical score from Clannad.

(b) There are shots and scenes of action, conflict, politics, and war. Unglamorized, these scenes are cruel, brutal, and chaotic. They tell of horror and anguish. But in themselves they are hollow. They are the shell of the action, awaiting meaning through the third mode of filming. These shots are never simply violent. Even that unprecedented scene in which Magua cuts out the heart of Munro and holds it up in triumph takes on a Shakespearian viscerality, not unlike the blinding of Gloucester in *King Lear*.

(c) There are reaction shots. It is hard to think of many other films that use such long close-ups of people's reactions to events. We see in the faces of all participants equal measures of uncertainty, bewilderment and determination. We see, as it were, into the depths of people, people who often struggle to speak. Their responses are bigger than their words. The result is an extraordinary humanization of all sides in the conflict—but to what end? To be measured against what?

We may answer that question by placing *Mohicans* back into the trajectory of Mann's work. Formed in the political cauldron of the 1960s, informed by a semi-hippie consciousness, Mann's key works are marked by two things in particular: a focus on *liminal* characters (that is, people who cross social thresholds), and his works' use to uncover social conflicts. *Starsky and Hutch*, for instance, was marked by the use of "low-life" contacts, especially (but by no means only) their black informant Huggy Bear. Many episodes were built around Starksy and Hutch having to explore the depths of their society because a good friend of theirs had been sucked into the depths. *Miami Vice* was built around street cops who both live in and police the ghetto. Speaking of one episode still important to him, Mann has said: "I took a cop and made him undercover as a migrant worker. Through what happens to him in LA—getting ripped off in sweatshops, working in restaurants in La Cienega Boulevard—it exposed the exploitation of migrant labor."[15]

This is the exploration of class relations through a liminal character. A rich humanism underlies this exposure. According to Mann, something is very wrong with a world that so degrades people. And the wrong is systemic, not grounded in evil individuals (hence his willingness to show the confusions and hurt in his problematic characters). But in *Mohicans*, there is a rub between Mann's intentions and the story, which results in a deeply reactionary and hopeless politics. The film displays the futilities of war and politicking. His characters are his witnesses to this. Their struggles with words, transformed from the stoic silences of the Western, are the awkward silences of bewildered people. Only Hawkeye, the liminal character, can find the necessary words. On behalf of the little men and women (the indentured servants, the small farmers) Hawkeye denounces greed. On behalf of harmony, he denounces exploitation, both natural and social. The idyll, therefore, is still the American idyll: a nation of small farmers honoring their land, with the depths of "nature" inside them. This is the hollow idyll Bill Clinton rode to power (also in 1992) as he shouldered aside the hard market ethics of George Bush's Republicanism. Its hollowness has been painfully exposed in the short and beleaguered presidency Clinton has enjoyed.

Michael Mann's *The Last of the Mohicans*, we would argue, is the fragile utopia of 1990s Democratic politics. Mann began elsewhere, forming his politics in the crucible of the anti-Vietnam War movement, in the radical ferment of the 1960s. He has here sunk away into a middle-American dream/nightmare. Partly, that is surely due to the progressive decline in American radical politics in the last thirty years. There is to us a symbolic irony about a "liberal" film being made under conditions that its work force have to strike to gain even the right to negotiate. But that isn't the sum of it. Something about the story of *Mohicans*, taken as the vehicle for Mann's radical vision, turns to constrain and defeat that radicalism. Exactly what that is must wait until our final chapter. The clue, perhaps, is in its bitterly anti-English strand. All the English characters are haughty, arrogant—and deceitful when need be. They stand opposite the simple, direct virtues of the ordinary colonials (who merge, at crucial points, with the native Americans). If the English in Cooper's story tend to represent a problematic strand in America, this opposition in Mann's film may be very significant and revealing.

Film is central to our tale, because film is so central to the way American culture talks to itself and to the rest of the world. It would be easy to devote great space to comparing these film adaptations. To do so could illuminate much. But we cannot. Instead, we are simply going to point toward some critical areas where such comparisons would be especially worthwhile. Our general question is this: Bearing in mind the tendency for everything in these films to tend towards mythmaking, in what ways, and with what results, does this happen with each of the following?

*The image of the English*: The "English" tend to symbolize the European connection, or the way other than the truly "American." And without much difficulty, "Englishness" can be associated with old aristocratic wealth. In each film, then, how are the English pictured? What motivates them? How do they react to the emerging Americans? What damage does being English do to characters or to situations?

*The image of the Wilderness*: The theme of wilderness has been the topic of extensive historical research, particularly (but not only) in relation to images in literature. But film works differently from literature, and the scenic is one of its preeminent capacities. How, then, is wilderness portrayed and evoked in each film? How are human beings set within or against it? What values, or dangers is it shown as presenting to us? And in particular how does Hawkeye relate to wilderness in each case? Is it part of his nature, or is he like everyone else out there?

*The image of Race*: "Race" is a social construct; we take that for granted. But it can be constructed in many ways. It is possible to show people as having fixed differences, or as grounded within cultures that may be different but compatible. Some people may be able to move between races or cultures. How does each film use the idea of "race" to explain, to justify, or to trouble our understanding?

*The issues of motives*: In Cooper's original book, we noted the presence of two co-present systems of explanation: the racial and the historical. Of course the two need not be sharply separate. But each film has to try to explain why people behave as they do. What image, then, are we given in each film of the motivations—the fears and hopes, the past experiences, the driving imperatives—of the key characters?

*The position of women*: Feminist writers rightly have shown how often it is possible to diagnose the state of a culture from the image and position of women within it. Yet there is a puzzle here. A good deal of important feminist work has unpacked the ways in which women are traditionally associated with "nature," as against male "culture." *Mohicans* seems to offer some sort of challenge to that, since the women are endangered because they leave culture to encounter nature. Yet at other levels the women clearly are the objects of sexual desire, romance, protection; they are the prizes over which men fight. How does each film deal with the position of women? What spaces, if any, do they allow for Cora and Alice themselves to be active and decisive?

The foregoing is not the sum total of our questions, but we think the issues are pivotal to understanding the different forms of myth our *Mohicans* films have proposed. In particular, we think that the answers to these questions might illuminate how the myth of the Mohicans relates to other myths about America. For America's myths about itself have shifted geographically around the continent. What we suggest here is drastically oversimplified, but we think there is a point to saying it, nonetheless.

In the early years of this century, much literature focused on the grimness of urban life, depicted in places like Detroit and Chicago. The novels of writers like Upton Sinclair portrayed urban America as a nightmare of suffering and corruption.[16] Opposite these were several parts: the West—clean and noble in works such as Owen Wister's *The Virginian*; and other wild places in the writings of, for example, Jack London.[17] In the 1930s, the mythic city stayed much the same (though Chicago came more to mean organized crime). There was a plethora of books and films about Prohibition, organized crime, and the struggle for life in the cities. But the countryside became more problematic, as the Oklahoma dustbowl, especially, seemed to typify rural America. Through the work of the Farm Security Administration and other New Deal activist groups, rural poverty was put on the national agenda.

By the 1950s, urban America had reverted to New York, that exciting, dynamic, but alienating city. Hollywood's MGM gave us films like *New York, New York*, while television's *The Naked City* told us "a million stories," each one balancing the positives and negatives of city life, many ending by reaching for the psychoanalyst. The rural "other" seemed to settle around Texas, though its "western" image collided with its reality as the biggest oil producing state.

During the radical questioning of the 1960s, a curious merging seemed to take place, with San Francisco representing the country within the city, the beautiful life on the streets. Often now speaking of and to the young through the medium of pop music, the image of "flower power" made the city tender and garden-like. But that did not last long, for by the mid-1970s the urban image was shifting a short distance south to Los Angeles. LA was a scenario for urban nightmares. The "city of the future," its skylines, smog, ethnic mix, and elaborate blend of tinsel and misery provided the setting for a large number of SF-ish films, from *Blade Runner* onwards. What is not so clear is what now constitutes the "other" of this. It has become a more indeterminate middle America: small-town, small-minded, and increasingly bitter. Or it has, very recently, headed north: the last few years has seen a crop of fictions set in and around Alaska, notably TV's *Northern Exposure*, which has become something of a cult program with its "utopia of diversity."[18]

Where does *Mohicans* fit into all of this? It doesn't seem to fit at all. Each film version, through its visual feel for the countryside and through its rhetorical account of the meanings of wilderness, seems to occupy a no-place. It is everywhere and nowhere. Its power seems to lie precisely in offering an abstract reconciliation of city and country, a way for America to return to itself through the secret wildernesses of the mind.[19]

CHAPTER 6    The Television and
             Cartoon Versions

Film seems in many ways to have been the ideal medium for working with the *Mohicans* story. The star system, the big budgets, the
need for wide appeal both within America and internationally all
contributed to the tendency of film to produce "types" and
"myths." Given the costliness of staging some of those outside
shots and fight scenes, it is not surprising that the most vital adaptations should be those in feature film. But not just these. Film also
achieved a central place in American ideology. Having become after
1915 very important economically, it settled into a clear niche,
speaking to "America" in the broadest sense.

When television arrived on the scene in the 1950s, its position
was quite different. Feared by the film industry because of its com-
petitive threat, soon a topic of concern about possible corruption of
the young, television was not a natural place for mythic storytelling.
And indeed if we examine the attempts to translate *Mohicans* into
media other than the feature film, it is soon evident that other

pressures have been at work. We will look, in turn, at the television versions and at two animated cartoons. Of the attempts at televising Cooper's story, only one is American, although the others have undoubtedly been broadcast in the U.S.

## Mohicans as wallpaper: The CBC version

The earliest, a Canadian series, ran to at least thirty half-hour episodes, and was first broadcast on American TV in 1957 and on British TV in 1957–58. The series was accompanied in both countries by considerable marketing. In America, among other things, Dell Comics produced a spin-off comic accompaniment.[1] In Britain Publicity Products, a marketing business, produced a book of the TV series, from which in turn came a series of pocketbook comics.[2] A number of other products, including a novelty wallpaper, were also produced.[3]

This Canadian series is curious in making insistent reference to Cooper, yet actually having almost no real relation to his story. For brevity's sake, we have only retold the first episode, since that is the only one to do more than nod to the original novel.[4]

HAWKEYE AND THE LAST OF THE MOHICANS (1956)
Director: Sidney Salkow
Starring: John Hart (Hawkeye), Lon Chaney, Jr. (Chingachgook), Michael Ansara (Ogana), Lili Fontaine (Marion), Dave Garner (Tommy Cutler)
Visions Productions Ltd. (1956) for the Canadian Broadcasting Corporation

The series opens with a series of shots culled from the 1936 film, over which an excited narrator announces: "The immortal pen of James Fenimore Cooper brings you thrilling tales of excitement, blazing action on the early American frontier and stirring adventures filled with the daring and courage of HAWKEYE—the first of the long rifles—and his blood brother CHINGACHGOOK, 'THE LAST OF THE MOHICANS.'"

*A cabin on the Iroquois trail.* Two figures, Hawkeye and Chingachgook, arrive at an old lady's cabin. It is Hawkeye's mother, who welcomes them and tells him his kid brother Tommy has grown up and joined the Redcoats. Cut to *Lake George, an isolated British outpost.* A messenger is being sent to warn the British of an impending British attack. Tommy (for it is he) is to be accompanied to a shortcut by a Mohawk scout, Ogana. But on the trail, and close by Hawkeye's mother's house, Ogana shoots Tommy in the back and takes his precious dispatch. Hawkeye and Chingachgook hear, and drive off the Indian before he can knife Tommy. They take him back to the house.

Ogana, returning to the fort, pretends that Tommy had been signaling to the Hurons. He, Ogana, had stopped him—and is now himself sent with the dispatch. Troops arrive to arrest Tommy just as he dies of his wound.

Hawkeye and the Mohican pursue Ogana and see him signal to a band of Hurons: "Brothers, I have come from the French camp. French general fool, have heart of woman. He say you get no Yankee scalps, no guns, no prisoners!" In order to be able to clear Tommy's name, the two scouts trick Ogana into letting them accompany him to the fort, where they see him fool the officers. The Colonel's young daughter, Marion, even thanks him for his help, and gets a leering look in return. It turns out there is a French officer passing as an Englishman. When Hawkeye and Chingachgook are forced to kill him as he is sending Ogana to tell the French to attack, they are arrested as traitors. But that night two people struggle into camp (by swimming the lake) to warn of Ogana's treachery and the impending attack. One of them is Captain West, Marion's sweetheart. Before our heroes can be released, however, the Hurons storm the fort and Ogana kidnaps Marion. Breaking out, the two companions pursue Ogana's group and overtake them just as Ogana is trying to persuade an Ottawa chief to marry him to Marion.

Hawkeye challenges Ogana to a fight to prove who is telling the truth. Finally, after a desperate struggle, Ogana falls dead at Marion's feet. The Ottawa chief keeps his promise to release them all. Back at the fort, the colonel asks Hawkeye to become his chief scout. Hawkeye declines: "That's a real compliment, Colonel. But I reckon, me and Army regulations just don't get along somehow. Besides, Chingachgook and I were plannin' on headin' out to the new territory, west of the big smoky mountain, where the grass is tall an' green an' there aren't any wars goin' on." To Marion's gently chiding warning that it only looks greener till you get there, he replies: "It seems that way, ma'am. But it doesn't stop a feller wantin' to find out for himself." And they depart, waving.

END

The question here surely is: what does this story gain by calling itself a version of *Mohicans*? Without question, this was a major international television production. To this day, it is fondly remembered by many who were children at the time. And its opening title sequence made strong claim for its origins in Cooper's writings.

Certainly in the course of this first episode (but in this one only) there are numerous small references to Cooper's original, among them the false Huron scout, the shortcut that goes wrong, the struggle by a small party to get through to the fort, the dispatches warning of attack that go astray, Ogana's lustful kidnap of Marion—

even, more weakly, the introduction of a chief of another tribe (in this case the Ottawas).[5] There are also hints of the 1936 film in, for example, the final invitation to Hawkeye to become a scout. Yet that is all they are: hints of a connection. It is as though the producers needed the license of the original story, its associations and resonances, to provide body and energy to all the subsequent episodes where they have traveled to the West. In those segments, they act much more like other Western heroes, such as the Lone Ranger and Tonto. They stop Indian wars, prevent injustices, and generally tidy up the frontier.

### "Major Heyward, an Indian is a reasoning man, whether he be varmint or friend."

The second TV version was a British one. Made as a Sunday teatime children's serial, it was broadcast in eight episodes in 1971.[6] Disappointingly, we have not managed to see all the episodes, though a lot can be learned from the five we have seen. Filmed mainly at Glen Affric in Scotland, the series earned high praise from virtually all reviewers, including the arts programs, and sold all over the world. The BBC has a notable tradition of turning great novels into costume dramas. Because of the BBC's own history, and because of the great importance that has historically been attached to the civilizing effects of literature, this tradition has always had to test itself against the criterion of doing justice to the original. Even here, though, there were distinctions. As director David Maloney told us: "BBC2 tended to do the more highbrow stuff, classic serials like Flaubert, but BBC1 had the tradition of Sunday teatime serials."[7] Maloney had come up through science fiction, directing many episodes of the BBC's groundbreaking series *Doctor Who*, and in fact returned to that field later to direct the science fiction series *Blake's Seven*.[8] A common thread through all the British reviews is how "convincing" the series *Mohicans* is. And that points us into the main determining discourse that dominated both its production and reception: the need to be "authentic." But that, as we can see even from part of the series, does not mean some mechanical reproduction. Rather, it means the creation of what is felt at its time to be an appropriate sense of period and a right way for us to relate to that period:[9]

THE LAST OF THE MOHICANS (1971)
Director: David Maloney
Starring: Kenneth Ives (Hawkeye), John Abineri (Chingachgook), Richard Warwick (Uncas), Philip Madoc (Magua), Patricia Maynard (Cora), Joanna David (Alice), Tim Goodman (Heyward), David Leland (Gamut)[10]

Episode 1: We first see Hawkeye and the Mohicans scouting outside Fort William Henry. As they return, two soldiers scornfully talk of them as "the Colonel's pets." There is an immediate clash of wills and knowledge between Hawkeye and a British major. Munro, at the fort, is longing to see his daughters, but "No, here I am and here I stay, among savages."

Cut to England, and a formal dance. Cora too is longing to see her father, but isn't allowed to travel on the troop ship that her admirer Major Grant will be going on. To the side, two unpleasant old women discuss the apparent romance: for all Cora's wealth, "Fools apart," says one, "there's no young man in the Western hemisphere who is a fit mate for Cora Munro. Of course in the Americas . . . but that's a horse of another *color.*"

At Fort Edward, Gamut enters, a sharp, collected young man who immediately starts teaching the soldiers his psalms. Inside, we see General Webb issuing instructions for the flogging of an Indian for drunkenness. Magua, watching angrily, is told it is only the rules: "White man has no rules." Heyward arrives with a request for troops to aid Munro. Webb, dismissively, reaches for his snuff. Now Cora and Alice arrive, seeking their father, to Webb's irritation. Heyward meets the girls for the first time, and in the ensuing conversation we see his growing attraction to Alice, and they and we receive instruction on the politics of North America at this time.

In the forest, Hawkeye and Chingachgook discuss the rights and wrongs of the white occupation of America, Chingachgook maintaining that the whites stole the Indians' lands, but Hawkeye responding that that is only what the Mohicans had done to their predecessors. Though there are two clear sides to the argument, Hawkeye seems to win—except on one point. The camera moves into a close-up as he accepts Chingachgook's criticism that the whites have abandoned a sense of tradition. Too much is book learning, and that is not the way: "A man should tell with his tongue what he's seen and done. And his face will then show the truth of his words," admits Hawkeye.

Back at his fort, Munro is ordering an execution party, for deserters fleeing the grimness of their situation. Munro can only bemoan his distance from his beloved Scotland. Now news of his daughters' proximity arrives. In the forest, Hawkeye watches Hurons hunting with the French. At Fort Edward, Magua is brusquely ordered to lead the women to their father by a back route. Webb again hears from Munro, this time detailing an attack by Montcalm. Again, Webb refuses to believe the intelligence.

These scenes are intercut with the women journeying with Magua, Heyward, and another soldier. We see them watched. Then, when they pause to eat, an attack by Hurons. Gamut and Cora in their own ways join the defense, until they are saved by Hawkeye and company. Magua, exposed as a traitor, escapes. Seeing the Mohicans scalp the dead, Alice shrieks. Hawkeye explains: "To them it is an act of mercy. They believe it sets the dead man's soul free." The episode closes as they journey on, led by Hawkeye and pursued by Magua's Hurons.

Episode 2: The long silent pursuit continues until the escaping party reaches the river, enters canoes, and reaches Hawkeye's island cave. Here they talk and Hawkeye explains Indian names and customs to the British. He then calls on Chingachgook to tell the tale of the Mohicans, a tale of the destruction of their culture by the Dutch.

A brief interlude at Munro's fort, then back to readying for the Hurons. Hawkeye argues the differences between forest fighting and standing battles. Heyward dismisses Indian skills as just "brutal and senseless savagery." Hawkeye puts him down firmly, stressing that he knows and trusts the Mohicans more than any Britisher.

Munro is worrying about the non-arrival of his girls, and Major Grant sets out with a search party. Intercut with the scenes at the cave, we see his party set out and be gradually whittled down by knives and arrows until Grant, the sole survivor, is surrounded and captured by Hurons. Meanwhile at the cave, Uncas looks long at the sleeping Cora. In the morning, woken by the screams of the horses, they prepare to fight. The Hurons attack, and as the defenders run out of powder, Cora insists that Hawkeye "waste" his last shot in an act of mercy on a wounded Huron. Disappointed, Hawkeye responds: "Those who live in the woods must learn the rules of the woods." With their powder gone, the Mohicans prepare to die until Cora persuades them to escape to get help (though Uncas, looking at her, is deeply unwilling). They do leave and soon we see them in the forest finding the dead body of Grant and, close by, his gun and ammunition. "We're men again," says Hawkeye. At the cave, the face of Magua appears ominously in the opening.

Episode 3: Magua captures the British and hunts frustratedly for "La Longue Carabine." They are taken down river by canoe, while we see the scouts following. Meanwhile a helpless Munro learns of Grant's failure. Elsewhere Webb has decided to send a token search party to cover himself. They find the cave, empty, and return to Fort Edward. Ashore, Heyward tries to persuade Magua to ransom the women. Magua dismisses him, and in a long scene makes his demand that Cora enter his wigwam. When she runs from his grasping hands to the others, they are all tied to trees. The Hurons taunt them, throwing tomahawks close to Alice's head. After Gamut, still free, has managed to shoot one Huron, Hawkeye and the Mohicans arrive to drive off the rest. They head for Fort William Henry, sleeping the night at the burial bunkhouse. Uncas has to be persuaded to approach by his friends, who assure him that the dead *were* scalped. In the night, a Huron war party approaches.

Episode 4: The Hurons retreat from the burial mounds, fearing the spirits. At Hawkeye's request, Chingachgook explains: "All Indians fear the dead if they are not scalped." There follows an important exchange:
Cora: "Scalping is barbaric!" Hawkeye: "So it is, ma'am, when it is done by British soldiers and colonials." Cora: "British soldiers? I do not believe it!" Hawkeye: "It is true for all that. White men take scalps . . . sometimes for the bounty, ma'am, or for trophies."

In the morning, they approach the fort and, using the fog, sneak through to Munro.

Meanwhile Webb bemoans their situation: "An outpost, by God. Never let us forget that we are nothing on the edge of nowhere, by the world forgot." He finally sends a scouting party to see if Munro is telling the truth about Montcalm's strength. When they confirm the siege, he sends dispatches advising surrender.

Cora and Alice decline the position of "ladies" within Fort William Henry, insisting on helping to nurse the wounded. Munro has hidden from them that Hawkeye and the Mohicans have not entered Fort William Henry. We learn what has happened when we see them tied to stakes, danced round in stylized fashion by Magua's Hurons. They are being tortured, preparing them for death. Montcalm with his soldiers intervenes to save Hawkeye, who refuses safety if it does not include his Mohican friends and his long rifle, to Magua's fury. Hawkeye is sent bearing Webb's captured dispatches, after which he joins the Mohicans in the woods to find healing herbs for their torture wounds. The episode ends at the parley, as Munro realizes he has been betrayed by Webb.

[Episodes 5–7 have eluded us to date.]

Episode 8 opens after Magua's departure with Cora from the Delaware camp. The opening scenes intercut three strands. Hawkeye and Chingachgook are planning a strategy for Cora's rescue, the former dismissing Colonel Munro's very "English" battle plans: "With, uh, respect, Colonel, this is not a regiment of infantry advancing on a regiment of infantry drawn up in line and waiting for us. You see, Colonel, this is an Indian battle. It's the Delawares who've declared war, not you and me. It just so happens we get something out of it—we rescue Miss Munro. . . . Oh yes, Miss Alice, we shall rescue her. But that ain't the object of the exercise for the Delawares. They aim to have a go at the Hurons because Magua's made bad blood." Alice is cool and deliberative.

Meantime Hawkeye has sent a young Delaware to recover his Long Rifle from a hiding place in the forest. We see the boy out scouting for it, being seen by one of Magua's Hurons who fires at him. Back at the camp he presents the rifle to Hawkeye, is praised as a man for his act, and falls, with a bullet hole in his back.

Magua is now getting a cool reception from other Huron chiefs, who fear that he is just making trouble for them. Why has he "raised a fire in the forest" that might burn them? Only when they hear of Chingachgook and "Le Cerf Agile" do they choose his side.

The war party is ready to set out. Hawkeye and Chingachgook both "seek the honor" of being accompanied by one of the white officers in their raid. In this way, the officers' honorable intentions are respected, but they have to acknowledge they don't know how to fight a war of this kind. Even David Gamut, looking like David of old with a slingshot, will go.

The Hurons prepare. Magua taunts Cora, who remains undaunted. Uncas calls upon the Manitou to bless their actions. His speech sees dark times ahead in the signs in the clouds. There follow long scenes of the Delawares advancing cautiously, then skirmishing with the Hurons. Now it is full scale fighting on the flanks, and Uncas's central group runs into action. Even the English officers join in the war whoops as they attack.

At the Huron camp, Cora taunts the two small boys left to guard her. Angered, they leave to prove themselves, and she escapes. Cora (looking for all the world like a 1960s flower child in ethnic dress) coolly steals a canoe and paddles herself away. Magua sets out in pursuit. Arriving, the triumphant Delawares pause to celebrate their victory. Restraining the over-eager Uncas and Munro, he argues: "In the dark, all men lie doggo." Alice: "And Cora—where must Cora lie?" And we see her alone, half-asleep in the bracken.

Next dawn, Munro is left behind wounded, and the others set off in pursuit. We see Cora still running, Magua's band tracking, and Hawkeye's group chasing behind in a canoe. Finally catching up, they lay an ambush for the Hurons, who have now recaptured Cora. Magua leads his Indians up beside a waterfall. Halfway up, Cora refuses. She will go no further; he can kill her if he chooses. "If I am to take a man, I will take Uncas." At that moment, Uncas jumps from above but, falling awkwardly, is stabbed by Magua. Another Huron kills Cora with his knife, and an enraged Magua slaughters him. Turning, he finishes off Uncas contemptuously, curses the Delawares, and turns to go. Chingachgook brushes aside Hawkeye's gun, and challenges Magua. After a deadly fight, Magua is hurled down the waterfall and dies.

In a final scene, the bodies of Cora and Uncas are taken back to be honored and buried, Tamenund declaiming the final speech like a Shakespearian actor. When Chingachgook calls out that now he is all alone, Hawkeye turns to him and swears to stay with him. They depart from the funeral gathering together.

END

The BBC version is an important one. It was an expensive and prestigious series, and it was produced with a clear eye to the American market. But it is in definite ways non-Hollywood. The action is slow and deliberative; there is no use of mood music—only an occasional drumbeat to signal tension. As to the narrative, just these five episodes of this adaptation make many small but influential changes. Major Grant exists only in this version. He not only serves as Cora's first suitor but by being there also enables us to hear the old women's color prejudice, and—quite differently—to explain how Hawkeye and company are rearmed after their escape. All the scenes with General Webb are additions, serving to make his British treacherousness evident. Many scenes and added dialogue play up the questions of appropriate "maleness" and "femaleness": the women's insistence on nursing, Cora's handiness with a gun, the episode with the Delaware boy, and many remarks by Hawkeye himself. Importantly, the killing of Magua now falls to Chingachgook, a change preferred in several versions as a more definite kind of narrative justice (the father revenging his son's death, risking his own life to do it).

There are other kinds of changes, too. Perhaps the most significant are those that reposition Hawkeye himself. He acts as interpreter in many ways. Chingachgook hardly speaks without Hawkeye's explicit request. It is Hawkeye who explains Indian customs and who especially explains, repeatedly, the reason for scalping.[11] He also, winning the argument with Chingachgook about the rights of occupation, marks down the wrongs of his own culture. But for all the changes, in all this version's *details* there is a real hunt for "authenticity." This is especially achieved through clothing and props, with the title sequence composed entirely of native American symbols, and with camera emphasis, for example, on the look of the old-fashioned rifles.[12] Wounds look bloody and painful—though all deaths, in the battle, take place just off camera (it *was* Sunday children's TV!). And the scenery looks just bleak and wild enough to satisfy without becoming an independent element in the story. In fact, nothing is allowed to rise above the BBC's commitment to make this a *classic* series.[13]

Yet this approach sits uneasily with the clear attempt to render a modern judgment on the events. Authenticity to the original book and time is married awkwardly with a wish to demonstrate an Indian way of life with its own logic and justification. As David Maloney put it to us: "There was a crusading attitude about the programme. You see, the Indian didn't have any concept of land-ownership. He saw it as a trust. Then, when he met the white man, the next thing he knew they'd put a fence up. Every single time this happened. It was terrible." Maloney felt that he got this sense of Indians being wrongly treated from the original book, but was also well aware of the sea change heralded in cinema by *Soldier Blue* and *Little Big Man*.

But this suggests that "authenticity" is not some simple quality. Consider the role of Hawkeye: he interprets the Indians to the whites, but he himself is not an Indian. The Indians have their ways, and we must respect them. They are not better or worse; they only have a different culture. How might we make sense of this mixture? The key, we believe, lies in two things: the date (1971) and the source (Britain). What was the main source of coloration of Anglo-American relations at this time? Without doubt, the Vietnam War.[14] British politics and culture at this time were riven by controversies and demonstrations over the war. Yet the 1971 version of *Mohicans* was a British series clearly intended for sale in America. The main British characters, then, all appear blemished. Webb is deceitful; Munro is prejudiced; Heyward is arrogant. What they have in common, though, is their reiteration of a sense of *being in the wrong place*. This is what is destroying them. Their attitudes, their tactics are all wrong. They can't survive.

One of the strongest "liberal" lines on the Vietnam war was that which declared it all to be a horrendous mistake. For whatever good motives America had let itself get involved in Vietnam, it was only hurting itself now and should get out and leave the Vietnamese to sort things out for themselves. This America could not do, because the Vietnamese (their traditions, their politics, their "reasoning") were just too different. It takes a go-between to tell the Americans this unpleasant truth.

It seems to us that just this structure of feeling is embodied in the BBC's series. A British version of an American myth, sold in America, presents the British as soured and spoiled by being in an alien land. The result is their embitterment and loss of self. Only the lone scout, Hawkeye, who is not at ease among the British, can mediate. There are no colonials in this version, not one apart from Hawkeye. The "true" America is present only in the character of Hawkeye. The British and French therefore take on the role of possible-

Americans; and Hawkeye has to teach them the error of their ways. With this *Mohicans* miniseries Britain thus offered America a view of its soul, a soul scarred by its "mistake" in invading Vietnam. Look at us, it seems to say, look what we did to ourselves when we fought over your land.

### "We each live by our own code of honor."

The next TV retelling is a curiosity. Made in 1979 for Pittsburgh Public Broadcasting Service, this version is embedded within a three-part series of *The Leatherstocking Tales*. PBS programming has long been the marginalized product of the heavily commercial American TV system—often maintained by a minor sense of guilt and to assuage critics. But among its notable achievements, of course, has been the success of *Sesame Street*, which was funded through the educational HeadStart program to help African-American and Hispanic children in particular.

This version, though, signals immediately that it is part of a different discourse. This is educational TV at its strongest, making fine literature available to a new generation.

THE LEATHERSTOCKING TALES (1979)
Pittsburgh PBS TV
Director: Mick Sgarro
Starring: Cliff de Young (Hawkeye), Roger Hill (Chingachgook), Faizul Khan (Reynard)
WQED Pittsburgh 1979, Metropolitan Pittsburgh Public Broadcasting, Inc.

This miniseries of three parts, each of two episodes, has a title sequence in which we see an illuminated book with the words "Once Upon a Classic" in medieval style. The book opens to show scenes from a series of costume dramas. Captions: *Written by John O'Toole. Based on the novels of James Fenimore Cooper.* Each episode ends with a presenter saying that "Once Upon a Classic has been honored by Action for Children's Television as an outstanding series for children and their parents."

The first episode establishes the character of Bumppo, as he is called, through episodes from the story of *The Deerslayer*. It opens with shots across a wild but pleasant-looking lake. (In general, the landscape depicted is uninhabited but unthreatening. It has a sunny remoteness.) Next into the woodland: two figures in buckskin running toward, then past the camera. They're being pursued by a "Mingo." One of them wants to shoot him. The other, Nathaniel Bumppo, stops him, in a calm steady voice telling him that to do so will bring down every Mingo in the neighborhood. More pursuit.

Finally at the lake, they make off in a canoe, and Bumppo shoots at one of the pursuing Indians, knocking his bow out of his hand without injuring him. Why didn't he kill him, demands the other? "Weren't no need to." "He was an Injun, warn't he?" "He was a man. I ain't killed one yet, and I ain't lookin' forward to the day I have to."

On the bank, the discouraged Indians discuss their need for rifles like Bumppo's. The Indians are presented in very human terms, seeming to reason and have feelings like anybody else. Bumppo meanwhile talks to his companion about the landscape as they go downstream: "It sure is purty. It's a holy place to the Indians, where the earth and the water come together. A gift from god to man." Now we meet a young Reynard, who will feature in the *Mohicans* episode. There is also a discussion of scalping, that acknowledges it as something that whites did. Bumppo attacks it: "Some tribes do, but it's against our nature. It's unlawful." We also meet Chingachgook. The story in this episode involves an attempt to rescue Chingachgook's beloved, Wah-ta-Wah, from the Mingoes, with the help of a young woman who is betrothed to Bumppo's companion. Their rescue attempt is virtually ruined by two whites' attempt to acquire Mingo scalps. This episode ends with Bumppo captured by the Mingoes after having outwitted Reynard's elder brother Le Loup Sauvage, and having been forced to kill the Indian against his own wishes. (Before he dies, Le Loup names Bumppo "Deerslayer.")

Episode 2 of *Deerslayer* sees Bumppo keep a promise he makes to the Hurons to return to their custody, even though it probably means his death. He explains that he owes it to himself to keep any pledge he makes. Eventually he is rescued because of the courage of Chingachgook and the young woman. It is she who gives him his long rifle.

Part 2, based on the first section of *Mohicans*, opens with the two women in the forest, accompanied by Heyward and two Indian guides (Magua, and an additional character called Singing Bear). Alice is complaining about the hardness of the journey, while Cora chides her gently. They decide to stop for the night and light a fire, while Cora makes a drawing of Magua. Alice can't imagine why she should want to draw anything so "horrid." In the night, Singing Bear disappears, as do the horses. Again Alice protests childishly. As they begin to walk on, the camera shows us an arrow in a tree, and a body—that of Singing Bear, clearly murdered.

At the next halt, Magua goes off on the pretext of having heard something. As they wait for him, Hawkeye comes up behind them. To their protests at his coming up so quietly, he replies: "No offense, ladies, but you'll find in these here woods your ears will save your lives more often than your tongues." He introduces Chingachgook to them, to Alice's dismay. She is presented as a frivolous Indian-hater, who sees all natives as savages. Chingachgook is presented, by contrast, as the one with the skills and knowledge to save them. (There is no Uncas.) Hawkeye sees the drawing of

Magua, recognizes him as Reynard, and reckons that Reynard is really after him, not the women. As they climb up to the cave where they must hide, Alice disparages the place they have come to: "Someone tell me why the French are fighting us for such an ugly and uncivilized place!" Hawkeye: "Well, ma'am, you're the first person I've heard call it ugly. Some folks think there's nothing more beautiful. Some folks think it was a right fine place till 'civilized' folks turned up."

In the night, from their hideout, Hawkeye and Chingachgook hear the Hurons calling Hawkeye's name. They reason that an attack won't come till morning, so Chingachgook will take first watch, then Heyward the second, with instructions to wake Hawkeye for his turn. He doesn't. In the morning, they discover that a Huron has managed to steal their powder. Hawkeye tells Heyward that they have to learn from the ways of the Indians if they are to survive. Alice again smarts at this suggestion, saying that there is nothing for whites to learn from Indians. Shouldn't the Indians be learning from them? So Hawkeye lists what the Indians have already learned from the whites: drinking whisky, stealing land, and so forth. Alice complains to Cora that he is rude, to which Cora replies; yes, but he is right.

With no powder, desperate remedies. Hawkeye and Chingachgook will leave to get help. Cora understands, but Alice bitterly complains. Inevitably the women and Heyward are captured, and Reynard/Magua learns that Hawkeye is not there. He takes the three as hostages. As they march out, Cora—on horseback, remembering things Hawkeye had said to her—makes a dash for it. As she runs, Hawkeye and Chingachgook arrive, and after a fight effect the rescue. Magua lies in a heap. Alice: "At least we're rid of the savage beast." Chingachgook: "Not a beast, a man." Alice: "I'm sorry, but an evil man." Hawkeye: "No, not an evil man, either, Miss Alice." Alice: "But he threatened us, and you said he wanted your scalp." Hawkeye: "That's because he'd sworn revenge on me, because I killed his brother." Then, after Magua has slipped away, obviously not hurt after all, Hawkeye philosophizes: "We each live by our own code of honor. I'll never like him, but I respect him. And I hope to keep to my ways as loyally as he keeps to his."

This part ends here, though installments from other Leatherstocking novels follow in the remaining episodes.

This is a doubly or even triply educational series. It is educational in being an introduction to Cooper's books, and the captions at start and finish make sure we don't forget whence all this material comes. It is also educational in terms of "manners." The quiet, soft-spoken Bumppo will not be ruffled. He gently reasons out what needs to be done and does so with a maximum of overt moral thinking. In his person he embodies the responsible frontiersman. And his chastening remarks seem to address us, the viewers, as much as they do the other characters.

But also, this version operates, even more perhaps than Michael Mann's, with an opposition between overcivilized urbanity and the meek and simple virtues of the wilderness. Even those whom Bumppo must fight, he respects. At heart is his code of honor. One of the things that most contributes to this effect—indeed, one of the most impressive aspects of this version as a whole—is the series' visual wildness. Working with what must surely have been very tight budgets, the makers have still managed to evoke powerfully a feel of early, empty forests. The woods are lush and green, dense and difficult to penetrate. The spaces are wide and unknown. The clearings look temporary and uncertain. Nonetheless, this version smells strongly of something to "do us good." We find it easy to imagine the series being shown in Pittsburgh's schools to black children, with teacherly discussion to follow on the dangers of gang warfare, on respecting each other, as we respect you. Natural camphor rub for the urban discontented?

As far as we know, there have been two animated cartoon versions. That there are any at all is surprising to us. We have not been able to determine much about the circumstances or motives for their making. The first was a product of the Hanna-Barbera Studio, the twenty-sixth in a line of full-length cartoons made for the American market. Like all the others, its animation is poor.

William Hanna began his career with MGM in 1937, soon teaming up with Joe Barbera to begin the series of cartoons from which they earned their (rightful) fame: *Tom and Jerry*. Over eighteen years, they directed more than two hundred *Tom and Jerry* segments. But in 1957 they formed their own company, Hanna-Barbera Productions, in particular to make cartoon films for television, and achieved early successes with *Huckleberry Hound*, *Yogi Bear*, and *The Flintstones*. This last series made them, for a time, the most successful cartoon producers, outstripping even Walt Disney. Unfortunately, rising production rates seriously undermined the production values of their work.

In 1966 they released the first of a long series of full-length cartoons: *Alice in Wonderland*. The series then ranged from comic book sources (*The Fantastic Four*) through classic and modern children's stories (*Jack and the Beanstalk*, *Charlotte's Web*) to classic novels (*Cyrano de Bergerac, The Count of Monte Cristo*). *Mohicans* was made in 1977.

THE LAST OF THE MOHICANS (1977)
Hanna-Barbera Studio (Turner Home Entertainment)
Adaptation from the book by Lewis Draper

The cartoon opens in the middle of the story. We see four characters (one Indian, two women, one man in military uniform) tied up in a forest. The Indian hears help coming; the officer says he can't wait for help. A knife cuts the officer's bonds. Then a little snappish dog that's with the younger woman starts yelping, awaking their captors. Now Hawkeye appears (or is identified) with a band of his "friends" the Delawares, and urges the freed captives to run. Battle (indistinct, notional) follows. From a shot of an arrow quivering in a tree, dissolve to titles and credits. Voice-over: "Fort Edward, New York State. August 1757." Shots of the fort. The major is mounting up and leading out the women to be reunited with their father. Cora is established as a contained, sensible woman. Alice complains about having to go on horseback because of Pip, her dog, which whines in sentimental union with her. Upon their departure, the gates shut behind them, seen from a high angle. The camera pans across the forest.

Shots of forest animals, to pleasant music. Cora: "In such magnificent surroundings as these, Major Heyward, it's difficult to believe that France and our own dearly beloved England are at war, to see which will finally possess the New World." Heyward warns her that "renegade Indians" could be lurking behind the beautiful facade.

Enter Magua. "There is something about him that I don't trust," says Cora. "Neither does Pip," replies Alice. Despite this, they seem to welcome Magua's guidance to a shorter trail, so they can reach their father quicker. Heyward hesitantly agrees, but first asks Magua which tribe he belongs to. "I am chief of my own tribe. We are small and bear no allegiance to any of the great Indian nations." Animal images again, as the group sets off down the new trail.

Dissolve to Hawkeye discussing with Uncas and Chingachgook why he prefers the English to the French, just for their "better food" and "geniality." "And the English girls . . . ah me!" (Generally the Indians speak semi-poetically, while Hawkeye's speech is "down-to-earth.") Three horses approach. Uncas puts his ear to the ground to identify them. Hawkeye jumps up when he sees them: "Magua, I told you that if I ever saw your ugly face again. . . . " Magua runs away, chased by Uncas. Hawkeye introduces himself to a cross Major Heyward, making a joke of his own real name. The travelers soon realize they've been misled. The women accept the blame for trusting Magua. Says Hawkeye: "We do not even think of him as a true Indian. He is a renegade, an outcast, followed by a band of equally loathsome outcasts—

the vultures of the forest." Uncas returns, warning them of approaching danger.

Leaving the horses, they take to Hawkeye's canoes, then down the river, over rapids, and into the lee of an island. Then, in a cave, the travelers sit by a fire. They are safe for the night because Magua will have "fear of the unnamed things of the night." After a while Hawkeye joins them. There are too many Indians out there, he tells them, so he and Uncas will swim to get help. The others will be safe because Magua is a greedy man who will want to ransom them. The rest of them retire into a back cave and hide. Cora wonders what her father would do about Magua, and declares he'd "trounce him spectacularly and probably drive him out of the New World." Hawkeye and Uncas swim out.

Cut to Magua figuring out where they are. In the cave the four wait. Daylight is coming. To calm Alice's fears, Chingachgook, who has remained behind, gives her his necklace with the turtle brooch, saying he wants it to bring *her* luck now. He's seen his people diminished "by war, pestilence and hardship," but with Uncas alive he still feels hope. "Through him the Mohicans will grow again, and once more take their place among the great Indian nations of the New World." They hear noises. Pip again yelps, and attracts Magua. Captured, they are led out. We see them walking in the forest, then Uncas and the Delawares following.

Now in Magua's camp. Heyward, acting like a coward, tries to persuade Magua to ransom them. Magua declares that what he wants is not money, but Cora as his squaw. Now we return to the scenes with which the film began: the four of them tied up; Hawkeye rescuing them; Pip giving them away; battle. At the height of the battle, we see Magua and Uncas fighting in silhouette on a clifftop. As Magua is about to kill Uncas, Chingachgook intervenes, and he and Magua plunge down the cliff. Dissolve to Uncas mourning his father.

Now Hawkeye, Uncas, Heyward, and the two women approach the fort, only to discover it has been sacked. We see Uncas and the women sitting in the remains, eating, Hawkeye and Heyward having gone scouting. They realize that Munro left the fort before it was burned and has gone to another fort. In the interlude, Cora and Heyward, amid suggestions of romance, discuss war and beauty. Heyward: "Conquest is man's genuine enemy, Miss Cora, conquest and ruthless ambition." Elsewhere Uncas and Alice meet and discuss Chingachgook's necklace. Alice grieves that perhaps her taking it killed him.

Enter a wounded man who has been trapped and tortured. They decide to hear his story in the morning. That night, while keeping watch, Uncas is grabbed from behind. In the morning as the wounded man is telling Heyward his story, Hawkeye enters to tell of Uncas's capture, and of the kidnapping of the two girls. It is Magua, who evidently didn't die after all.

Uncas, Heyward, and Hawkeye set out into Canada to rescue the women. Shots of their journey are intercut with scenes of Magua traveling with his prisoners. There is a huge storm at night. Next morning, the rescuers reach Magua's camp, where Cora is being held. Uncas goes to rescue Alice from the place they guess she is being held, nearby. We are told that the tribe holding her is not bad by nature but is "under Magua's control." Nighttime. Hawkeye steals into the camp, disguised as a medicine man, to rescue Cora. He is surprised by Magua. They prepare to fight, but the next thing we see is Magua tied up and being brought out.

Now we see Uncas and Alice tied to the stake, preparing to face "the test of the long knife." Cut back to the others, planning their next move. Back to Alice and Uncas; the necklace is discovered, and we learn that its amulet was given to Chingachgook as thanks and promise of future help for saving the life of the Delaware chief. Freed, Uncas readies to go help the others, with the Delawares helping him.

A chase scene. We see the Delawares waiting to help, and Hawkeye, Heyward, and Cora being pursued towards them by Magua's band. As the leading Indian is shot by one of the Delawares, the others turn and run, defeated.

Now at Fort Ticonderoga, the travelers finally reach Colonel Munro, who greets his daughters and thanks their saviors. At dinner that night, Hawkeye makes it clear that he won't stay; he is a woodsman, and to the woods he must return. Uncas: "I am the last of the Mohicans. I must begin again to gather a tribe around me. Who knows, perhaps there are other Mohicans somewhere out there, in the vast New World." Alice protests at his plans, but accedes.

In the morning, Hawkeye goes his own way. Uncas also rides out, as Alice cries. Then she declares her love for him, hugs her father and sister (handing Pip to her), and runs after Uncas. Pip struggles free and runs to catch up with them. Uncas lifts the dog onto his saddle, and they ride off together.

END

We must confess that it is hard to see much logic at all in the form of this version. So many changes are made to Cooper's story, with no new unity emerging: the introduction of the wretched dog, who whines and sniffles as much as his Penelope Pitstopp owner; the saving of Uncas, who is left with the task of rebuilding his people; the emptying of the fort, and the loss therefore of a good quarter of the story; and so on. Much work has gone into the moralizing— Heyward speechifying to Cora about the wrongs of war, Hawkeye making sure that we don't think of Magua as a "typical Indian." Couple these points with chronically poor animation and an ending that would disgrace the most sentimental B-movie; and nothing more needs to be said. The one puzzle that remains is: Why was it done? On that question, in the absence of any direct evidence, the file must remain open. But if we had to guess, we would point to the American Bicentennial.

The second cartoon version suffers equivalent levels of silliness, but at least is graced with an (accidental?) sense of humor. Produced in 1987 by a small production company, Family Home Entertainment (whose only other listed work, according to the British Film Institute's database, is licensed cartoons of the Transformers toys), this cartoon was in fact made in Australia at Burbank Studios. It brings to the fore the real problems of trying to capture in words the flavor of a visual mode of expression. The best way we can prepare the ground for proper understanding of this version is to indicate that any character who is going to play a minor and probably daft role is drawn with an extremely long and pointed Pinocchio-style nose, and this is generally associated with a foolish voice and a foreign accent. Bear these things in mind when following the narrative. (We have given hints on nasal elongations at necessary points.)

THE LAST OF THE MOHICANS (1987)
Burbank Studios for Family Home Entertainment
Screenplay: Leonard Lee

The film opens with titles and credits superimposed over scenes of mountains and rivers. Narrator: "Back in the 1700s, the British colony of America was a troubled land. First, there was Injuns fightin' Injuns," of which we see shots. Chingachgook, seeing himself surrounded, says to his son: "My son, you must leave here. The Huron dogs are too many. We cannot win." Uncas: "Father, a Mohican warrior does not run. I will fight till they take my skin." But an arrow pierces Chingachgook at that moment: "You, my son, are the last of the Mohicans," he gasps, and dies. Uncas too is surrounded by Hurons, but as they close in, led by a villainous Magua, a bullet takes the knife right out of Magua's hand: "Hold it right there," says a skin-clad hunter. To Uncas he says, "I'm a friend of your pappy's. Sorry I couldn't have got here sooner. Magua, take your men, and git!" Together, Hawkeye and Uncas bury Chingachgook.

Narrator: "Now if that weren't enough, there were the British fightin' the French. Now the Americans didn't want the French even more'n they didn't want the British. So they joined in alongside and gave the Redcoats a helpin' hand." In a fort, Colonel Munro is addressing a Captain Washington, asking if there is news of a relief column. No, replies Washington, nor of your daughters.

Cut to Magua acting as guide to a white party. We meet the very English Heyward (high nose-index); a cool and Scottish Cora; and a childish Alice (diminished, turned-up nose), who bats her eyelids at Heyward. That night, the women sleep while Heyward promises to stand guard—but doesn't. Come morning, Hawkeye creeps up on him and takes his gun. He'll shoot him if he's French! But Uncas stops him: "Wait! The red-jacket speaks with a truthful tongue. Let him live." Hawkeye introduces himself: "Ma real name's Nathaniel Bumppo but I reckon that's not much of a name. Ma friends call me Hawkeye." He's also an old friend of Munro's. When they learn the truth about Magua, Alice faints. (There are attempts at humor in the dialogue. When Cora says they had better hide if the Hurons might be around, Uncas replies: "Dark eyed woman speak the sense of ten white men!" "He kinda means yes," interprets Hawkeye.) They set out. Magua, finding the trail, swears "by the Great Spirit" to take Uncas's scalp.

We see Magua tracking them, over narrator's comments on his villainy. They pause to allow Hawkeye to scout ahead. All are immediately recaptured. Magua turns on Uncas: "Die as you have lived . . . like a dog!" Heyward is to die too, the women to become Magua's slaves. As before, as Magua's knife rises, there's Hawkeye: "Not so fast, Magua."

Montcalm's (maximal nasal-index) tent, as bombardment recommences: "That's eet. Let 'em 'ave eet. More beauteeful boom boom." He goes back into his tent, to a giggling "Josephine." In the fort, a stern (low nose-index) Munro refuses Washington's (equally serious nose) suggestion of surrender.

Another stage of escape and pursuit, this time on a raft, then a cave to hide. Magua, following, displays deep rationality to guess their whereabouts: "Hmm. Trail stop here. Mohican dog and paleface cannot fly like eagle. Must be they hide like bear!" Hawkeye and Uncas jump hundreds of feet into the water to escape and get help. The others, hiding inside, are found when Alice screams at a spider.

Emerging from the river, Uncas goes for help to old Tamenund, who agrees to help (when reminded that Chingachgook had once saved his life) but then only if it will not lead to conflict among Indians. Uncas promises that no one will die, not even the Hurons. So, as Magua and the Hurons are manhandling the prisoners along the way, suddenly all are caught in traps. Uncas to Magua: "You have brought great shame to a great Indian people. Only by my promise to the wise chief Tamenund do you live." Magua, humiliated, departs, telling Uncas that the next time they meet, they will fight to the death.

At the fort, rising fog causes confusion, with British sentries firing blindly at Hawkeye's party and hitting Montcalm's chandeliers. In the confusion, the party slips into the fort. Munro greets his daughters. Now, Montcalm sues for truce—he has intercepted the message saying no help will come. Munro refuses to surrender, but accepts Montcalm's offer to let women and wounded go safely. Out ride Cora and Alice and a few men, to be ambushed by Magua, who kidnaps the two women.

The truce over, Hawkeye and Uncas leave to catch up with the women, only to find one surviving wounded soldier, whom they send back to the fort on Hawkeye's horse. They rush on to try to rescue the women.

Back at the fort, after a weary night (during which Montcalm, nose to the fore, has serenaded his Josephine), battle commences. But when the English try to fire, nothing happens. "Cloek, cloek, cloek?" chortles Montcalm in delight. Washington to Munro: "I'm sorry, Colonel Munro, but enough lives have been lost. I'm going to order my American troops to surrender. We may need to fight another day." Munro (in a wise Scottish accent): "Aye, perhaps ye're right, Washington. Next time, we could be on opposite sides." As the surrender is signed, in comes the wounded soldier, and Montcalm apologizes for Magua's behavior. The French will come to help rescue the women.

At the Huron camp, the women are forced to work in terrible heat, Alice weeping piteously. The Hurons are worried that their crops are dying; are the captives bringing bad luck with them? Enter a witch doctor to do a rain dance in front of puzzled Hurons. But his mask slips off. It is Uncas, who is seized. This time, when Hawkeye tries his "Not so fast . . . ," Magua turns the tables and captures him too. They are to be burned at the stake. The traditional tomahawk dance round the fire in silhouette begins. But at that moment, Tamenund arrives, and learns from Hawkeye of Magua's promise of a fight to the death. Tamenund insists that this happen.

On a high cliff, Magua and Uncas struggle, until Magua falls to his death. As the other Hurons prepare to attack, French troops arrive with Munro and Heyward to rescue them. Munro says of Montcalm: "I hate to admit it, but he's an honorable man." Montcalm preens himself (but not his nose) gently.

Final scene. Asked to stay with the British, Hawkeye declines: "With respect, General, an American like me don't need no French or British soldiers holdin' his hand." Uncas: "I too will stay. These lands are my home and the home of my ancestors." As the British party departs, Tamenund, seated on a high throne of rock, hears the final thoughts. Hawkeye: "Maybe it's time we all made a little peace with one another. One day there'll be no French and no British, just us, and we're all just gonna have to get along." Uncas: "My friend Hawkeye is right. We cannot be free in this land until we make peace." Tamenund: "It is good. Uncas, last of the Mohicans, you must stay here with your Indian brothers, and cleanse the land of the bad blood between you. And you, paleface warrior, tell your people to treat us with respect. Only then can we talk as equals, one nation to another." Hawkeye:

"I'll try, Tamenund, but it won't be easy. Goodbye, Uncas, my Mohican friend."

END

Sometimes, when considering a presentation like this, it is hard to get past the sheer badness of it, its shallow, cheap and ill-considered techniques. But here, the awful combination of poor jokes and high-minded moralizing is part of the meaning. For this version of *Mohicans* surely shares much with another American television tradition of exactly this time: the tradition typified by *The Muppet Babies*.

When *The Muppets* appeared in the 1970s, they offered outrageous and anarchic characters joyously introducing simple skills: reading, writing, counting, classifying, reasoning. An animated trashcan puppet show, it worked by never patronizing. Instead it linked TV to children's urban culture through surreal presenters like Kermit. But in the mid-1980s came their baby selves. Now everything changed, as the show's agenda resonated with moral stories of American history. Each story was prettified, sentimentalized, and made "good" in its teachings by the appearance of one of the Muppet Babies asking "childlike" questions. Let one episode from 1986 illustrate: "Kermit Goes to Washington."[15]

In the nursery, the babies are playing a game with a toy boat in the bath. But Miss Piggy keeps changing the rules whenever she loses. As all the others get annoyed with her, Nanny arrives to tell them they must agree to the rules and stick to them—and to make Miss Piggy say "sorry!" There follows a series of scenes in which different babies fantasize about being able to make the others play by their rules, until Gonzo proposes they play to his preference: no rules. Re-enter Nanny just in time to stop the anarchy and to make the babies sit still and think about what they are doing. A song routine ensues in which, realizing they have been punished, they imagine what jail must be like, with them in it. Now Nanny brings them a book from which they can learn how to make rules properly, a book about "democracy." And now they play at politics, learning about the secret ballot, nominating candidates for the presidency, and voting in the cupboard. Kermit is elected! and off they go to Washington, to find out what the president does. Kermit has to give a press conference, then goes off to a cabinet meeting to decide what he should spend (on toys, clothes, computers, ice cream, sweets). With all the money gone, "reality" returns, and they begin to wonder how easy democracy is. So they decide to make laws, and Miss Piggy jumps in fast to propose a law that everyone should give her a present on her birthday. To her amazement, they all vote for it: "Gee, I guess democracy is pretty good stuff, after all!" she says plaintively. With love and harmony restored, they are back in the nursery, being praised by Nanny and promising that the nursery will *always* have secret ballots in future. . . .

This is history made anodyne, palatable and safe for little minds. Gone is the anarchic fun in learning and learning through fun. Now, a smell of holy goodness permeates the nostrils, carried by the very innocence the characters had achieved in their earlier phase. What better analogy for the noses of this pitiful version of *Mohicans*! Stuffed with moralizing, sneaking in the American icon Washington, making cheap historical points about future conflicts upon which America would be founded, and with an ending that is like the start of a teacher's activity sheet. "Right now, children, let's talk about how *we* could all make it easier for Hawkeye to bring peace to the world." We can't resist completing the analogy. This sort of moralistic politics, taught by a nanny, simply does remind us of the debates about the "Nanny State" in the era of Reagan and Thatcher, just about the time this pap got produced.

Perhaps the most important thing to say about the nonfilm versions of *Mohicans* is that they are not just different from each other, but crucially different from the film versions. And the most important distinction is that each of these versions has a specific job to do: whether it is to be a "classic series"; or to be a derivative Western, filling the schedules; or to prove that television can be good for education; or to teach simplistic morals. In each case, the version has been penetrated and overtaken by a particular function. But that suggests that the main film versions, though we have shown the ways in which they resonate with the concerns and assumptions of their times, nonetheless remain first and foremost versions of Cooper's story. If this is right, it reemphasizes what we (and of course many others) have suggested about the central role of film as the elaborator of American culture.

There is a good test of what we are saying. At the very time that we were revising the manuscript of this book, Sky TV in Britain announced a new series, to begin in March 1995, called "HAWK-EYE: The First Frontier." To be honest, we were surprised.[16] Despite our own arguments, we had felt that the Michael Mann film was so definitive that it would surely bar, at least for some time, further uses of the "Mohican tradition." Intellectuals shouldn't prophesy! Sky TV's multipart series is still underway as we write, but enough of it has been broadcast to allow us to form an opinion.

HAWKEYE: THE FIRST FRONTIER (1994)
Stephen J. Cannell Productions; created by Kim LeMasters
Starring: Lee Horsley (Hawkeye), Rodney A. Grant (Chingachgook), Lynda Carter (Elizabeth Shields)

It is not appropriate to give detailed plot synopses since, even more than the 1956 series, this series is only loosely related to Cooper's *Mohicans*. However, there are definite links. The most obvious is that the title sequence (for the early episodes) uses clips from three different parts of Michael Mann's film: the opening shot across the mountains, the parade outside the fort during the truce, and the second massacre.

Outside these visual references, the plot is largely separate. The setting is 1755, amid the conflicts between English and French. The stories revolve around a fort in the middle of Huron country, often visited by Hawkeye and Chingachgook, to which come Elizabeth Shields and her husband Samuel. Samuel's brother commands the fort and is supposed to have set up trading contracts with the English military. Instead, jealous of his brother, he has set a snare so that Samuel is captured by the Hurons, tortured, and disappears. Elizabeth is left to tend for herself, while still hoping for Samuel's eventual return.

After the pilot episodes established these characters and outlined their relations, subsequent episodes build a story that explores some aspect of "life on the frontier." The second post-pilot episode, for instance, explored two related themes: the difficult position of women on the frontier, who are seen by the English as sexual servants yet are discarded for lack of virtue even if raped; and the question of "honor" in men.[17] This was signified by having Hawkeye rescue a young woman from abduction by a Frenchman living with the Hurons. Having killed the Frenchman, he is seized by the Hurons, who offer him a choice: either marry the widow and thus redeem her future, or suffer torture and death. Hawkeye is prepared to die for his beliefs, and is vindicated when the Huron chief acknowledges his "honor"—something the English conspicuously seem to lack.

What is interesting to us is the way the series is using the reputation of *Mohicans*, the Michael Mann film, and indeed of its three leading actors[18] to create a space for exploration of a range of moral issues. This is possible because the series can play between two poles: authenticity versus romanticism. As the production notes say:

To bring the world of HAWKEYE to life, the producers have assembled an extraordinary team of designers, historians, and craftspeople. "While we're recreating life in the 1750s for the series, we're keeping in mind that James Fenimore Cooper wrote his novels nearly 100 years later," says Production Designer Phil Schmidt. "Cooper, as well as the Hudson River Valley school of painters in the mid-1800s, had a romanticized vision of life on the frontier before the American Revolution. In reality, life during the French and Indian Wars was difficult, dirty and dark, but the art and literature of the next century portrays it with a sheen or glow, symbolizing the spirit of the 1700s and the heroism of the frontiersmen who helped forge a new nation. We're going to great lengths to create sets, costumes and props authentic to the Hudson River Valley region in the mid-1700s, but the series will also have a gorgeous rich look in keeping with the heroic vision of Cooper and the other artists of his time."

This balancing act produces a collision in the series. Filmically, the setting (near Vancouver) is stunning, rich, warm, and tranquil. Yet the *talk* all the while is of the "savagery" of the frontier. In the narrative, there is a sharp delineation of who is and isn't a "good" character. Yet the *talk* is all about the difficulties of life on the frontier and the problems of learning and making choices. Because we have access in this case to the producers' own account, it is possible to see why this tension exists: " 'America in 1755 is a rich and vivid backdrop for a romantic adventure series like HAWKEYE,' said executive producer Stephen J. Cannell. 'Striking parallels exist between that time and our own. Today, questions about the intent, character and future course of our country are at the forefront of national debate, these same questions raged as armed conflict 240 years ago. Like our ancestors, we are living in times of uncertainty, when a new order is emerging from diverse claims to our culture and natural resources.' "

At the time of writing, this approach has resulted in story lines that shift restlessly between adventure and moralizing. The first post-pilot episode is almost pure adventure, involving renegade English trying to sell gunpowder to the French. The second, as we've seen, instructs its audience on men's honor and the treatment of women. The third returns to adventure (Hawkeye prevents the besieging French from bringing a massive gun to their aid) but manages to work in some appropriate moralizing: when Elizabeth despairs over why the French and English need to fight over a land with space for all, Hawkeye portentously replies, "For some nations, there are never enough riches." The most effective episode to date[19] returns to moral dilemmas with a vengeance, as an orphaned white baby is stolen by the Hurons to compensate for the death of one killed by whites. Elizabeth, risking her own life and a "mourning war," steals it back. Hawkeye declines to stop her, believing she must make her own decisions (a powerful theme in all the episodes). But when they argue over the ethics of the situation, Hawkeye quietly trumps her final, religious argument. Elizabeth: "She should be raised to know the word of God, so that when she dies, she'll go to heaven." Hawkeye: "Your God must be smaller than mine, because my God could find a child in a Huron village." Elizabeth returns the baby to the Huron village, into the arms of a loving "mother".

What once more drives a Cooper-based story is a moral imperative to "draw lessons" from a past acknowledged to be romanticized, yet which—with appropriate attention to "authenticity"—can be made to bear the load of thinking: What is proper behavior? How to resolve the ethical dilemmas of our time? But once more, in a TV version, we can see compromises being struck that make this series a *dependent* one, unable in itself to create a new interpretation of the Cooper myth.

# CHAPTER 7    Comic Books: The Hidden Tradition

Comic book versions raise quite different issues from the films. First, the history of comics in both Britain and America is a history of nervousness about their cultural position. When, therefore, a comics publisher decides to do a version of a classic book, there has almost always been a hint of genuflection to "serious culture." Comics have thought of themselves as second-class citizens, and their treatment of books, especially classics like *Mohicans*, is essentially reverential. Therefore the comics rarely, if ever, change the main elements of the plot or the sequence of events. Particular moments may get eliminated, as we will see; and the special "grammar" of comic books means that in complicated ways they can shift our understanding of characters' motivation. But the fear of offending means that, with the American and British comic versions at least, the book rules.

But there are more complicated factors from the history of comics that determine how they will treat a book like *Mohicans*. To understand these factors, we need to look briefly at some of that history. Standard histories of comics will tell you that comics began around the turn of the century. Such histories are only telling part of the truth. In his history of comics and narrative art, David Kunzle has shown comics have important continuities with woodcuts and other forms of illustrations.[1] And in particular in the nineteenth century, in satiric books and magazines, a group of innovative artists laid down a basic grammar of comics. Gustav Topffer, Gustav Doré, and others created a great variety of stories, from the overtly political to the simply humorous. This was an international tradition, in which for example the Paris *Charivari* helped to produced the London *Punch*, and in which artists could move from country to country.

But in the late 1880s, a variety of forces broke down this internationalism, and set in motion an increasing link between comics and nationalism. In Britain, this nationalism took a number of forms: in the ironic but ultimately deeply patriotic Ally Sloper, whose royalism was never so deep than when he was drunk. Roger Sabin recalls the forgotten story of just how popular Sloper was, he whose name meant "the one who nips down the back alley when the rent man cometh," but whose nature was a celebration of lower-middle-class jingoism.[2]

There was also the imperialism of the boys' books and papers. Aside from the general chauvinism and racism that characterized the work of boys' writers such as G. A. Henty, R. M. Ballantyne, and Rudyard Kipling, perhaps the most revealing connection is supplied by Henry Newbolt, author (in the 1890s) of one of the most famous poems associating war and empire with sport. Most significantly, the poem made direct associations between war and sport, boldly summed up in the repeated line "Play up! play up! and play the game!" It was Henry Newbolt, as we saw in chapter 4, who in 1921 chaired a government committee on the role of "English" in the curriculum. This committee established the teaching of "literature" (and that word must always resonate and roll round the tongue to extract all its meanings) as that which could do most to encourage a "sense of nationhood."[3] Comics were decidedly outside that process. For younger children, there was an emphasis on stories being "innocent," free of any taint of politics or adult emotions (hence the rise of anthropomorphic characters inhabiting safe, homely worlds in the early comics in Britain).

In America, the same move away from internationalism was associated with different processes and hence had different results. First was the rise of cartoons in newspapers as part of the rise of yellow journalism. Two New York publishers, Randolph Hearst and Joseph Pulitzer, battled for ownership of a cartoonist, R. F. Outcault, and his character, the Yellow Kid. Cartoons, and then comic strips, collectively know as the funnies, were to play a rising role in the fortunes of American newspapers. There was also a new role for cartoon characters in advertising and merchandising, the best-known example being Buster Brown, whose image was first associated with a boot polish but quickly expanded to include everything from dolls to ashtrays.[4]

But for us the most important strand was the role that the funnies were asked to play in overcoming ethnic diversity. America, in the period up to and after the First World War, saw waves of immigration especially from southern and eastern Europe; the absorption of these peoples became a highly contentious political issue. Whatever their political orientation on issues of immigration control and the "threats of racial degeneration" (common themes in this period), newspaper owners had a vested interest simply in selling papers to all ethnic communities. Les Daniels, among others, has shown clearly how the comic strips responded to this need. The funnies showed two big changes, going from displaying ethnic diversity to middle-American anonymity, and from satirical intensity to domestic sentimentality.[5] Comics were, of course, ideally suited to play this role. Their visuality meant that they could appeal to people with limited fluency in English; and the speech balloon, along with the stabilization of visual conventions, enabled the pictures to convey more and more of the meaning.

In 1929 King Features, the largest syndication agency, sought out writers and artists to create a new line of adventure strips. From this initiative came Buck Rogers (later transferred to film) and a number of others. Collected reprints of these strips stirred the first attempts in the 1930s to produce books of comic stories, culminating in the launch in 1938 of *Action*, with the character who summed up the tendencies at work here: Superman.[6] Publishers of pulps, seeing the success of comics, abandoned pulps with enthusiasm, and from the late 1930s much dodgy money was transferred to hiring bad writers and artists and pumping out inferior comics, to a bemused but enthusiastic public.[7]

These were inauspicious beginnings for comics. The primary

genres were boys' adventures and pseudo-mythological fantasies; the orientation was toward "entertainment." Comics were categorized either as Saturday fun or as low culture—not a rich ground for attempting serious treatment of books. Any attempt at being serious was bound to be greeted with suspicion, if not outright hostility. This was not what "comics are." Their image was compromised. It fell to one Albert Kanter to attempt the brave, eggshell-walking task.

Kanter was the son of Eastern European immigrants. He was one of many such who believed they had a role to play in developing a specifically American culture. It is no accident, given the role assigned to cartoons and comics in the early years, that quite a number of immigrants came to contribute to many aspects of American visual culture. Kanter, born in 1897, moved through a variety of jobs until, after bankruptcy in 1929, he found employment selling books for the Elliot Publishing Company in New York. His job was door-to-door sales, at which he was very good. In 1940, he conceived the idea of a line of comics devoted to making great literature accessible to the young. Very much an "improving" idea, it was intended to lead young readers to the books themselves. Two friends provided the initial financial backing. They bought the name and property of a bankrupt company, Gilberton, and prepared the first issue—a version of *The Three Musketeers*—adapted by Kanter himself. This issue was sufficiently successful that it financed issue two. Thus was born the line of Classic Comics (later Classics Illustrated) which lasted until 1971. Issue two was *Ivanhoe*, issue three was *The Count of Monte Cristo*, and issue four was *Mohicans*. Gilberton's *Mohicans* went through twenty-four reprints during the company's lifetime, being given (as were many other titles) a complete new adaptation and artwork in the late 1950s.[0]

Rather like Disney in the 1920s, Kanter took risks to ensure that his company would remain independent. So, when Woolworth's offered to carry his line on condition that they be its sole distributor, he rejected them. He preferred to toil at building up local sales and did not agree to a national distribution deal until 1950. In that year he formed a link with Curtis Circulation Company, who persuaded him to increase his cover price to fifteen cents, 50 percent more than any other comic of the time. It was a risk, but for a time paid off. For the period 1948–55 was the high tide of the campaign against comic books led by Dr. Fredric Wertham, who particularly targeted what he called the "crime comic books." But he was not averse to having a go at the Classics Illustrated line as well. In his *Seduction of the Innocent*, he attacked Gilberton's *Julius Caesar* and *The Mysteries of Paris* (Eugene Sue), among others.[9]

Kanter's response was to ignore Wertham and to insist on his complete separation from the "bad comics." Increasing the cover price was one way of marking this distinction; the Classics were now priced to be bought by parents and teachers rather than by children. They were printed on heavier paper stock and had painted covers (as opposed to their own earlier line-drawn covers), trying to look more like books than comics. For the time being this strategy paid off. Sales took off through the 1950s, while many other comics publishers were being driven out of business by Wertham's campaign. Ironically, Kanter's policy would backfire fatally in 1969 when the U.S. Postal Service took seriously his claim that he published books rather than magazines and withdrew his right to use second-class postage. That decision, in concert with declines in sales because of the rise of television plus the growth in the paperback book business, spelled the end for Kanter. In 1969 he sold the company to Patrick Frawley, owner of a multitude of businesses from a film company (Technicolor) to a Catholic newspaper.

Kanter rarely articulated his philosophy in writing. The most direct statement of the goal of his series comes in the testimony of one of his colleagues, Meyer Kaplan, to the Joint Legislative Committee on Comic Books Control in 1951:

The taste for good literature and fine art must be cultivated in a child slowly. . . . By forcing him to read the truly heavy and none-too-easily understood language of the classics while still too young to appreciate it, a dislike of good reading will be cultivated rather than an interest. But a pictorial rendering of the great stories of the world which can be easily understood and therefore more readily liked would tend to cultivate that interest. Then, when he grows older, if he has any appetite at all for these things, he will want to know more fully those bookish treasures merely suggested in this, his first acquaintance with them. He will more eagerly read them in the original form because he will already have a mind's eye picture of what the author was trying to portray in words.[10]

Kaplan couldn't really know that his sincere defense was just the kind of thing calculated to infuriate his literary opponents, to whom "easy understanding" and "picturing in the mind's eye" were the equivalent of destruction of the thing he claimed to be helping.

Kanter sought respectability for his series. In 1950 when he tackled his first Shakespeare project, *Julius Caesar*, he sought advice and comments on the adaptation from scholars at New York University, at a cost of $14,000. But acceptance was at best tentative from parents, educationalists, and local authorities, who found it hard to make distinctions among comics. And there was a price to be paid, as has been shown by Joseph Witek in his study of one Classics issue on the American Civil War.[11] Analyzing three different tellings of the first shot in the American Civil War (one prose narrative and two comic book versions) Witek shows how the Classics version strives painfully to achieve an ideological neutrality with no hint of taking sides. The story even has onlookers weeping desperately as if aware of the historical significance and pity of the events. The comic limits itself to a visual rigidity and static mode of presentation, even though it was the work of Jack Kirby, possibly the artist who did most over a thirty-year period to demonstrate how visually dynamic comics can be. The point Witek is making is that Kanter did not dare offend anyone, especially given that he issued this comic in 1961, the centennial of the start of the war between the states.

To date we have traced eight American direct comic book adaptations of *Mohicans*, of which we have managed to obtain complete copies of five, substantial parts of a sixth, and a seventh that is a completed excerpt.[12] Four of these (the 1942, 1959, 1977[b], and 1992 versions) owe their provenance directly or indirectly to Gilberton's line. The other three (dated in 1940/1, 1954/5, 1957, and 1977[a]) come out of quite different orientations and traditions. Although, as we've said, they are together unlike the films in remaining faithful to the narrative, in every other way they differ from each other. They are also extraordinarily variable in quality. Gilberton's 1942 edition, with artwork by Ray Ramsey, vies with the 1940 version in the comic *White Rider and Super Horse* (whose artist wisely preferred anonymity) for sheer awfulness. Perhaps the best is Marvel's 1977 version, with artwork by Sonny Trinidad. But setting aside our subjective preferences, there is real significance to the differences.

How can we analyze comic books' meanings? Comics are like and unlike other visual media in their components.[13] There does not yet seem to be an agreed-upon language for distinguishing comics' graphic and textual elements. The following rough catalogue of elements is enough for our purpose:

(a) *Visual story-moments*: each story-moment has a boundary often indicated by a drawn border but that can be indicated in a number of other ways. A single story-moment is generally known as a panel (hence the term "panelologist" for someone who studies comics). But a single panel does not necessarily mean a single event. Within one panel, the event may be single, but may commonly freeze transitions of time or movement. On the other hand, some single panels might just as well contain collages of many events.

(b) *Narration*: generally (but not always) carried in a box at top left of a panel.

(c) *Titles*: which frequently include both text and visual, and which often cross over onto visual story-moments.

(d) *Dialogue*: generally (but not always) carried in balloons attached to their speakers and sequenced within a panel from top left to bottom right. The style of balloon as well as the manner of the lettering form part of the meaning being created.

(e) *Effects*: sound, movement, and emotion effects, conveyed by an indefinite number of visual/textual devices within the visual display, from movement lines to emotion-markers and onomatopoeic words drawn in ways that signify the sound they "mean."

(f) *Sequencing*: there is a requirement to "fill in" meanings in the gutters between panels, to create a continuous story from the frozen moments of each panel. These frozen moments are augmented by such things as pace of movement between panels, shifts of angle of vision, and so forth.

(g) *Page layout*: the relation of panels to each other, by virtue of size, dimensions, separation/overlap, nature of borders, and so forth.

But perhaps the most important feature of the grammar of comics is the way these elements can fuse and become part of each other. All the levels are permeable by each other, without exception. Thus, a piece of dialogue will be written or, perhaps better, drawn to be also part of the visual meaning. Dialogue can be continued, or responded to, by a piece of narration rather than another character. It can flow into a title. Its placement on the page can become part of the flow of meanings. It can become the container for some of the visual elements. It can even become part of the object-environment (the equivalent of the filmic mise-en-scène) of the visual story-moments. Only by conscious abstinence on the part of a comic's creators are words ever simply words. The best creators are aware of this full palette of possibilities. This general lexicon of devices can of course be used with more or less skill by particular creators. But they can't help being used. As we will see with Pendulum Illustrated, even a version that tries to deny its comic-ness acknowledges the devices in its very denial.

How, then, to identify the main differences between the comic book versions of *Mohicans*? Begin with the exclusions. All versions bar one omit two important moments in the plot: the killing of the colt during the flight to the river and the dialogue at the fort during which we learn of Cora's mixed race. These cuts surely must be motivated by the same protective sensibilities that led to much the same exclusions in most book abridgments. In the first case, it would have to do with the perceived sentimental relations that children are felt to have with animals. The second case is more complicated.

Now compare how the versions shape the beginnings. We begin with the opening of the story itself. In date order this is done as follows:[14]

*1940/1*: "Introduction—DURING THE FRENCH AND INDIAN WAR, MAJOR DUNCAN HEYWARD WAS ESCORTING CORA AND ALICE MUNRO TO THEIR FATHER, COLONEL MUNRO, COMMANDER OF FORT WILLIAM HENRY, WHICH WAS BESIEGED BY THE FRENCH. ON THE WAY THEY WERE JOINED BY DAVID GURMET [*sic*],[15] A PSALM SINGER. THE TRAVELERS DID NOT KNOW THAT THE FORT WAS IN DANGER, NOR THAT THEIR INDIAN GUIDE WAS TREACHEROUS. HE WAS A HURON AND UNFRIENDLY TO THE BRITISH. HE ALSO WISHED REVENGE ON COLONEL MUNRO, WHO HAD CAUSED HIM TO BE FLOGGED." This text is written, as though on a piece of pegged-out cloth, within a panel showing an Indian walking towards us through a wood followed in the distance by three figures on horseback, one declaiming something. The book's title appears across the top of the panel, as though made up of shavings and scratchings of words on bits of wood. Responding subjectively, we can't help feeling that the whole thing has a cheap and thrown-together look.

*1942*: This version devotes a whole page to its introduction, including (down each side) small insets giving us little portraits of the cast of characters. The central picture shows a stylized Indian catching a deer by the horns, partially superimposed on a small line-drawn map of the area of New England where the story is set. Above these are the title and author's name (with, to the side, "Illustrated by Ray Ramsey"). And below, to start the story: "THERE IS GREAT ACTIVITY AROUND FORT EDWARD. WORD HAS JUST COME BY INDIAN RUNNER FROM COLONEL MUNRO, COMMANDANT AT FORT WILLIAM HENRY, OF IMPENDING DAN-

GER. MONTCALM, WITH AN ARMY OF FRENCH AND INDIANS, 'NU-
MEROUS AS THE LEAVES ON THE TREES,' IS MOVING DOWN LAKE
CHAMPLAIN TO ATTACK HIM.

"GENERAL WEBB, IN COMMAND AT FORT EDWARD, HAS OR-
DERED A BODY OF SOLDIERS TO MARCH THE TWENTY MILES SEP-
ARATING THE TWO FORTS, TO THE RELIEF OF COLONEL MUNRO.

"IT IS 1757, THE THIRD YEAR OF THE FRENCH AND INDIAN WAR.
SINCE BRADDOCK'S DEFEAT IN 1755, THINGS HAVE GONE BADLY
FOR THE ENGLISH AND THE COLONISTS." Our reaction: a glaring mis-
match between careful impression-management in the choice of words and
an almost perverse lack of care over the quality of the artwork.

1954/5: This excerpted version begins in fact by acknowledging its limita-
tions, and hymning the original: "THE FOLLOWING PICTURES HAVE
BEEN EXCERPTED FROM A STORY BY JAMES FENIMORE COOPER,
THAT TOOK PLACE DURING THE FRENCH AND INDIAN WARS!
THEY CONCERN A WHITE SCOUT CALLED HAWKEYE . . . A MOHI-
CAN CHIEF CALLED CHINGACHGOOK . . . HIS SON UNCAS . . . AND
THEIR PERSONAL FEUD WITH THE HURON INDIAN TRIBE: THESE
SIX PAGES ATTEMPT ONLY TO GIVE A TANTALIZING GLIMPSE INTO
THAT GREAT CLASSIC . . . *THE LAST OF THE MOHICANS!*" The retell-
ing then begins well into the story, with our first sight of Hawkeye and the
Mohicans. Let us save discussion of this point for a moment. The first
impression, though, is of a homage to a great story—but a story that is,
without embarrassment, conceived pictorially. If it is just a glimpse, it will
be one that will seek nonetheless to evoke a whole mood and atmosphere.

1959: The introductory page of this version is dominated by a powerful
visual image of two Indians wrestling, with legs interlocked (see chapter 8
below for a discussion of this image) over and against the backdrop of a
scene of a lake, hills, forests, and sky. The two figures appear almost giant
size and out of proportion, like mythic creatures that do not belong in the
landscape. Above their heads, but with an ax almost puncturing it, the title
and (much smaller) the name of Cooper. Below, as though on an old un-
scrolled parchment: "IN THE SUMMER OF 1757, FRANCE AND EN-
GLAND WERE IN THE MIDST OF A WAR FOR POSSESSION OF NORTH
AMERICA. IN THIS FIERCE STRUGGLE KNOWN AS THE FRENCH
AND INDIAN WAR, MANY INDIANS WERE ALLIED WITH THE
FRENCH. THEY WERE OF DIFFERENT TRIBES, BUT THE COMMON
NAME FOR THEM WAS MINGO.

"THE OTHER EASTERN TRIBES EITHER SIDED WITH THE BRITISH
OR WERE NEUTRAL. BUT ONE TRIBE HAD BEEN SO BADLY DISPOS-
SESSED BY THE FIRST EUROPEAN SETTLERS THAT IT HAD ALL BUT
DISAPPEARED. THIS WAS THE TRIBE OF THE MOHICANS." First re-
sponse: there is a strength about the visuality of this version that helps to

"place" the introductory words, and in some ways to contradict them. It seems to project us into a past we are hardly connected with.

*1977(a):* Here the introduction is made up of several distinct elements. First, there is a page that greatly resembles a film poster. It is a collage of figures and faces: a woman (Cora?) sitting at bottom left in a revealing dress, a wild and dangerous Indian bursting out from behind her, another Indian above standing as though invoking the spirits; behind again, the figure of Hawkeye looking off to the left with his gun at the ready; and so on. The words of the title are shown three-dimensionally, again like an old film poster, scaling away to the bottom right, where we see in miniature a troop of English soldiers riding away from a distant fort. A small band, hand-drawn and lettered, carries Cooper's name. It is a busy, suggestive panorama, hinting at multiple conflicts and relationships, including romantic/sexual.

But on turning the page, the first thing one encounters is a paragraph of bare typed text—in fact the first paragraph of the book: "It was a feature peculiar to the colonial wars of North America that the dangers of the wilderness were to be encountered before the adverse hosts could meet. A wide and apparently impervious boundary of forest separated the possessions of the mutually hostile provinces of France and England—and perhaps no district of the frontier could more vividly host the fierceness of savage warfare than the region between the headwaters of the Hudson River and the adjacent lakes of Champlain and 'Horican' (or Lake George). . . . " And here the text peters out, as we suddenly enter the world of the story. The first panel is a high angle shot on a troop of soldiers leaving a fort, with the narration: "FORT EDWARD, 1757: SINCE GENERAL BRADDOCK'S DEFEAT IN 1755, THE ENGLISH HAVE FARED POORLY IN THE FRENCH AND INDIAN WAR. NOW, HAVING RECEIVED WORD FROM COLONEL MUNRO—COMMANDANT AT FORT WILLIAM HENRY—THAT MONTCALM'S FRENCH AND INDIAN FORCES ARE MOVING DOWN LAKE CHAMPLAIN TO ATTACK, GENERAL WEBB DISPATCHES A BODY OF SOLDIERS TO MUNRO'S AID. . . ."

The story then flows on through a further four panels on the same page. First impression: some sharp shifts of genre going on here, a quick mention of Cooper, and then let the real show begin!

*1977(b):* In a smaller booklet size and black and white on higher-grade paper, this version has the look of a school-play edition. A double-page spread introduces the story. To the left, along with printed title and author's name, identifying faces of the main characters. To the right, against a virtually static picture of soldiers outside a fort (all midshot to distant), and typeset onto a scroll background: "In the 1750s, the English colonies in America were ruled by Great Britain. But France also claimed a large part of North America. The French and Indian War was fought between the French and the English to settle the matter. Some Indian tribes sided with the French, others with the English. Much of the fighting took place in the land that was to become New York State." Below right, in a ruled circle: "One summer evening, an Indian runner brought an important message to the British Fort Edward by the Hudson River."

First response: this version is almost embarrassed at having to be visual at all.

*1992*: Presented in black, white, and grays, the opening page of the story is set opposite a full page of a single sketch of battle with a stripe of editorial information down its middle. The first page itself is composed of a scroll of text (hand-lettered, and identical to the dialogue), and three subsequent cross-page panels. The text reads: "IT WAS A FEATURE PECULIAR TO THE COLONIAL WARS OF NORTH AMERICA THAT THE TOILS AND DANGERS OF THE WILDERNESS WERE TO BE ENCOUNTERED BEFORE THE OPPOSING HOSTS COULD MEET. IN JULY OF 1757, THE FRENCH AND INDIAN WAR ENTERED ITS THIRD YEAR. IT WAS THE FINAL, TITANIC STRUGGLE BETWEEN FRANCE AND ENGLAND FOR POSSESSION OF THE CONTINENT, AND GENERAL BRADDOCK'S DEFEAT IN 1755 HAD PLACED THE ENGLISH FRONTIER AT THE MERCY OF THE FRENCH—ESPECIALLY ALONG THE HUDSON RIVER OF UPSTATE NEW YORK, WHERE ONLY TWO SMALL FORTS FACED OVERWHELMING ODDS." Then, below the scroll but above the first panel: "ONE DAY, UNWELCOME NEWS WAS RECEIVED AT FORT EDWARD: GENERAL MONTCALM, AT THE HEAD OF 10,000 FRENCHMEN AND INDIAN ALLIES, WAS MARCHING ON NEARBY FORT WILLIAM HENRY!" The panel shows an Indian striking his palm in a singular gesture as he looks away from us toward four bewigged English officers sitting in a bunkhouse, with guards behind them (in gray-shadow). We "hear" the newsbringer: " . . . NUMEROUS AS LEAVES ON THE TREES." The officers debate: "CAN WE BELIEVE HIM?" "AYE, GENERAL WEBB. MAGUA IS ONE OF COLONEL MUNRO'S BEST RUNNERS."

First response: a version that is working very hard, deploying all kinds of artistic devices and narrative techniques, to make a comment—to what end?

Six versions of the opening, then. Of course, they overlap in the information they provide. But already it is possible to distinguish quite different manners of communicating that information. First, there is a clear disjunction in the extent to which the versions feel the need to acknowledge the bookishness of Cooper's original. The 1940/1 version does not do so at all, whereas 1977(b) is the most constrained. 1959 has managed to stage the book as a drama, so that while the source is acknowledged, it is included but surpassed. In a different way, that is true of 1977(a). Here, though, there is a tension between the poster collage, the dry literariness of Cooper's opening words, and the plunge into comic format. The 1992 opening is the oddest. The words are from the original, indeed have the feel of antiquity. When we enter the panels, Magua is in the middle of speaking a snatch of rather literary words. It is a bookish version, yet very much in comic book format. What this portends, we shall see.

How do the different versions prepare the ground for the story? The 1940/1 version is careless and throwaway, setting the scene with such uninvolved factuality that the story is comatose before it leaves page one. For the 1942 version, the emphasis is clearly going to be on the action, to which the historical circumstances are attached as a rider. We are to read an "exciting story"! Can the English survive yet another attack!? The 1959 version is curious. Against the backdrop of those mythic giants we learn that one tribe, the Mohicans, with whom we are clearly meant to sympathize, had suffered greatly at the hands of the first settlers. But that was long ago, of course, not our responsibility now. . . .

The 1977(a) comic starts with the bang of its poster collage, pauses to remind us that this was "literature," and then slaloms off the dots at the end of its quote into a fast-moving, vibrant page of action. The 1977(b) version feels it must first give us a lesson, a school lesson, in the facts of history. In short, clipped sentences, it takes us there. First, who was involved, then when it was, then where it was. Now that we have got that straight, we can learn about an "important message." There is a pedantic, almost condescending tone to this version. The 1992 version, meanwhile, seems to work at establishing a different kind of seriousness. A sense of period authenticity is invoked in which the period might be that of the book (hence of Cooper's own intentions) or of 1757 itself.

These are, of course, just openings. If the cues and clues were not followed up, there would be little point in such close attention to how our first impressions are managed. Consider, then, how we meet the second set of characters. What can we learn from these introductions? How do they continue the agendas set by the openings we have already considered? (See page 158.)

First of all, let us eliminate the 1940/1 version. Its miserable emptiness speaks for itself; there is no attempt to achieve anything. We have real difficulty finding anything of interest to say about these panels. Compare, instead, the 1942 and 1977(a) versions. The

**Our first introduction to Hawkeye and the Mohicans.**

THE FOLLOWING PICTURES HAVE BEEN EXCERPTED FROM A STORY BY JAMES FENIMORE COOPER, THAT TOOK PLACE DURING THE FRENCH AND INDIAN WARS! THEY CONCERN A WHITE SCOUT CALLED HAWKEYE...A MOHICAN CHIEF CALLED CHINGACHGOOK...HIS SON UNCAS...AND THEIR PERSONAL FEUD WITH THE HURON INDIAN TRIBE: THESE SIX PAGES ATTEMPT ONLY TO GIVE A TANTALIZING GLIMPSE INTO THAT GREAT CLASSIC...

# THE LAST OF THE MOHICANS!

"Where are the blossoms of those summers - fallen, one by one: so all of my family departed, each in his turn, to the land of spirits. I am on the hilltop, and must go down into the valley; and when Uncas follows in my footsteps, there will no longer will be any of the blood of the Sagamores,* for my boy is the last of the Mohicans."

\* Sagamores – Mohicans and Delawares

© EC Comics, 1954

ON THAT SAME DAY, NOT FAR AWAY, TWO MEN WERE LINGERING BY A SMALL STREAM, DEEP IN DISCUSSION.

MY PEOPLE, THE MOHICANS, WERE HAPPY, HAWKEYE, UNTIL THE PALE-FACES CAME. THEN, WE WERE DRIVEN BACK FROM OUR LAND, FOOT BY FOOT, WE WERE DRIVEN BACK FROM OUR LAND.

I AM WILLING TO ADMIT, CHINGACHGOOK, THAT MY PEOPLE HAVE MANY WAYS OF WHICH I CAN'T APPROVE

*Classics Illustrated,* © and ™ Classics International Entertainments, Inc., 1959

(Left:) *Marvel Classics*, © Marvel Entertainment Group, Inc., 1977
(Above:) © *Pendulum Illustrated*, 1977

*Dark Horse Classics*, © Dark Horse Comics, Inc., 1992

first is a bare introduction, with just the textual information necessary to follow the story. It tells us which side *they* are on and,
therefore, which side *we* are presumably supposed to be on. Visually,
the 1942 version is uninformative, the two characters seeming pas-
sive and uninvolved, not even meaningfully still. The most additional information we are given is the lack of "civilization" suggested for Chingachgook. His grunt-like response, nakedness, and
proximity to the ground all signify near-animality. Contrast that
with the 1977(a) version's picture of both characters: Hawkeye is
visually powerful, outtopping the very borders of the panel, but not
because of any implied superiority. He is listening, attentively, to
Chingachgook's funereal philosophizing: overblown language, with
gesture to sustain it. The narration tells us firmly that these very
different men are bonded, beyond race and heritage. Chingachgook is
a tragic figure, and their conversation is essentially for our benefit.
After all, if they have been close friends this long, how come
Chingachgook is only telling Hawkeye these things now? Surely he
would already know; but for the purposes of the story, Hawkeye here
participates in Chingachgook's sense of tragedy. It is his, too.

The sharp difference between these two versions can alert us to
milder alternatives. Look, now, at the others. The 1959 version,
interestingly, continues the apologetic tone of its introduction.
Hawkeye distances himself from the white maltreatment of Indians
that was hinted at in the beginning. But the price is a sense of slight
distance, of formality, between the two men; they are not "as one."
The 1977(b) version is different again. Here, there is tangible tragedy
in the noble features of Chingachgook, but it has no location, no
cause. It is merely that there is no future for his tribe. Why? We do
not know. The conversation seems to be for our benefit, and once
again Hawkeye is like an onlooker: detached, like us.

The 1954/5 excerpt, of course, begins at this point, therefore immediately associating the striking title lettering with the central
image of despair in Chingachgook. And, unusually for these publishers, the handwritten quality of the dialogue combined with
the footnoting secures a powerful mix of visual strength and literary
authenticity. Without overstatement, we are witnessing great
events.

Now consider the 1992 version, the one we have already noted as
curiously different. Here, in a grainy image suggesting the earthi-
ness of nature, two diminished figures again talk, for the benefit of

our overhearing, but now Hawkeye is admitting the partiality of his own understanding. Once again, we drop into the middle of a conversation. We can guess what is meant by "what my people teach." It is the standard version of the history of whites and Indians. Chingachgook's account is different. Its tone has the serious but poetic tone of a fine story. The faces are expressive—still, but lined and containing character. There is a pervasive sense of immobility, partly but not entirely a function of the particular strengths of the writer/artist. Here, then, is a "noble" version, one whose politics of Indian life are looking to be very different from the others.

With these comparisons in mind, let us consider each version in turn, the circumstances of its production (where we have been able to determine this), and the overall nature of its textual rendering of *Mohicans*. We do not mean to spend long on the 1940/1 version, simply because it is so poor. That poverty is not accidental or incidental. The story first appeared in early issues of *Target Comics* (Funnies Inc./Novelty-Star Publications) and later in the shorter-lived title *White Rider and Super Horse* (Novelty-Star), which folded before completing the reprint. The publishers were typical of those described by Matthew McAllister in his essay on the political economy of early comics: "Many early comic book organizations, especially the smaller companies, were owned by people who had earned sizable amounts of money during Prohibition, not always legally, and sought to invest this money in easily accessible and successful industries. The philosophy of many of these early publishers was 'do it cheap. Find cheap labor, pay cheap prices. Low overhead. Tie up as little money as possible. Take out as much money as possible.' The results were predictable—in a few years the bad drove out the good."[16] Enough said. All the other versions, however, are differently interesting. Let us take them in historical order.

*1942: The Mohicans Go East.* This version was Kanter's first attempt at a comic book adaptation of an American novel—itself noteworthy. The 1942 comic went through some twenty reprints before being readapted and redrawn in 1959. The most striking thing about this edition is its dehumanization of the Indians, even the good ones. (Hawkeye to Uncas: WELL, UNCAS, WHAT SAW YOU? Uncas: NO SEE, NO HEAR NOTHING!) If the Mohicans are reduced to grunts, the Hurons become bestial. Magua is variously described as a "snake," a "painted fiend," a "slippery savage." It is hardly surprising, then, that there is not a hint of Uncas's attraction to Cora, let alone her counterdesires. All reason for the virtual disappearance of the Mohicans has gone. Magua's intense desire for revenge is reduced to a virtual threat of rape because he was whipped for getting drunk. And when, at the camp of the Delawares, he rails against the whites for stealing Indians' land, this is scaled down to his being "crafty."

This version is constructed around so sharp and hard a distinction between the whites and the Indians that when Uncas dies, nothing remains of Tamenund's moving closing speech. The final panel hurries Alice and Duncan off to be married and Hawkeye back to the woods; there is not even a glimpse of the bereaved Chingachgook. This white/Indian opposition is unargued. There is no trace of discussion or philosophizing in the entire story—because, perhaps, it was unarguable. Consider the time of its production: August 1942. America had just experienced the shock of its history: Pearl Harbor. The "little Yellow Devils" had turned, against all predictions, and done what they were supposed to be incapable of: they had outwitted and beaten American forces. In a startling study of this period, John Dower has shown the way American images of the Japanese shifted during the Second World War.[17] Up until Pearl Harbor and the defeats in the Pacific, a deeply-ingrained general hostility to the Japanese had them pictured as small, virtually subhuman monkey-like myopics—an image so strong that Dower is able to quote substantial evidence that sections of the American military believed the Japanese incapable of skills such as night flying. Therefore when the attack on Pearl Harbor took place, some American commanders insisted that the attack must have been led by Germans. Once the realization sank in, the image of the Japanese changed. They became much larger, more threatening, more gorilla-like. That they had an unhealthy liking for white women was increasingly postulated.[18]

In the 1942 *Mohicans* we see the Indians functioning symbolically as an Enemy, subhuman, incapable of any but the basest emotions, desirous in a crude way of white female flesh. So much so, that the differences among whites themselves must pale into insignificance. So, as a noble-looking Montcalm is preparing to receive the surrender of the English troops, he encounters a still-bloodthirsty Magua. Contrary to all that Cooper says, the 1942 version excuses Montcalm with his worried response: "THAT RED-SKIN MEANS MISCHIEF. WE MUST BE ON THE ALERT." In *Mohicans* the Indians always signify more than just themselves. They

are the good and evil that "America" must take or reject. No wonder Chingachgook disappears at the end—he must have been interned as an enemy!

*1954/5: The Last of the ECs!* The early 1950s were a torrid time for comics, what with Wertham's attacks, the New York legislative and U.S. Senate hearings into comic books and delinquency, and frequent local campaigns and even mass bonfires of comics. No publisher was targeted more than William Gaines's EC Comics. Equally, no other company in this period took as much pride in its products as did EC. Transformed when Gaines inherited the company after his father was drowned in a boating accident, EC attracted many of the best writers and artists, who were given substantial editorial and artistic freedom to express themselves.

Jack Davis, who adapted and drew our excerpt in the penultimate edition of *Two-Fisted Tales*, was one of EC's leading artists. His drawing style was very personal—something encouraged by EC's system—and emphasized the expression of emotions through the stance and movement of bodies (with a tendency towards the bizarre and the gothic, encouraged by his love of dark shading). *Two-Fisted Tales*, one of two EC war titles, was noted for its attention to detail and for its generally critical attitude towards war. Not quite pacifist, still, it always stressed the anguish war caused.

In Jack Davis's homage to Cooper, the griefs of war are captured through the very physicality of the action. Faces and bodies share every mood and emotion. Few other versions are so faithful to the original text, and no other version so confidently asserts the visuality of the story. What a shame that Davis never attempted an unabridged rendition of the story! It leaves us a fragment that once again demonstrates how much was lost when EC withdrew from comics production only a month after the publication of its *Mohicans*. Bruised by the batterings of the anti-comics campaigners, Gaines closed down his horror, crime, war, and science fiction lines, maintaining only *MAD*. What was lost, arguably, was the greatest individual achievement in American comics' history. Its influence lived on, bursting forth in particular into the Underground Comix of the late 1960s. But in Davis's fragment of *Mohicans*, we see a gleaming indication of what could happen when novel and comic meet on equal ground.

*1959: Classic Reconciliations.* In 1959, as part of raising their status, many of the early *Classics Illustrated* were readapted and redrawn. *Mohicans* was readapted by Stephen Addeo (about whom we know nothing) and drawn by one of the ex-EC artists, John Severin. This new version was produced in a much different climate. America had passed through the nightmare of McCarthyism into a more tolerant and self-critical mood. The first elements of the civil rights movement had emerged. In this more relaxed climate, this second version allows some gentle reflection on ideological tensions. America was becoming unsure of its Dream.

It is remarkable to be able to compare two such different versions from the same publisher. If in 1942 Indians were subhuman savages (metaphors for nonwhites everywhere) by 1959 they are different human beings. They have laws and customs of their own, with their own validity. Where the Delaware law that Cora belonged to Magua was inexplicable in the earlier version, in the later it has taken on a force of its own ("UNABLE TO INTERFERE WITH THE STRICT TRIBAL LAWS OF HOSPITALITY, UNCAS WATCHED ANGRILY"). Where the earlier version could not even hint at a mutual attraction between Cora and Uncas, the 1959 version acknowledges it, but transforms it in the process. Alice speaks to Cora as they try to rest in the cave, guarded by Uncas: "CAN YOU SLEEP WITH SUCH A SENTINEL?" Cora: "HE IS A FEARLESS LOOKING YOUTH. I THINK HE WILL BE A BRAVE AND CONSTANT FRIEND." Sex is kept firmly out of the picture. So when Magua makes his demand that Cora become his squaw, and she rejects him it is not with the look of distaste and sexual horror that characterized the 1942 version. She defies him, and his response is to feel that his status, not his race, has been insulted: "SO THE DAUGHTER OF MUNRO IS TOO GOOD FOR MAGUA! WE WILL SEE."

But of course an attentive reader knows already that Cora has no such objections to Indians in general; she can admire them as much as any other. What takes the place of sexuality in this retelling is a sharp separation of gender roles. Through the manner of drawing as much as anything else, an image is created of what real men and real women are like—and it is against this measure that Magua fails. A real man protects a woman; she will feel safe with him. Cora is "high-souled," "courageous," and "noble" (words from her funeral oration), and the reconciliation with the dead Uncas will be a protective one: "FEAR NOTHING, NOBLE MAIDEN. THE GREAT WARRIOR UNCAS WILL BE AT YOUR SIDE ON YOUR TRIP TO THE GREAT SPIRIT. HE WILL PROTECT YOU FROM EVERY DANGER," says the mourning Delaware woman.

This time the end unites Hawkeye and Chingachgook in grief, even sharing the words of mourning originally assigned to Chingachgook. This easy reconciliation would not seem so easy two years later, after a black woman named Rosa Parks, refusing to leave her (white-designated) seat on a bus in Montgomery, Alabama, gave a clear impetus to the civil rights movement. From that time on, it

**How comics tell stories: the threatening of Alice. Is she
(a) a Hollywood heroine in distress, (b) overcome with
terror, or (c) a lesson in firm resolve?**

*IT CUT SOME OF THE RINGLETS FROM HER HAIR. MADDENED BY THE SIGHT, DUNCAN TORE HIMSELF FREE.*

*Classics Illustrated,* © and ™
Classics International Entertainments, Inc., 1959

*THE SAVAGELY HURLED TOMAHAWK NARROWLY MISSES ALICE'S HEAD, CUTTING SEVERAL RINGLETS OF HER BLOND HAIR...*

*THE SIGHT MADDENS HEYWARD AND, WITH SUPERHUMAN EFFORT HE RIPS FREE OF HIS CAPTOR--*

(Left:) *Marvel Classics,* © Marvel
Entertainment Group, Inc., 1977
(Above:) *Dark Horse Classics,* ©
Dark Horse Comics, Inc., 1992

would not be so easy to fudge issues of black/white relations and pretend there was no controversy.

*1977(a): A Marvelous Myth.* It does not surprise us that there is a twenty-year gap in virtually all versions of *Mohicans*—film, TV, comic—since the 1960s were in many ways an anti-mythic period. Nor is it surprising that the return to the myth so nearly coincides with the bicentennial of the Declaration of Independence. But such returns to past stories are never simply returns: they have to take account of the changes wrought in the period between. So, the two 1977 comic versions (as also the TV movie we have already explored) do go back to the myth, but in the light of new tensions and problems that have to be negotiated.

First, let us consider the Marvel Classics Comics edition. Between 1976 and 1978 Marvel produced thirty-six adaptations of classic texts. The first twelve (which included staples such as *The Time Machine, Moby Dick*, and *20,000 Leagues under the Sea*) were reprints from the artwork of Pendulum Illustrated, a company that had broken away from the wreckage of the old Classics Illustrated line. Number 13, the first to be based on separate adaptation and artwork, was *Mohicans*. There is an untold story here, since Pendulum also published a version of *Mohicans*: our 1977(b). In this period Marvel was undergoing a severe shake-up following a downturn in sales in the early 1970s. We do not know why this split took place, or why Marvel produced this line at all.[19]

Marvel's version, adapted by Doug Moench and drawn by Sonny Trinidad, is dramatic and dynamic, owing much to Marvel's general comics style. The comic has a penchant for explosive fight scenes, emotion-charged faces, for wild filmic shifts of perspective, and for text that is both verbally and visually dramatic. As we have already argued, these are not add-ons; they are part of the meaning of the adaptation that Marvel offers. Having made their gesture to literariness, thereafter they are once again the world's leading comic book company, and they know it. Nothing will make them compromise that position. So, their cover is pure Marvel. Grimacing fighting Indians spill across it, with this lettered guarantee: THE THRILLS AND EXCITEMENT OF THE ORIGINAL CLASSIC—IN A POWERFUL, NEVER-BEFORE-SEEN COMICS ADAPTATION! (See chapter 8 for a reproduction of this cover.)

This unashamed comic-ness shows in many ways. In the panel introducing Hawkeye and the Mohicans, notice the punctured border, as a way of indicating strength and status; and the visual arrangement to suggest relationships among characters. Marvel uses the full range of visual-textual effects: enlarged type for loudness or urgency, fading size for uncertainty; jagged balloons for emotional emphasis, and dotted balloons for whispered conversation. The boundary between dialogue and narration sometimes dissolves. When Uncas is brought before the council of the Delawares and is denounced as a renegade, the following transition takes place: Narration: AS THE INCENSED DELAWARES SAVAGELY SPRING UPON UNCAS, THE MOHICAN'S TUNIC IS RIPPED FROM HIS BACK . . . REVEALING . . . Tamenund: "THE TORTOISE—! HE WEARS THE SACRED SIGN OF THE TURTLE CLAN!" The narrator is part of the action, part of its atmosphere and emotions. In these ways, Marvel brings the story to life in a way rarely achieved by the other comic versions.

To what end? What version of the myth does Marvel offer? It is unashamed about the possibilities of sexual attraction between Cora and Uncas. Marvel rises above the prejudices that afflict Cooper's story and so many other adaptations. Indeed, it revels in doing so. At the cave: HAWKEYE IS AMUSED AS HE WATCHES UNCAS ACTING AS ATTENDANT TO THE FEMALES—ESPECIALLY THE DARK-HAIRED CORA—WELL KNOWING THE INDIAN'S MIXTURE OF DIGNITY AND ANXIOUS GRACE IS CONTRARY TO THE CUSTOMS OF HIS PEOPLE . . . CUSTOMS WHICH FORBID THEIR WARRIORS TO DESCEND TO MENIAL TASKS, ESPECIALLY IN FAVOR TO WOMEN. BUT THEN, THIS CORA IS A MOST STRIKING WOMAN. . . . And three panels later, as Cora and Alice settle to sleep, guarded by Uncas, Cora begins: "LOOK AT THIS UNCAS, SISTER—SUCH A NOBLE, HANDSOME, AND FEARLESS YOUTH HE SEEMS. I THINK HE WILL PROVE A BRAVE AND CONSTANT FRIEND." Alice: "PERHAPS MORE THAN A FRIEND, SISTER CORA, OR DOES THE LIGHT IN YOUR GAZE DECEIVE ME—?" Cora: "WHAT OF IT ALICE, DO YOU NOT HAVE STALWART DUNCAN TO ATTRACT YOUR EYES . . . ?" The open admission of attraction is bold and novel, and is maintained right to the death, literally. Uncas dies because he loves his Cora. To that extent, this telling passes out of myth and symbolism into a realism of emotions. But at a wider level, it remains a myth. What kind?

In a way *Mohicans* becomes one among a thousand other Marvel

Marvel absorbs Cooper's novel into its own canon of superheroes (*Marvel Classics*, © Marvel Entertainment Group, Inc., 1977)

myths, belonging to the same plane as Spiderman, or Thor (in the Marvel Universe version), or the Thing. But that is not the whole. For whereas in each of those cases, stories are always fragments of a larger whole, and characters always have the potential to step beyond their own world into each others' (usually for the purpose of a good brawl), *Mohicans* signals its self-containedness and completeness. Its end is final. We have, as it were, visited Hawkeye's world,

Marvel-style, but we leave it to return that world to its classic, literary status. The end is striking. We quote it at length:

GRIEVING, BUT AT LAST FINDING PEACE, MUNRO, ALICE, HEYWARD AND GAMUT DEPART FOR THE OUTPOSTS OF THE BRITISH ARMY. AFTER A TIME, WHEN THE STING IS LESSENED IF NOT FORGOTTEN, ALICE AND DUNCAN HEYWARD WILL WED. . . . BUT FOR NOW, THEY CAN THINK ONLY OF THE LOSS—OF CORA . . . AND OF TWO FRIENDS WHO KNEEL OVER A MOUND OF FRESHLY TURNED EARTH . . . Hawkeye: "HE WAS GOOD; HE WAS DUTIFUL; HE WAS BRAVE. THE GREAT SPIRIT HAD NEED OF SUCH A WARRIOR, AND HAS CALLED HIM AWAY." [New panel. Close-up on the two mourning faces.] Chingachgook: "YES, HAWKEYE, HE HAS GONE AWAY . . . LEAVING ME A BLAZED PINE IN A CLEARING OF WHITE MEN . . . I AM ALONE" (this last in reduced lettering). [Final panel. Side by side, bent over the grave, with Hawkeye comforting Chingachgook.] "NO, CHINGACHGOOK—NOT ALONE. THE GIFTS OF OUR COLORS MAY BE DIFFERENT, BUT GOD HAS PLACED US BOTH TO JOURNEY ON THE SAME PATH . . . THE BOY HAS LEFT US FOR A TIME . . . BUT SAGAMORE, YOU ARE NOT ALONE." Narration: AND NOW, THE TWO WOODSMEN WILL BOW THEIR HEADS TOGETHER, WHILE SCALDING TEARS FALL BELOW THEM . . . WATERING THE GRAVE OF UNCAS LIKE DROPS OF SLOWLY FALLING RAIN . . . [Final lettered paragraph of text.] AND THERE WILL BE NOTHING LEFT BUT THE AWFUL STILLNESS AND THE BURST OF FEELING IN THE WORDS OF WISE, ANCIENT TAMENUND: "GO, CHILDREN OF THE DELAWARES, FOR THE ANGER OF THE MANITOU IS NOT DONE. THE PALEFACES ARE MASTERS OF THE EARTH, AND THE TIME OF THE RED MAN HAS NOT YET COME AGAIN. MY DAY HAS BEEN TOO LONG. IN THE MORNING I SAW THE SON OF CHINGACHGOOK HAPPY AND STRONG; AND YET, BEFORE THE NIGHT HAS COME, I HAVE LIVED TO SEE THE LAST WARRIOR OF THE WISE RACE OF THE MOHICANS." END. Facing these words of closure is a black-and-white page montaging the figures of Hawkeye and Chingachgook onto a statuesque drawing of James Fenimore Cooper.

There is a way in which the comic, with its overdrawn emotions, its deluge of tears and caring, is saying, "This is a cleansing. Experience with us, through our comic, this great story and the great tragedy it encompasses, and by the end you will be purged of the wrongs it encapsulates. The 'mystery of race' will have been overcome. The mythic figures will be back in their still place in the landscapes of our imagination. 'America' will be right again." This is the good that Marvel sets itself to do. Its comic is an enactment. It itself is the remedy to the evil that the story encodes. By the end, we may say we feel better for that.

*1977(b): Suffer the little children. . . .* The contrast between Marvel's version of *Mohicans* and the other 1977 version—Pendulum Illustrated's Now Age Book, illustrated by Fred Carillo—could hardly be greater. If Marvel lets rip, Pendulum is tense and cautious as a school primer—which it precisely tries to be. This version even ends with a page headed "Words to know," then offers questions treating us as pupils who have been reading the story as a piece of history: "Why was the French and Indian War being fought? On whose side were General Munro and his daughters?" and so on. This textbook reestablishes the story somewhere between fact and fiction. It is school reader size, printed on good paper, and bound, not stapled. It has been prepared by "qualified reading consultants." There is a self-conscious appeal to teachers:

Children are motivated to read material that satisfies their quest for knowledge and understanding of their world. In this series, they are exposed to some of the greatest stories, authors, and characters in the English language. The Series will stimulate their desire to read the original edition when their reading skills are sufficiently developed. More importantly, reading books in the NOW AGE ILLUSTRATED Series will help students establish a mental "pegboard" of information—images, names, and concepts—to which they are exposed. Let's assume, for example, that a child sees a television commercial which features Huck Finn in some way. If he has read the NOW AGE Huck Finn, the TV reference has meaning for him which gives the child a surge of satisfaction and accomplishment.

To read the Pendulum *Mohicans* is a kind of sponsored self-improvement. This double appeal, to teachers and children, is nicely shown in the text on the back cover, headlined "Bringing the Classics to Life . . . : Discover reading and enter the exciting world of adventure and mystery. Turn the pages of history and look into the frontiers of tomorrow. Live among timeless heroes as they spring to life in the NOW AGE ILLUSTRATED SERIES. The unique format of these books is designed to stimulate interest in reading, build and strengthen vocabulary, and improve reading skills. Most of all, NOW AGE ILLUSTRATED verifies that reading is fun!" One can just about imagine children saying "Yes!" to entering exciting worlds of adventure and mystery, but it strains credibility a bit to hear them saying "Wow!" to building and strengthening their vocabulary. The teacherly address is very evident.

How does this educationalism affect the form and content of the story? The look of this version is all important. With its avoidance of speech balloons and its use of upper- and lower-case type for the narration and dialogue, it refuses the comic conventions which have allowed comic book text to be heard rather than spoken. As a result, and because Pendulum avoids anything smacking of lived speech (instead aiming to suggest "fine speech"), the dialogue seems to float awkwardly above the panels in which it occurs, as in this example.

© *Pendulum Illustrated*, 1977

It is as if the words are spoken by actors, not characters.

Pendulum removes all hint of the romantic attraction of Uncas and Cora; indeed, more than that, it removes almost all hint of why characters do anything at all. All we know even of Magua is that he was whipped, and wants revenge—revenge carefully couched in terms of demanding that Cora "draw my water, hoe my corn and cook my meat." We learn nothing of Hawkeye or the Mohicans' feelings, of Heyward's desire for Alice (let alone Munro's feelings about Heyward's apparent rejection of half-caste Cora). Only once, right at the end, is Cooper's rhetoric allowed small rein. Even here, Tamenund's closing eulogy is carefully edited and framed: "The palefaces are masters of the earth, and the time of the red men has not yet come. My day has been long. I have lived to see the last brave of the wise race of Mohicans." Narration: "And it was many years before the Indians stopped telling of the white maiden and the young Mohican who had gone together to the happy hunting ground. THE END." Any judgment on the passing of the Indians is headed off, and the story ends in that fairytale world where, even if not living happily ever after, the tale lives on, but as an *Indian* tale.[20]

It seems to us that this inheritor of the Classics Illustrated mantle has found itself caught between increasingly incompatible demands. American education has become increasingly politicized since the 1970s, with battles over textbooks,[21] the aftershocks of 1960s radicalism, and with, of course, the deep conflicts and uncertainties over "race."[22] The results are an almost squirming embarrassment. If Joseph Witek identified a will in 1961 not to cross any opinion on the Civil War, here one can positively hear a flinching from offense.

*1992: In Other Words. . . .* Not so the 1992 version. Published by Dark Horse Comics, a publisher that has mainly made its name and money from licensed products (especially comic adaptations of films), this version was adapted and drawn by Jack Jackson. Jackson's previous record is relevant here. First appearing in one of the Underground Comix, *God Nose* (1964), Jackson is best known for later stories in which he challenges traditional attitudes toward native American peoples. From his early "Nits make lice" (published in *Slow Death* 7 [1964]), he moved on to full-length graphic novels: *Comanche Moon* (1979) and *Los Tejanos* (1982).[23] Jackson brought to *Mohicans* his position as an author of comic books on Indian issues. He turns *Mohicans* into a vehicle for an argument about white treatment of Indians.

Compare four versions of the moment when Cora and Alice realize they are to have an Indian guide to the fort as shown on pages 176–177. These mini-debates among the whites about "dark skin" position us differently. The 1942 version sets up a bald clash. Magua is a loathsome, hardly human figure, and Cora will surely pay for her trusting attitude! The 1959 version cautiously deletes the race issue; the only question is Magua's "reliability." The 1977(b) treatment makes a flat statement of the correct attitude: dark skin is not the issue, is that clear, children? The 1992 rendering, however, is more complicated. A question mark is put over the attitudes of the white people. There is a division between Cora, whose anger suggestively arises from "rich blood," and Alice, whose response to scolding is flighty and impetuous. The eye of the author is outside the white point of view, which is shown to be limited and partial.

Consider the scene in which Magua tells Cora of his flogging. Cora: "AM I ANSWERABLE THAT UNPRINCIPLED MEN EXIST, WHATEVER THEIR COLOR?" Taking almost three pages for this one scene, the comic does not spare us the sight of Magua's back savagely scarred by the whip. When Magua finally makes his demand of her, interestingly, there is a conflict of principles at work. Cora: "WHAT WOULD YOU HAVE OF ME, HELPLESS AS I AM?" Magua: "THAT THE DAUGHTER OF MUNRO SHOULD LIVE IN MAGUA'S WIGWAM, FOREVER! . . . LET THE GREY-HAIR SLEEP AMONG HIS CANNON. WITH YOU IN MY WIGWAM, I HAVE HIS HEART WITHIN REACH OF MY KNIFE!" Cora: "MONSTER! WELL DOST THOU DESERVE THIS TREACHEROUS NAME! NONE BUT A FIEND COULD MEDITATE SUCH A VENGEANCE!" Narration: "THE INDIAN ANSWERED THIS DEFIANCE WITH A GHASTLY LEER, BRINGING A BLUSH TO CORA'S CHEEKS." This Cora is strong, both visually and verbally. This is not a white woman fearing rape by a savage. Magua, too, is humanized—but part of his humanization is to be shown *as an individual* to be capable of rape and brutality. Even Alice, pretty Alice who has spent most of her time in adaptations moaning, recoiling, and fainting, is firm in her choice of death over dishonor.

It is no surprise, then, that this is the only version to include (and indeed feature, over a page and a half) the exchanges between Munro and Heyward over Cora's mixed race. Narration: "MUNRO SPOKE OF A LOVE LEFT BEHIND IN SCOTLAND, DUE TO HER FATHER'S OBJECTION, THEN OF A MARRIAGE IN THE WEST INDIES TO A WOMAN OF MIXED, CREOLE BLOOD. . . . " Heyward: "CORA'S MOTHER! . . . " Munro: "AND YOU, SIR, SOUTHERN-BORN AS YOU ARE, SCORN TO MINGLE THE HEYWARD BLOOD WITH ONE CONSIDERED INFERIOR—

**How comics tell stories: Cora and Alice's first reactions to Magua invite subtly different readings of their emotions and the rightness of their reactions.**

Classics Illustrated, © and ™ Classics International Entertainments, Inc., 1942

Classics Illustrated, © and ™ Classics International Entertainments, Inc., 1959

But he is an Indian! Can we trust him?

He was once an enemy, Alice, but he is now a friend. If I did not believe so, I would not trust him with your safety!

If there are enemy Indians nearby, they will follow the troops, hoping to pick up scalps. The secret way will be safer!

And it is wrong not to trust the Indian just because his manners are different and his skin dark.

© *Pendulum Illustrated*, 1977

Alice Munro had her doubts about their guide, whose warpaint scarcely masked his sullen fierceness.

I LIKE HIM NOT, DUNCAN.

Major Duncan Heyward, entrusted with the safe delivery of Colonel Munro's daughters, tried to reassure them.

THOUGH A CANADIAN, AND THOUGH HE ONCE WAS AT ODDS WITH YOUR FATHER, YET HE SERVED WITH OUR FRIENDS THE MOHAWKS. HE IS NOW ONE OF US...

Fair Alice, still alarmed by Magua's menacing look, turned to her elder sister.

IF HE HAS BEEN MY FATHER'S ENEMY, I LIKE HIM STILL LESS! CORA, WHAT THINK YOU?

Cora answered coldly, her complexion charged with the color of rich blood ready to burst its bounds.

SHOULD WE DISTRUST THE MAN BECAUSE HIS MANNERS ARE NOT OUR MANNERS, AND THAT HIS SKIN IS DARK!?

At that, Alice gave her Narraganset the lash, and plunged into the tangled brush after Magua.

*Dark Horse Classics*, © Dark Horse Comics, Inc., 1992

LOVELY AND VIRTUOUS THOUGH MY CORA BE?" The issue of Uncas's and Cora's mutual attraction poses no problem for Jackson. We know well that had they lived, they would have become lovers. At the end, after their deaths and before an emotional presentation of Chingachgook's mourning, the narration underscores the matter for us: "ALTHOUGH LIFE NEVER PERMITTED THEM AN EXPRESSION OF THEIR LOVE, CORA AND UNCAS WERE UNITED IN DEATH ACCORDING TO DELAWARE CUSTOM." This is a wholesale change in the issue of interracial sex. Now the problem is in those who fear it.

The 1992 comic contains no easy prettification of native Americans. In fact this is the only comic version we have found that includes the slaughtering of the colt during the flight to the river. This moment becomes an emblem of the harshness of life and a measure of the dangers that threaten the characters.

But there is a price to be paid for this virtual reversal of the meanings Cooper installed in his book. Jackson has to work hard to remove the excitement of the action, so that the energy of concentration can shift to reading motives in more complicated ways. An illustration: when Cooper wrote *Mohicans*, as we have noted, he built in two long chase sequences—one for each published half of the book. All other comic book versions virtually eliminate the post-massacre pursuit into Canada, in some cases condensing it to a single panel. Not so Jackson; he has a use for it. Over still illustrative panels, the narration and dialogue tell us: "THEY SPEND THE NIGHT AMID THE BURNED-OUT RUINS, AS SCAVENGING WOLVES PROWLED THE PLAIN BELOW . . . A SKULKING ONEIDA FIRED ON THEM FROM THE DARKNESS. THOUGH HIS TRIBE WAS ALLIED TO THE BRITISH, UNCAS BROUGHT BACK HIS SCALP." Hawkeye (holding the scalp): "HE SHOULD HAVE BEEN FRIEND, YET HE WAS FOE. IT IS TO BE EXPECTED, WHEN NATURE'S ORDER IS THROWN INTO DISARRAY . . . WHEN FRIEND IS ARMED AGAINST FRIEND, AND NATURAL ENEMIES ARE BROUGHT TOGETHER TO FIGHT SIDE BY SIDE. . . . I LIKE NOT THIS UTTER CONFUSION OF NATIONS, AS RESPECTS FRIEND AND FOE . . . RED NATURE IS NOT LIKELY TO ALTER WITH EVERY SHIFT OF COLONIAL POLICY . . . TO FORGE BONDS WHERE NONE BELONG—SAY BETWEEN MOHICAN AND MINGO—IS LIKE THE LOVE ATWIXT A WHITE

MAN AND A SERPENT." Narration: "THE CONVERSATION GREW SPIRITED, AND LASTED LATE INTO THE NIGHT." Hawkeye: "IT IS WHITE CUNNING THAT HAS THROWN EVERYTHING INTO DISORDER!" Heyward: "PART OF OUR NATURE, I SUPPOSE YOU'D SAY." There follow two further pages of almost freeze-frame images of them undertaking the tedious pursuit.

Jackson downplays every element that other versions have developed, so that his version will be opposite in all senses. But the result is therefore only interesting if you recognize it as different and if you are interested in reading an oppositional version. It is a complex, secondary adaptation whose life is dependent on its argument with the primary versions. The price to be paid for its oppositional politics is that myth can't come alive. Only once does Jackson slip the reins, and that is right at the end when our attitudes, willy-nilly, are set. Then, in the last three pages, he shows the death of Magua in a sequence of six panels whose silent cinematic quality is a slow-motion inevitable resolution of all that has gone before. There follow two moving pages of mourning and departure, ending with Tamenund's prophetic and unforgiving valediction.

The most obvious general truth about the comic book versions is, with two exceptions, their apologetic nature: they have to bow to the bookishness of the original so as not to offend those who "own" the classics. They dare not tamper with the story. All include the death of Cora (which some films change). All hold to the strict sequence of events (with which the films frequently tamper). None add scenes (again, a common filmic ploy). The most they dare do is to leave out awkward bits. But deploying the conventions and generic devices of comic books, each version differently recasts two things: the organization of motives of the characters; and the organization of our relationship to them, through their visual and textual image. Perhaps most interesting is Jack Jackson's difficulty in making a counterreading of the myth. The price of his attempt is near-sterility, a still dryness that demonstrates how strong the tendencies are in the original. Once again, that poses a question that we can only answer in the final chapter.

Before closing this chapter, we want to add a word on the use of comics as a source. Comics are a much neglected medium, yet in many respects they are an ideal medium for study. Because of their history and cultural marginality, they have a certain transparency, which means that, considered carefully, they can illuminate cultural processes very well. They also have the very real advantage that they stay still while you study them or reproduce them!

*"A myth may be defined as an inconsistent story whose inconsistencies are not perceived by its receiver."*[1]

CHAPTER 8    # In the Matter of the Mohicans

Having considered the history of the reception of Cooper's book; having examined and compared the book, film, TV, and comic book versions; having examined the relationships among various adaptations, abridgments, transformations, and reworkings of the *Mohicans* legend to see how they might relate to the specific context of their production and appearance; and having thought about the status of a story like this as a "classic". what does it add up to, and what does it leave? It leaves, for us, the most difficult question of all, the significance of the story in itself—its sheer ability to survive many retellings, to go on providing for different people over a very long time a story that in some way stirs them and is worth retelling. It is, of course, a good yarn, at least once one gets past some execrable writing. But to us, that enjoyment is possible because of the power of the story to symbolize. It offers us figures in a landscape who always speak of more than themselves. What do they symbolize, then? What, if anything, is continuous *behind* all the changes?

If there is anything, for whom does it speak? If *The Last of the Mohicans* is a myth, whose myth is it?

A word, again, about *myth* as we mean it here. The study of myths has progressed enormously in this century. For us it does not mean something "unreal" or "fictional"; instead, myths can be studied for their capacity to speak a society's view of itself through symbols. Indeed, real events and characters can become mythic in this view.[2] In early societies, the myths of the gods offered ways of making sense of the uncertainties, quirks, and hopes of human life. They mixed symbolic accounts of natural processes (seen as alive, as agents) with pictures of the social order (who held power and how, the relations of men, women, and children), and with those things that held ritual importance to people. As human control over the environment increased, so myths reflected more and more the social arrangements, stored them in the coded language of narratives, and offered them back as stories. But also, as societies became more complex and divided, so the stories fragmented.

In recent times, where social life is lived increasingly through the publicity machines of commercial capitalism, our myths have become more and more like a shattered mirror. A million fragments of story-glass, each refracting small elements back to our lives. Advertisements, films, speeches, every circulating story: each one contains chips of images about our place in the world, small fragments— sometimes despairing, sometimes utopian—of ideas about our lives, our past and our future. Some have argued that this slivered windshield of images represents an end to ideology in the sense of any unifying image of the world. The present is the postmodern, they say, the dissolution of society into a million mutually glancing images. We doubt that this view is correct in general, but we are sure it is not true of Cooper's *Mohicans*, even in the face of the wide diversity of uses to which his protagonists have been put. Let us therefore ask some questions about continuities, as well as changes. What we have to say is ambitious and therefore risky, and perhaps hard to follow. We hope readers will bear with us as we try to knot together the many strands we have handled individually till now.

### Cooper's landscapes

In 1826, while *Mohicans* was actually at the printers, Cooper readied his family for what was to be a seven-year sojourn in Europe. The greatest American author yet to appear was deserting his native shores, a fact that became a stick in the hands of his conservative opponents. Just days before the family's departure, Cooper's beloved "Bread & Cheese Club" organized a farewell dinner in his honor. Charles King delivered the main valedictory panegyric to the club's most famous member. Cooper, he said, was living proof that democratic America could produce noble writing, something that had long been doubted:

To the works of Mr. Cooper we may in like manner refer as evidence that if fine, vigorous, and original conception, a quick and happy perception, and exquisite delineation of the beauties of nature—a power hardly surpassed of portraying the deep and strong passions of the human heart—a capacity to excite and to sustain the most breathless interest in the fortunes of those whom he brings upon the scene—if any or all these constitute genius, it may be claimed for him. . . . To have sprung thus full-grown into existence, and to have taken a place at once, if not beside, at least in close approach to, the Great Master of the art [Walter Scott], *proximus a primo*, is glory enough. It would, indeed, seem that the great events of our revolutionary contest, the wild and peculiar habits of our early settlers, and the deeply interesting, and alas! rapidly vanishing aboriginal race of this continent have inspired the pen of the American novelist, and that he has looked with a poet's fancy and a painter's eye upon the grandeur and magnificence of our mountain scenery, the varied tints and glorious sunshine of our autumn skies and woods, our rushing cataracts, and mighty rivers, and forests coeval with nature.[3]

Take this florid prose as more than flattery, more than metaphor. Cooper is novelist, poet, painter. He is the living proof that America, with its democracy, can achieve nobility of conception, high art. Taken seriously, it should not surprise us that our "painter of nature" should have become a significant source for the emergence of America's first major landscape painting tradition.

As we've seen, at least three major painters took up the invitation they perceived in *Mohicans* to figure America. Thomas Cole (in several paintings), Asher Durand, and John Quidor all rendered the American landscape through Cooper's vision. Cole's paintings in particular reveal the symbolic universe of nature that he and Cooper shared. Like many of his other landscapes (it didn't seem to matter whether they were overtly fictional or not) Cole's *Mohicans*-inspired landscapes are vast and overwhelming. This is more than nature untamed, it is untameable. Human beings within it are di-

Thomas Cole, "The Council Gathering," 1827

minished into the middle distance, to become temporary occupiers of small spaces. Wild places were far, not near; enticing, but thunderous; lush, but without crops; and like echoes of a storm gone by, the traces of the alas! vanishing natives could be seen.

But if this nature was vast and untamed, it could be brought close and made safe through imagining, even through the owning of books and paintings depicting it. It could thus belong in full to its new, white owners. Thus was born an autonomous American tradition of landscape painting that continued through the 1830s and '40s. Then, like raw lightning, it flickered and shifted to the West. And in entering the plains and savannahs of the new territories it changed. Rarely pastoral as in the English tradition, the West was depicted as a contrast. There were dangerous Indians, noble enough to be painted (later photographed) in headdresses. But they were dangerous for all that, therefore best shown as old and wrinkled, immobile, passing away, leaving the scene, blending back into it like a dream. And there was arable land awaiting its fences, its houses, its people working (something Indians apparently never did, except in the buffalo hunts). Only the cowboy, romancing the ranges on his horse, comes close to bridging the Indians and the land. But in all these images, Cooper's sense of the overwhelming has departed.

Where did this image go? It died back, to await regrowth as monied Americans again began to celebrate wild places, the last virgin forests, the "wildernesses of the mind," in the 1890s. But it was not the same. Now wilderness was something to be captured differently. Not in oils, primarily, but in silver iodides, in film and photography. This is an odd shift, difficult to grasp. While Cole, Durand, and Quidor had been content to interpret nature for us, in the manner of Cooper, later artists let nature "speak for itself." And nature, speaking through the camera, spoke once more of the departure of the Indians. In the dry West, they dissolved like shadows into the mesas and canyons.[4]

It was as if wilderness had become holy, something of which one might not make a graven image. Nature could be painted but could not be envisioned in its vastness. If painted at all, it was in fragments. This can be seen in the work of the most famous interpreter of Cooper's *Mohicans*: Newell Convers Wyeth. Born in 1882 in Needham, Massachusetts, N. C. Wyeth became, in the early years of

"Vanishing Americans," 1903. Edward S. Curtis's photograph shows ghostly Indians disappearing into a dry landscape.

Two of N. C. Wyeth's classic illustrations for Scribner's (1919) edition of *Mohicans*. Note the way the lighting of the pictures makes the wilderness a dark surround.

this century, the leading illustrator of book classics. His work covered Mark Twain, Robert Louis Stevenson, Daniel Defoe, Jules Verne, and James Fenimore Cooper. Wyeth's illustrations for *Mohicans* were prepared for Charles Scribner's Sons' 1919 edition. They need to be considered both for what they are and for their subsequent influence.[5]

Wyeth traveled to the Adirondacks to prepare himself for his paintings. But he did not see the mountains as Cole, Durand, or Quidor had. On the contrary. In Wyeth, the wilderness is the darkness closing in on the characters who are, in their turn, lit by shafts of light breaking through. Cooper's figures are caught in tableaux, lit in ways suggesting stage lighting. This is most evident in his "The Fight in the Forest," in which a fierce footlight competes with dry ice to reveal or mask the figures frozen in battle. These are, indeed, classic images for a new generation. And of course tableaux were regular drawing room entertainment in the homes of the wealthy, cultured northeasterners, such as Theodore Roosevelt, to whom Wyeth "spoke."

For us, Wyeth's most relevant illustration was "The Battle at Glenn's Falls." Magua and Heyward struggle at the brink of the falls, legs interlocked. Uniformed civilization meets the raw muscle of the savage, who surges out of the dark at bottom left. It is a most dramatic image. And it was used subsequently in many of the comic book versions of *Mohicans*—but with a difference. Always "correcting" the book, these unashamed swipes swapped Heyward for one of the Mohicans. Compare the various comic books uses as shown on page 188.

What can we learn from these images? We learn, of course, that the artists drawing the various comic book versions recognize a powerful composition when they see one. Yet not one subsequent use holds to the white/Indian combination, though Scribner's edition has remained in print as a source ever since. It is not as if they would only have depended on other comic book versions.

We are suggesting that an image of this kind reveals something rather important about the tradition of *Mohicans*. It seems important to *have* continuities, to acknowledge sources, to gain the authority and resonances of past versions. But it seems to be equally important to change and adapt. We might represent the differences between Wyeth's original and the subsequent derivations as follows: while Wyeth venerates the book anew, the comic book versions

Establishing continuities: four comicbook covers or splash pages rework Wyeth's illustration, replacing Heyward with a Mohican in each case.

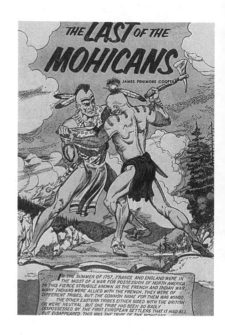

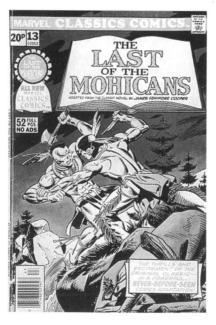

bring it "up to date." Whereas Wyeth renews the link to 1826, tapping into its energy lines again, subsequent versions assume that line to have been reestablished and fix their focus on more local needs. Wyeth's paintings—and it matters that they *are* paintings—return Cooper to his rightful owners. The others picnic at will.

We want to argue for the significance of these kinds of continuity. Up to this point the stress of this book has been on changes. But we think there are equally important ways in which it matters that each version knows itself to be a version of something that continues.[6] The continual reuse of Wyeth is not the only example. Let us baldly list some of the others. Griffith's final death-dance faithfully reproduces a hundred contemporary photographs of The Disappearing Race. Tourneur and Brown's 1920 version borrows the common photographic "plot" of Glacier Rock in Yosemite Valley,[7] and of course is itself in many ways a reply to Griffith's *Birth of a Nation*, which had borrowed from Cooper the death-rather-than-rape scene. The 1926 spoof borrows the very idea of the book to mock the pretensions of the middle class. The 1956 TV version borrows clips wholesale from the 1936 film version to establish its credibility in its title sequence. The 1992 version honors Philip Dunne's 1936 screenplay (though, as we know, it was hardly Dunne's at all). But in its turn the 1992 version has provided filmic ammunition for the new TV series. These are some of the most obvious continuities. What can we learn from them?

What happens when we "quote"? To quote another source (be it a person, a book, a film, or whatever) is the most ordinary thing in the world. But though ordinary, it is still an important way in which cultures hand on their meanings. In quoting, we remind and renew, but also place into a new context. And not all acts of quoting are the same. Compare Charles Lamb's *Tales from Shakespeare*, Tom Stoppard's *Rosenkrantz and Guildenstern Are Dead*, and Mel Brooks's *To Be or Not to Be*. Each "quotes" Shakespeare, but with different aims and results. Lamb, working in the nineteenth century, was making Shakespeare safe for minds that might not filter out immoral materials in the Bard. He is therefore very dependent on Shakespeare, but nervous of the dangers that lurk in such greatness. Stoppard takes a minor moment from *Hamlet* and asks: who were these minor characters and what happened to them after? It is, in effect, a drama on a footnote. Its relation to Shakespeare therefore is quite different: Shakespeare provides the justification and a surrounding significant context; the rest is Stoppard's. Mel Brooks happily pillages an instantly recognizable title for a film that thereafter owes nothing else to Shakespeare. It is disrespectful burglary at its most knowing.

Here we have three very different relations of reference and continuity.[8] We might develop this into a thesis by drawing in a largely forgotten but useful book on film. Jay Leyda studied the history and uses of stock footage and how meanings are "transported" by that footage into different contexts of use.[9] Such footage entered use as early as 1898, when Francis Doublier organized a film on the Dreyfus affair almost entirely through borrowed materials. Leyda argues that such materials were quickly perceived as offering new ways of telling history. What was crucial was how they were edited in. This could be done subversively. In the 1930s in Holland, for instance, Joris Ivens was borrowing newsreels from Dutch cinemas on a Saturday, reediting them and showing them to working-class audiences on Sunday, then returning them to their original form and owners on Monday. But the subversion was effective to the extent that it was obvious what had been done. It had to be seen to be a remake, not an original.

Leyda's argument is that the development of film archives put a premium on developing skills of editing, cutting, overlaying, sequencing, and narrating, in order to facilitate propaganda and counterpropaganda. It also made crucial the ownership and control of archives. But in documentaries the hunt was always on for *novel* footage, something new and surprising to startle an audience's perceptions. Arguably, the opposite is true in our case. While novelty is important, it seems that in many ways the recognizable motifs are the guarantees of the groundedness of each version. It may be new, but it belongs to the tradition. The assurance of this conclusion lies in the images that resonate from previous versions. If there is truth in this, it suggests that the continuities between versions of *Mohicans* are part of its guidance system, guiding how we are supposed to read the story.

## Intellectual Properties

We need to go back again in time. James Fenimore Cooper is most remembered now for his Leatherstocking novels. But of course he wrote far more than these. His writing might be seen as falling into two broad groups. There are his romances, those novels (including the Leatherstocking Tales) that use ideal/typical characters to *represent* his society in symbolic terms; and there are his other, more polemical writings, through which he tried to intervene in the political debates of his day.

Cooper's political views were balanced delicately between two poles. Born to a politically powerful landowning family, and marrying deeper into the same social group, he nonetheless embraced Jacksonian democracy, a strand in American politics that enthusiastically embraced the "common man," but only if he was white. Andrew Jackson, perhaps more than any other American president, hymned three things in the "American Dream": the frontier; homesteading for all; and the removal—by force, if necessary—of native Americans from the "land of the Free." In fact Jackson's aim was the overcoming of the Frontier and the *abolition* of wilderness. In 1830 in his presidential address to Congress, he asked: "What good man would prefer a country covered by forests and ranged by a few thousand savages, to our extensive Republic, studded with towns and prosperous farms . . . and filled with the blessings of liberty, civilization, and religion?"[10]

Cooper's Jacksonianism is a puzzle. Jacksonian Democracy was also very hostile to the old families of the Northeast, the early wealth and money that was seen to represent a virtual aristocracy: in short, Cooper's, his wife's, and his friends' families. Cooper in fact vented his political views very frequently. He spent years in dialogue with those who objected to his "taking flight" to Europe, and the way he there used the "American experience" for apparently radical ends. For example, during his 1826–33 stay abroad, he wrote his *Notions of the Americans* virtually at the request of the French liberal leader LaFayette (a famous figure in America because of his aid during the War of Independence). In that work, he argued for the benefits of liberal democracy. He even published a "statistical demonstration" of the financial benefits of democracy over centralized government. These kinds of arguments deeply antagonized conservative forces in America. Among these, newspaper editors were not slow to condemn Cooper in print.

His response was to mix writing political tracts with writing polemical fictions. *The Bravo* (1831), a fictional justification of his

*Notions*, was followed in 1834 by *A Letter to My Countrymen*, in which he responded to criticisms of his supposedly revolutionary views. In fact his enthusiasm for "democracy" waned severely shortly thereafter, particularly perhaps as a result of the "Three Mile Point incident." The Cooper family owned a stretch of land that was very popular with picnickers. In 1837, complaining about its misuse, Cooper erected "No Trespassing" signs. The ensuing controversy gave new opportunity for assaults on him as an "aristocrat." These attacks were soon linked with another issue. In 1839, and for several years after, tenants in the great New York estates agitated with considerable success for reform of their leases and for the dissolution of the estates themselves. In response, Cooper not only railed publicly against this anti-landlordism, but went on to write three of his polemical novels in defense of the landlords: *Satanstoe* and *The Chainbearer* in 1845, and *The Redskins* in 1846. This last will concern us greatly in a moment.

So what were Cooper's political views? They are best summarized in his 1838 tract *The American Democrat*. Cooper was a poor political theorist, given to weak little homilies and instances to make his points. In part, this style must surely stem from a deep fissure in his beliefs, which needed continual papering over. The core of his beliefs is the centrality to civilization of private property—but at a price: there *must* be private property or there will be tyranny. But he also recognized that property itself could become a basis for financial despotism. As the editors of one edition of these writings put it: "In his discussion of property in *The American Democrat* there is always a powerful tension, verging on contradiction, between his absolute commitment to the defence of property and his conviction that it ought not to rule."[11] But however fearful he was of the dangers of financial despotism, Cooper nonetheless knew ultimately where he stood. Discussing the opposition between individuals' property rights and any claim of "public good," he placed his standard clearly: "As between the publick and individuals, therefore, the true basis of a democrat . . . is to take sides with the latter."[12]

How did he resolve these tensions? In his polemical novel *The Redskins*, they come as near to resolution as possible, but in peculiar fashion. *The Redskins: or, Indian and Injin* is a vehicle for Cooper's views about anti-rentism. The movement centered on the rights of tenant farmers to own the land they used. The anti-renters accused landlords of incipient "feudalism" and "aristocracy"—an accusation that stung Cooper, with his commitment to democracy. Yet Cooper, son of a judge who had amassed tens of thousands of acres of land, and married into the DeLancey family (which represented "Old Money" even more), hated the anti-renters, and particularly loathed one aspect of their campaign: their use of the legislative process to harass and press "patroon" landlords to sell their land to tenants. In *The Redskins*, all of this loathing is expressed through clumsy attempts to turn around the meaning of "democracy." The anti-renters are accused of subverting rights through combinations and of using liberty to overthrow property. *They* are the aristocrats, ruling through public opinion. In *The Redskins*, these arguments are clumsy and unconvincing, and it takes much authorial manipulation to make sure the "right side wins."[13]

One way this is done explains the subtitle of the book: "Indians and Injins." "Injins" refers to the practice of anti-renters (and indeed others) who carried out house-burnings and the like but disguised themselves as Indians to pass off the blame. But then who are the "Indians"? The fact is, they do not appear in the book, except as one very minor character. But the *idea* of the "Indian" inhabits the book. It is as if Cooper believes that, in the absence of actual Indians, the mantle of their natural inheritance of the land could fall onto the "natural aristocrats" among whites, those with higher feelings—in short, those for whom Hawkeye was the ever-present symbol.

How did this belief show in Cooper's defense of property? He asserted a kind of theory of ancestry:

[H]ere is a citizen who has got as much property as he wants, and who wishes to live for other purposes than to accumulate. This property is not only invested to his entire satisfaction, as regards convenience, security, and returns, but also in a way that is connected with some of the best sentiments of his nature. It is property that has descended to him through ancestors for two centuries; property that is historically connected with his name—on which he was born, on which he has lived, and on which he has hoped to die; property, in a word, that is associated with all the higher feelings of humanity.[14]

There is a striking resonance between this passage, and what Cooper wrote in a letter in 1828: "It is not enough simply to be the son of a great man; in order to render it of essential advantage, some portion of his merit must become hereditary, or the claim had better be suppressed."[15]

Our argument is this: Cooper's quite contradictory political views were only resolved through the construction of a nonsensical idea: the idea that holding property could induce a form of nobility. But though bizarre and nonsensical when stated in this way, the idea *lent itself to expression in his mythic novels.* There, he could stress the special qualities of each race. And he could, without any possibility of a charge of "aristocracy," endow with full nobility a frontiersman, one who, because he is in tune with the wilderness, would live out the rich relation of man-to-land. In sum, Hawkeye in *The Last of the Mohicans* is a living myth of private property. He inherits at its end, through his relation to Chingachgook, the once-perfect relation of the "good Indian" to the land.

For Cooper, then, "wilderness" was not itself a source of rights, but an estate where those attuned to it could and would demonstrate their higher humanity. Not just anyone could walk into a primeval forest and become ennobled. Only those in tune with, and with a calling to, ennoblement could do so—and thus, the preternatural importance of the myth itself. The myth of Hawkeye and others like him is itself the test. Anyone can read it, of course. But, like texts that preach predestination, perhaps, only some—the already-chosen—will know and respond.

In support of what we are arguing, consider the following triangle:

(1) Cooper publishes *The Last of the Mohicans*, to become the best remembered of his five Leatherstocking Tales.[16] In it, a noble man "inherits" all the fine qualities of the Indian, through his association with the last of the ur-Tribe.

(2) But that tribe, in reality, never disappeared. The Mohicans (or Moheakunnuk, as they came to call themselves) lived on, as has recently been told in fascinating detail by Patrick Frazier.[17] Frazier details the long period in which the Mohican people sought to live with and alongside white settlers, including fighting on the American side in the War of Independence, only to find their land gradually stripped from them through political machinations and legal maneuvers.

(3) Among those who played fast and loose with dubious titles to the Mohicans' lands was one John van Rensalaer. The van Rensalaers were classic examples of the old wealth that assembled in the northeastern states and became just the patrician class that the tenant

farmers attacked in the 1830s. They are also the *very family* whom Cooper himself used as illustrations of the rights of property in his *Redskins*.

This triangle, to us, neatly illustrates the relations of myth to politics in Cooper's writings. *The Last of the Mohicans*, accordingly, we read as a mythic expression of the fundamental rights of private property, embodied in the nobility of the "man of the wilderness." Only such a man as he can contain and symbolize the virtues that turn property from ownership into the embodiment of natural virtue.[18]

## After Cooper

With this in mind, perhaps we can make better sense of the career of Cooper's book. Cooper fell out of favor very quickly after his death. There were complicated reasons for his decline, among them the antagonism toward his political views plus (soon) the attack on his literary qualities. But still his books remained in print, and his themes (of the frontier and the frontiersman) became more popular than ever after 1860. But they did so in a form that was at odds with everything that Cooper represented.

For the 1860s saw the rise of the dime novel Western. By this time, the literary version of the frontier (usually published as double-decker or even triple-decker expensive novels) was everywhere in decline. But in 1860 the New York firm of Beadle and Adams released *Malaeska: or, the Indian Wife of a White Hunter*. Written by Anne Stephens, this cheap and self-contained story sold 65,000 copies within a short time. Stirred by their success, the publishers launched a whole series—and began a publishing phenomenon that only died in the 1920s, with the arrival of film and of the pulp magazines. Beadle and Adams were soon joined by competitors: in 1863 by (George) Munro's Ten Cent Library, in 1867 by Robert de Witt's series (which ran to 1,118 titles in his first ten years), in 1870 by Munro's brother Norman's series, then the two most successful publishers: Frank Tousey and Street & Smith. Indications of the scale of popularity can easily be gleaned. One of the earliest dime novels, Edward S. Ellis's *Seth Jones: or, The Captives of the Frontier* (1860) sold more than 600,000 copies in all. And by 1864 an aggregate of more than five million Beadle and Adams novels had been put into circulation.[19]

Daryl Jones's study of the dime novels properly begins with the fast-changing world of industrialization America faced after 1864. As he argues, there was a growing tension between declarations of optimism and increasingly harsh, urbanized, alienated realities. He sees the dime novels as evolving in response to this loss of optimism and as containing within their formulae the tensions of their times. For example, in the earliest dime novels, "Nature" shifts between being Paradise, a place where people can rebuild their spirits and receive a true education, and being hostile, savage, and "Indian." Hence, *Quindaro: or, the Heroine of Fort Laramie* (1865) explicitly calls the wilderness the Garden of Eden, but poisoned by the "serpent," the Indian. This is pure Jacksonianism: the wilderness as the Manifest Destiny of whites, to be cleared and tamed. But by the mid-1870s, Nature has become a landscape for other, social clashes.

Again, in the early days, the hero is the backwoodsman, in the model of Hawkeye. Often ugly, incapable of living within civilization, these figures are rarely even recuperated through marriage. In *White Slayer, The Avenger: or, The Doomed Red-Skins* (1870), the man of the frontier is in fact rejected by the heroine, Mary Dawson, in favor of a peaceable young settler. But within a few years, the hero-figure has changed, either into "factional" figures such as Wild Bill Hickok, or Kit Carson, around whose romanticized lives the myth of the West was generally rewritten; or into young easterners who have to encounter the frontier to reeducate themselves into the proper values in order to be worthy of the heroines; or—importantly—into the figure of the Outlaw. The Outlaw, whether wholly fictional (as Deadwood Dick, for example) or fictionalized (as were the real James Brothers) is motivated and driven by revenge on the greed and brutality of bankers and range enclosers. In simple terms, these later dime novels embody the rising social tensions and class conflicts of the East through a refiguring of the frontier. Hardly surprisingly, Street & Smith, the main and most successful publisher of these Outlaw stories, came under increasing pressure to kill these series, a pressure to which they finally succumbed in 1903, withdrawing seventy-five titles.

What Jones underplays about this whole dime novel tradition is the class nature of these publications. If Cooper was by birth, culture, and manner of publication a writer for the wealthy and the intelligentsia, the dime novels were for the people. Cheap and throwaway, easy to read and sensational, they were written by eastern authors for an eastern audience about the West. And once they began to express the discontents and anger of their mainly working-class audience, so they were attacked (interestingly, in the name of "protecting children").[20]

As Cooper goes out of the center of attention, then, the myth of the frontier moves into other hands and begins to be used for other purposes. What happens to bring Cooper back? The turnaround begins in the 1890s. In 1893, Frederick Jackson Turner delivers an address to the World Congress of Historians. Turner considers "The Significance of the Frontier to American History." His argument is that America owes its democratic spirit primarily to westward expansion and the creation of a freeholding farmer tradition. But the frontier is, for all intents and purposes, now closed. American history, therefore, is about to enter a second phase; it is not one about which Turner is fully happy. A new capitalist spirit will spread from the East, undermining the "independent freeholders." Turner's thesis, it seems to us, is most important not for any truth it contained but for the fact that it was said and heard so widely. For this begins the period in which, as never before, the "frontier" would be lived in the imagination.

If Turner is important, it is for the intellectual respectability he bestowed on a sentiment that was felt by many besides himself. Perhaps its most important exponent was in fact Theodore Roosevelt, who was a historian and became president of the U.S. Richard Slotkin has shown that Roosevelt held to a frontier thesis every bit as powerful and influential as Turner's.[21] His was a thesis based on "race," conceived as that amalgam of forces which had made America dynamic and expansionist. America had benefited from the waves of diverse immigration because the frontier experience had welded together a new kind of people. Roosevelt was a great admirer of Cooper's Leatherstocking novels, to the point that he didn't regard himself as "complete" until he finally killed a man in the Spanish-American War.[22] From Cooper he derived a picture of noble struggle. Conflict with the Indians had provided the test and measure of early Americans. Indians had been worthy opponents, great fighters; to defeat them, therefore, Americans had had to develop special qualities.

But now that the western frontier was closed and the native Americans were defeated, there were two resources that could replace them: international expansionism (with the Philippines as the first target) and hunting in the wilderness. But as Slotkin shows, these options were not for everyone. It was for the new ruling elite, a new cultured aristocracy who were "destined to lead."

No surprise then that only one year earlier the first of the great wilderness organizations had been set up. The Sierra Club, founded in 1892 by John Muir, was to be involved in the creation of the U.S. Forest Service and in the founding of the national parks—one of the earliest of which was Yosemite Valley, where Tourneur and Brown would then film their *Mohicans* so brilliantly. A celebratory history of the wilderness movement, published by the Sierra Club, summed up this love affair in striking terms: "Wilderness was the frontier and Progress celebrated its retreat. As we destroyed wilderness, it built us. If the warp of our national fabric was traced in the threads of our move westward, the weft was the wilderness we moved over and under and through. Without it our fabric would have been a flimsy thing, transparent, too easily tattered to meet the tests that came."[23] But by a curious reversal of intentions, "wilderness" now becomes a *public* concern. Wilderness has to be preserved, for the general good, even against the private interests of owners. Increasingly, "wilderness" came to be understood not just as undamaged areas, but as Nature, as the last repository of values. The men who participated in these movements included Roosevelt, and his friend N. C. Wyeth, who became in 1919 the most celebrated illustrator of *The Last of the Mohicans*. The Wilderness Movement, while it did indeed save huge tracts of American landscape from commercial exploitation, did so in the name of a curious ideology. It is an ideology that seeks to save wilderness for "the people" by making it as hard as possible for actual people to enter it.[24]

As we have already discussed, this was also the period of the rise of the Progressive Movement, that period of outright dominance by businessmen who fought for the introduction of "rational" modes of administration, "rational" curricula in schools—but all within the framework of the urgent building of a "sense of America." It is within these political and ideological contexts that Cooper's *Mohicans* returns to prominence. It becomes, we want to argue, a new statement of what "America" is or should be. In different ways, in different hands, it still is, because of its nature, a fundamentally capitalistic myth. The dime novels could skirt the edges of subversion. In response to the dangers of them, *Mohicans* returns to restate the safe myth of the frontier.

## Class and the West

In making this claim, we are pointing towards the ideas and arguments of Alexander Saxton—and perhaps extending them. Saxton is one of a group of historians who have recently argued powerfully that America's myth of the frontier has to be understood in *class* terms.[25] In early nineteenth-century America, class positions were notably fluid. Within a few years, a man (and it would mostly be males, of course) could find himself variously an employee, then an employer of a small number of tradesmen, then involved in small-scale commerce, moving to become a farmer, but usually also (except for those in the few emergent cities) supplementing his food with some hunting.

This fluidity was certainly associated with great suspicion of those leading settled, wealthy lives, who were able to manipulate to their own interest the institutions to which the insecure might need to turn, especially the banks and the monetary systems. (Hence the incredible political turmoil aroused by the founding of a national Bank of America.) In this situation, it might be argued, two tendencies will be accentuated. First, there will be a great sensitivity as to how one's social position is described and defined, because how one is labeled can determine the chances of mobility, who one is seen to be associated with, what future is mapped out. And one of Saxton's fellow historians has in fact depicted very well just such sensitivities, over what a "wage laborer" might be called. Historian David Roediger shows in great detail how, especially in the key eastern centers from New York to Philadelphia, working men argued over their title. There were no masters and servants, they insisted. Only "Negers" could be servants:

As the masters sought greater production and lower costs in a post-revolutionary and slaveholding society, their motivations were closely scrutinized by journeymen whose reactions mixed republicanism and whiteness. It was particularly difficult to be mastered by someone who was not a master of his craft. Thus the Philadelphian General Trades Union in 1836 complained that the "merest *botch*" among craftsmen too often assumed "*kingly supremacy* to himself the very moment he becomes a 'MASTER MECHANIC.'" Earlier and smaller labor organizations had made similar points. During 1806, in the Philadelphia journeymen shoemaker's conspiracy case, a labor appeal referred to "these masters, as they are called, and who would be masters and tyrants of the world." Well before the term *wage slavery* came into common use, journeymen criticized *masters* as "so-called after the slavish style of Europe." A very early carpenters' organization scorned the "haughtiness and overbearance" of masters as more appropriate to those who "give laws to slaves . . . depriving free men of their just rights."[26]

Therefore it is not surprising that race riots could be sparked by a fear of being made into "slaves and tools," by the admission of black people into trades.

This politics of language links rising labor protests, the turn to racism, and the felt need to avoid being seen as "unfree." But given this politics, a second tendency might be just as important. In a fluid, unstable world of social relations, great importance may come to be attached to the *stories* that are told to try to make sense of the world. If the social world is a maelstrom in which one's place is constantly at risk, then it is all the more important that there be stories, myths that show how that world works.

Saxton therefore argues that in early nineteenth-century America a process began in which class differences were allayed by being transmuted into racial ones: that the battle between Jacksonian democracy (with its unification of southern planters and northern urban workers) and its enemies found its resolution in (a) the great drive westward, requiring a vision of wilderness to be tamed and mythic "Americans" to do the taming; and (b) the restructuring of attitudes towards slaves. He further proposes that various forms of mass culture, from blackface minstrelsy to the lived stories of the Frontier, played a necessary role in encouraging and enabling white workers to define their futures in terms of their color, rather than their class.

Within this framework he suggests that Cooper's Leatherstocking embodies a version of these requirements. There are many strands to his argument, and he catches hold of Cooper's texts in novel ways. For example, he attaches significance to the peculiar ways that Natty Bumppo talks, constantly shifting between a very educated eloquence and a vernacular manner. This observation links with Daryl Jones's point that in the early dime novels the heroes mainly talk bad dialect but are soon derided for this. As the dime novels progress, their heroes begin to speak a purer language: they empower themselves through their speaking.

Saxton also discusses the crucial role of relations with the English. This isn't simply a matter of the historical conjunction within the narrative. The "English" represented one strand of American politics, the opposite, in fact, to Jacksonian national democracy. And as Roediger shows, "Europe" was a symbol of forms of mastery that were being resisted mightily. This raises important questions about how different subsequent reworkings of Cooper's story picture the English. Is Heyward an arrogant fool or a noble young blood? Who, out of Montcalm or Munro, represents wisdom and goodness? There is a clear tradition in America of associating the Old Wealth of the Northeast with England. This is surely the reason why George Bush went to such lengths to represent himself as a Texan instead. "The West," by contrast, is pure, virtuous, and American.

Finally, Saxton argues that even as early as the 1820s a process was underway in which real individuals were being turned (and in some cases turning themselves) into mythic ones—especially, but not only, Daniel Boone, Kit Carson, Davy Crockett, Bill Cody, and Bill Hickok. Saxton's argument is that America was literally living out its class/ideological tensions through these individuals. But of course central to his argument is precisely the displacement of class onto race. This displacement, more than anything else, is what we share with him. Where perhaps we stray from his argument is in seeing Cooper's *Mohicans* as having a particular class quality as a text.

This takes us back to the very beginning of this book. There, we asked the question: why has this story survived so successfully? What qualities did it shape within itself that have kept it going so effectively? Put at its simplest, why is it *The Last of the Mohicans*, and not another of Cooper's novels—or other books altogether, say, *Nick of the Woods*, arguably a better-told story—that survived and flourished? It is hardly *Mohicans*'s literary qualities. Nor is it, it seems, some inherent narrative power (otherwise people would not have gone to such trouble to change the narrative so often).

We are suggesting that *The Last of the Mohicans*, because of the particular circumstances under which it was written, balances with great precision on top of a nest of contradictions. Born on the cusp of a contradiction in Cooper's own politics, born at a time of very fast transition in the image of Indians and of the wilderness, *Mohicans* holds within itself, in tension, a wealth of possibilities for subsequent use. To be brutally paradoxical, it has a coherent incoherence.

But that does not mean it can be used for anything. It retains, like a birthmark, like Achilles' heel, the signs of its birth, and therefore lends itself best to certain uses. It is not that it can't be turned to purposes other than Cooper's. But to the extent that subsequent users have tried, they have had to work against the grain of the narrative. It *is* possible to turn it into an anti-racist narrative; but then, like Maurice Tourneur and Clarence Brown, you have to lard your film with the right rhetorics, and so organize your death scenes that your audience is pulled with you. You *can* make it into an impassioned plea for the common people and the simple virtues (against greed and commercialism); but then, like Michael Mann, you have to change significant features in the narrative, and Magua has to undo himself in the great speechifying at Tamenund's council. In fact, curiously, it is not too difficult to make what is in many senses a racist text into an anti-racist one. Marvel Comics did it, albeit it by peppering their version with the right phrases. But hardest of all would be to turn the story into one that questioned the equation of "naturalness" with "respectability" with "virtue," because that would be to challenge the very sources of the story's power. If, as Alexander Saxton has argued, race is a deformed substitute for class, then wilderness is a beautified substitute for property. And that argument suggests that one of the things that emerges when a myth is formed—almost accidentally, because of the particular requirements and pressures and possibilities of its time—is something akin to a cultural organism: a story-form which makes its own demands, resists perverse uses, and lingers on in the imagination long after its primary uses have passed away.

We began this book because we had picked up the scent of an unexplored body of materials. Raking them all together, then making sense of them, has given us untold pleasure. But it has also pushed us to ask some disturbing questions. It couldn't all be innocent fun, all entertainment. For those very categories are deceitful.

If this book has a value, it may be in one of two things. It may simply be in the insights it offers into one story, its tradition and its ability to survive. For that in the end is what we most want to say: *The Last of the Mohicans* has survived because it speaks on behalf of a class, and a class whose interests are not ours. The devil may not have all the good tunes, but the wealthy and powerful have certainly cornered a large part of the market in good tales! But whether we are right or wrong about this particular conclusion, we are sure that the question needed asking. Aside from sheer narrative thrill (of which there is some, but in truth not so very much in *Mohicans*) something has worked to keep the carcass moving. And if the question can be asked of our story, it can surely be asked of others. Maybe our method can be applied elsewhere. What we have done is to search the many versions symptomatically, tracing back to a core of meanings. In the case of *Mohicans*, it has turned out, we believe, that the most important symptoms are the press of images of wilderness and the overlay of political rhetorics. There are of course other components, but perhaps these are the magnets around which other elements (images of the Indian, of women, of the English, and so forth) revolve.

It is unlikely that the same would be true if someone were to study, say, the many versions of Dumas's *The Count of Monte Cristo*, or Stevenson's *Treasure Island*. But we believe that the same fundamental orientation might help. It may of course be that some of this work has already been done, and we did not know of it. In which case, like David Gamut, we can only raise our heads and sing like two possessed, and hope that the savage critics will pass us by. . . .

# APPENDIX

## Mohican-ography

*What follows is a list of all English and American versions of Cooper's story that we have been able to discover. Inevitably, this list is incomplete. Both the British Library and the Library of Congress have very incomplete collections (and indeed listings) of editions—especially of abridgments, which were often produced and distributed in quite cavalier fashion. For some of the versions and editions listed below, we have incomplete and (we suspect) sometimes unreliable information. To all readers who can tell us of versions we do not know, or who can correct the information we present here: we would be delighted to hear from you.*

### Stage, Film, TV, and Radio Versions

*Note: We have not included in this list film versions from other parts of the world, although we know of at least three such versions. We also lack any information of American radio adaptations, although it seems likely that there have been some. We have not included the recent spate of audiobook versions, as our research on these versions is incomplete.*

1842    *The Last of the Mohicans: a tragedy, in five acts, founded on the novel of that name,* by J. F. Cooper. John Blurton, Sheffield. [Copy held in the Library of Congress]

1909    Dir: D. W. Griffith, *The Leatherstocking* [Single-reeler, Biograph. Paper copies held at both the Library of Congress and the Museum of Modern Art, New York]

1911    Dir: Pat Powers, *The Last of the Mohicans* [Single-reeler, now probably lost]

1911    Dir: Thanhouser, *The Last of the Mohicans* [Single-reeler, now probably lost]

1911    Dir: Unknown, *In the Days of the Six Nations* [Two-reeler, now probably lost]

1920    Dir: Maurice Tourneur and Clarence Brown, *The Last of the Mohicans* [Print held at Photoplay Productions, London]

1924    Dir: George B. Seitz, *The Leatherstocking* (compilation of *The Last of the Mohicans* and *The Deerslayer*) [Now probably lost]

1926    Dir: Unknown, *The Last of the Mohee-cans* [Print held at the British Film Institute, London]

1931    *The Last of the Moe Higgins* (Buzzell, Edwards, USA) [Only known through a reference in the *International Film Index*]

1932    Dir: Reeves Eason and Ford Beebe, *The Last of the Mohicans* (Mascot Films, twelve-chapter serial) [Available on video through dealers, catalog number not known]

1936    Dir: George B. Seitz, *The Last of the Mohicans* (United Artists) [Video Late Show 220–1007]

1947    Dir: George Sherman, *The Last of the Redmen*, released in Britain as *The Last of the Redskins* (Columbia) [Columbia/TriStar Video 26883]

1950    *The Iroquois Trail* (United Artists) [loosely based on *The Leatherstocking Tales*]

1953    Excerpts presented in play form, BBC Radio Home Service, 12 November. [Now probably lost]

1955    Six-part adaptation, BBC Radio Light Programme, beginning 22 August. [Now probably lost]

1956    Dir: Sidney Salkow, *Hawkeye and the Last of the Mohicans* (CBC) [ITC Video 0331]

1966    *The Last Mohican* (Leaf, Paul, USA) [Only known through a reference in the *International Film Index*]

1971    Dir: David Maloney, *The Last of the Mohicans* (BBC TV, eight-part serial, shown in America in thirteen parts) [Copy held in the Museum of Television, New York]

1977    Dir: James Conway, *The Last of the Mohicans* (Schick Sunn) [Castle Vision Video CAS 9046]

1977    Adapted: Lewis Draper, *The Last of the Mohicans* (Cartoon, Hanna-Barbera) [Turner Home Entertainment Video HB 1104]

1979    Dir: Nick Sgarro, *The Leatherstocking Tales* (a compilation of parts of *Mohicans* along with *The Deerslayer* and *The Pioneers* (Pittsburgh PBS TV) [MasterVision Arts Series Videos 714 & 715]

1987    Screenplay: Leonard Lee, *The Last of the Mohicans* (Family Home Entertainment) [Available on video through dealers, catalog number not known]

| 1990 | Adapted by Ted Moore, BBC Radio 4, 2 July [BBC Sound Archive] |
|---|---|
| 1992 | Dir: Michael Mann, *The Last of the Mohicans* (Morgan Creek) [Warner Bros Video S012619] |
| 1994 | Creator: Kim LeMasters, *HAWKEYE: The First Frontier* (Stephen J. Cannell Productions) [Sky TV] |

## Comic and Picture Book Versions

*There are large numbers of shops, markets, and other exchange systems for comics, especially American. A large but not complete set of British comics is held divided between the British Library and the British Newspaper Library.*

| 1930s | The British boys' story-paper *Rover* (D. C. Thomson) contained a half-version of Cooper's story, under the title "Hawkeye the Redskin Detective." (We have not managed to locate this precisely.) |
|---|---|
| 1940–41 | *Target Comics* (Funnies, Inc.), Vol. 1, three parts of this reprinted in *White Rider and Super Horse* (Accepted Publications, USA), 4–6, 1950–51. |
| 1942 | *Classic Comics* 4, reprinted as *Classics Illustrated*. Art by Ray Ramsey, script by Alfred Kanter (Gilberton, USA) |
| 1947 | Promotional coloring book of *The Last of the Redskins*, to accompany the 1947 film (UK) |
| 1949 | "David Baxter and Hawkeye," artwork by Ron Embleton, in *Big Hit Comic* (Scion, UK). |
| 1952 | "The Last of the Mohicans," *Thriller Comics* 15, art by Geoff Campion (Amalgamated Press, UK). |
| 1954/5 | *Two-Fisted Tales* 40, contains a retelling of an excerpt from *Mohicans*. Adaptation and artwork by Jack Davis (EC Comics, USA). Reprinted in *The Complete Two Fisted Tales* (West Plains, Mo: Russ Cochran Publishing, 1980). |
| 1958 | "Hawkeye and the Last of the Mohicans", *4-Color* 884, adapted from the 1956 TV series (Dell Comics, USA). |
| 1958 | *Hawkeye and the Last of the Mohicans*, adapted by J. Paton from the 1956 TV series (Publicity Products, London). |
| 1958–9 | "Hawkeye and the Last of the Mohicans," *TV Picture Stories* 1–6 (Pearson, UK). |
| 1958–60 | Serial version of "The Last of the Mohicans" carried in *TV Heroes* (L. Miller, London). |
| 1958 | *Hawkeye and the Last of the Mohicans*. (Annual no. 1.) Adapted by M. Holt, artwork by Ron Embleton. (Adprint, London). |
| 1959 | New version of *Classics Illustrated*. Art by John Severin, script by Steven Addyeo (Gilberton, USA). |

| 1964–65 | "The Last of the Mohicans," twelve-part serialization in *Look And Learn* 147 (7 November) through 158 (23 January) (Fleetway Publications, London). |
| 1977 | *The Last of the Mohicans*, script by Doug Moench, art by Sonny Trinidad. (Marvel Classics Comics, USA). |
| 1977 | *The Last of the Mohicans*, adapted by Naunerle Farr; illustrated by Fred Carrillo (West Haven, Conn: Pendulum Press). |
| 1977 | *The Last of the Mohicans*, adaptation and artwork unknown (King Classics, 2, USA). |
| 1992 | *The Last of the Mohicans*, adaptation and artwork by Jack Jackson, cover by Sam Yeates (Dark Horse Comics, USA). |

## Published Editions

*It should be noted that, especially in the twentieth century, many publishers have continued to reissue editions over a long period. Perhaps the most notable reissue of* Mohicans *is Scribner's 1919 edition, illustrated by N. C. Wyeth, which is still in print today. It should also be noted that some abridgments have reappeared several times under different publishers' imprints.*

The Last of the Mohicans. A narrative of *1757*.

Carey & Lea, Philadelphia, 1826.

J. Miller, London, 1826.

L. Baudry, Paris, 1826.

Philadelphia, 1836.

London, 1852.

*The last of the Mohicans; a narrative of 1757*. Revised, corrected, and with a new introduction by the author.

Henry Colburn & Richard Bentley, London, 1831, 1834, 1836.

Edward Ravenscroft, London, 1838.

G. P. Putnam, New York, 1849.

Thomas Allman, London, 1850

Routledge, Warne & Routledge, London, 1862.

James G. Gregory, New York, 1864.

George Routledge & Sons, London, 1867.

Frederick Warne & Co., London, 1867. [Abridged edition]

D. Appleton & Co, Philadelphia 1872.

Groombridge & Sons, London, 1875.

Houghton, Mifflin and Co., Boston, 1876.

Cassell & Co., London, 1886.

Ward, Lock & Co., London, 1887 (abridged).

Frederick Warne & Co., London & New York, 1888.

George Routledge & Sons, London, 1889. [Arranged for youth]

McLoughlin Bros., New York, 1890.
Cassell & Co., London, 1890.
Society for the Propagation of Christian Knowledge, London, 1893. [Abridged]
George Newnes, London, 1898.
Macmillan & Co., London, 1900.
Collins, London & Glasgow, 1902.
James Nisbet & Co., London, 1900.
Blackie & Son, London, 1906.
J. M. Dent & Co., London, 1906
E. P. Dutton & Co., New York, 1906.
T. Nelson & Sons, London, 1906.
"Penny Popular Library," W. Stead, London, 1908.
Cassell & Co., London, 1908.
Thomas Nelson & Sons, London, 1908.
Macmillan Co., New York, 1909.
American Book Co., New York, 1909. [Adapted for schools by Margaret N. Haight]
George Bell & Sons, London, 1909. [Adapted by Margaret N. Haight]
W. & R. Chambers, London, 1911.
George G. Harrap & Co., London, 1912. (Adapted by Margaret N. Haight)
Cassell & Co., London, 1911.
Constable & Co., London, 1911.
Charles Scribner's Sons, New York, 1919.
T. Nelson & Sons, London, 1919.
Hodder & Stoughton, London, 1920.
George G. Harrap & Co., London, 1925.
Houghton Mifflin Co., Boston, 1930.
Readers Library Publishing Co., London, 1933.
Dean & Son, London, 1936.
Philip & Tracey, London, 1940. [Retold and edited by Constance M. Martin]
Mellifont Press, London, 1946. [Abridged]
E. J. Arnold, Leeds, c 1948 [Abridged by J B Marshall]
Collins, London & Glasgow, 1953.
J. M. Dent & Sons, London 1957.
E. P. Dutton & Co., New York, 1957.
W. Foulsham & Co., London, 1957. [Abridged]
Murrays Abbey Classics, London, 1957.
Thames Publishing Co., London, 1957. [Abridged]
Dean & Son, London, 1959. [Abridged]
Longmans, London, 1963. [Simplified by Margaret May Maison]
Parents' Magazine Press, New York, 1964. [Classics to grow on]
Golden Pleasure Books, London, 1964. [Adapted by Richard Sadler]

Peal Press, London, 1965. [Abridged by Gavin Gibbons]
Harper & Row, New York, 1965.
Fearon Publishers, Palo Alto, California, 1967. [Abridged and adapted by John M. Hurdy]
Bancroft Books, London, 1967. [Abridged]
Barnes & Noble, New York, 1969. [Abridged by Jack B. Moore]
Greenwood Press, New York, 1969.
Studio Vista, London, 1973.
D. McKay Co., New York, 1976. [Abridged by Robin S. Wright]
Purnell Books, London, 1976. [Abridged]
Franklin Center, Pa., Franklin Library 1977.
Pan Books, London, 1977. [Retold by Alan Robertshaw]
Illustrated Classic Editions, I. Waldman & Co, New York 1977. [Abridged]
Ward, Lock 'Take Part' Series, London, 1978. [Adapted by Sheila Lane & Marion Kemp]
Franklin Center, Pennsylvania, 1981. [Limited edition with designs based on head-work of Eastern Woodland tribes]
State University of New York Press, Albany, 1983.
Ladybird Books, Loughborough, 1983. [Retold by Raymond Sibley]
Reader's Digest Association, Pleasantville, N.Y., 1984. [Abridged]
Penguin Books, New York and London, 1986.
New York, Oxford University Press, 1990. [Edited and introduced by John McWilliams]
Wordsworth Classics, 1992.
New York, Random House, 1993. [Abridged by Les Martin]
Wheeler Pub., Hingham, Mass., 1993. [Large print]

## Other versions

Cooper's *Leather-Stocking Tales*: comprising *The Deerslayer, The Pathfinder, The Last of the Mohicans, The Pioneers,* and *The Prairie.* 5 pts. George Routledge & Sons, London, 1868.
*The Novels of James Fennimore [sic] Cooper, Esq. Comprising The Pilot . . . The Spy . . . The Last of the Mohicans . . . Lionel Lincoln . . . The Pioneers . . . The Prairie . . . The Red Rover . . . The Water Witch . . .* Complete in one volume. W. M. Clark, London, 1844.
*Scenes from The Last of the Mohicans.* Edward Arnold, London, 1899.
*The Redskin Omnibus (The Last of the Mohicans; The Deerslayer* [by James Fenimore Cooper], *The Scalp-Hunters* [by Mayne Reid]), 3 pts. Collins, London & Glasgow, 1935.
*The Red Indian Omnibus Book . . . The Last of the Mohicans. The Pathfinder. Deerslayer.* (Abridgments.) 3 pts. Blackie & Son, London & Glasgow, 1939.

*Twelve of the World's Famous Books* ("Condensed to about 20 minutes reading time each"), Keep-Worthy Books, New York, 1945.

*The Leatherstocking Saga. Being parts of The Deerslayer, The Last of the Mohicans, The Pathfinder, The Pioneers and The Prairie* (Edited by Allan Nevins) Collins, London, Kingsport, 1955. [This book was adopted as an alternate choice by the Book-of-the-Month Club in the same year.]

*The Leatherstocking Tales.* Literary Classics of the U.S. Distributed to the trade in the U.S. and Canada by Viking Press, New York, c. 1985.

*Classic Adventure Stories*, Derrydale Books, New York, 1987.

*Eight Classic American Novels*, Harcourt Brace Jovanovich, San Diego, c. 1990.

# NOTES

## Preface

1. One of these, the December 1911 *In the Days of the Six Nations*, is only known to us through Denis Gifford's *Books and Plays in Films, 1896–1915* (Jefferson, N.C.: McFarland, 1991). Gifford's attribution of this film to the Republic Production Company looks to us to be a mistake since (as far as we can tell) this company did not emerge until the 1930s.

2. Daniel Francis, *The Imaginary Indian* (Vancouver, B.C.: Arsenal Pulp Press, 1992).

## 1. The Mohican Myth and the American Dream

1. The name "Hawkeye" will, of course, be for many people the most obvious first memory connection, because of the TV series *MASH*. There is much to be said, though not here, about this ironic reference to *Mohicans* in a "frontier abroad."

2. Raphael Samuel's opening essay, "The figures of national myth," in his edited volume *Patriotism: The Making and Unmaking of British National Identity*, vol. 3, *National Fictions* (London: Routledge, 1989) lists and explores a large number of such British mythical figures.

3. A good discussion of these tendencies is David Bordwell, Janet Staiger, and Kristin Thompson, *The Classical Hollywood Cinema: Film Style and Mode of Production to 1960* (London: Routledge, 1985).

4. We do acknowledge that we have hunted harder for versions of *Mohicans* than versions of these other works, so some versions of the others may have passed us by. But the discrepancy is real nonetheless.

5. Brian Street, *The Savage in Literature: Representations of "Primitive" Society in English Fiction, 1858–1920* (London: Routledge, 1975).

6. A reader of our manuscript has pointed out to us that Mason is, of course, well known for another of his books, *The Four Feathers*, which has itself been the subject of more than one film treatment. We accept and acknowledge the correction. But the point, we feel, remains. There is a difference between studying books which *in their time* were undoubtedly influential, and studying the history of the influence of books that have continued to speak to subsequent generations. And we are pretty sure that though one of Mason's books has indeed survived, it does far less to conjure up his name as author than does Cooper's *Mohicans*.

7. Jack Zipes, *The Trials and Tribulations of Little Red Riding Hood* (London: Heinemann, 1983).

8. Martin Barker, *Comics: Ideology, Power and the Critics* (Manchester: Manchester University Press, 1989) chapter 6.

9. There have been, to our knowledge, two such records: one, a rare compilation for which we do not have production details; the other, strictly a post-punk humorous piece by Otway and Barrett, *Last of the Mohicans* (VM Records, Bacon Empire Pub. Ltd, 1987).

10. Geoffrey Wagner, *The Novel and the Cinema* (Cranbury, N.J.: Fairleigh Dickinson University Press, 1975).

11. Derek Elley, *The Epic Film: Myth and History* (London: Routledge, 1984) 1. Emphasis in the original.

12. Robert A. Nowlan and Gwendolyn Wright Nowlan, *Cinema Sequels and Remakes, 1903–87* (Jefferson, N.C.: McFarland, 1989). One does, though, one wonder about their completeness when the Nowlans do not even mention Cooper at all!

13. See, for example, Dick Hebdige, "Towards a Cartography of Taste," in his *Hiding in the Light* (London: Comedia, 1988), 45–76; Dominic Strinati, "The Taste of America: Americanisation and Popular Culture in Britain," in Dominic Strinati and Stephen Wagg, eds., *Come on Down? Popular Media Culture in Post War Britain* (London: Routledge, 1992), 46–87; and Duncan Webster, *Looka Yonder! The Imaginary America of Popular Culture* (London: Routledge, 1988).

14. Recently, in the field of cultural studies, a (sometimes heated) debate has been taking place over the extent to which audiences are free to arrive at their own interpretations and uses of media messages. On the one hand, as it has often been put, readers and viewers are able to "negotiate their own meanings." On the other hand, critics have replied that there are there are "preferred readings" or "limits to interpretation." While we very much agree with the criticisms, we feel that the way they have been posed largely misses the point. The problem is that *both sides* seem to give precedence to those media audiences who are the least motivated to do anything with their reading and viewing. They do not seem to pass on their ideas, they do not much share their pleasures. These are the most disengaged and casual

audiences. What we have been studying are those who *want to reinterpret,* who *feel the need to communicate their reinterpretations,* and who therefore have to *put their reinterpretations into a coherent shape and communicable package.* Perhaps this book can also contribute a new angle to these debates.

15. See R. H. Fossum and J. K. Roth, *The American Dream* (London: British Association for American Studies, 1981).

16. In a sense, this promise was bound up with a figurative America even before that continent was discovered. Columbus imagined that a new kingdom of God might be established in the land to which his navigational mistake had led him.

17. Turner's essay is cited more often than it is reprinted. However it was included in Ray Allen Billington, ed., *Frontier and Section: Selected Essays of Frederick Jackson Turner* (Englewood, N.J.: Prentice, 1961), 37–62.

18. See Daniel Francis, *The Imaginary Indian.* Of course, the "Indian" was the invention of the European, and it could be argued that the adoption of this term was the first step to stereotyping native Americans. As Francis says: "When Christopher Columbus arrived in America 500 years ago he thought he had reached the East Indies so he called the people he met Indians. But really they were Arawaks, and they had as much in common with the Iroquois of the northern woodlands as the Iroquois had with the Blackfoot of the western plains. In other words, when Columbus arrived in America, there were a large number of different and distinct indigenous cultures, but there were no Indians" (4).

19. Dee Brown, *Bury My Heart at Wounded Knee: An Indian History of the American West* (New York: Holt, Rinehart & Winston 1970). We should acknowledge here the previous work of historians in academia, especially that of W. Washburn, whose *The Indian and the White Man* (New York: Doubleday, 1964) was an important precursor to Brown's book.

20. It is significant that some big Hollywood stars lent their names to the "red cause." The most famous was Marlon Brando, who with activist Russell Means set up the radical pressure group AIM (American Indian Movement). Means later went on to play the role of Chingachgook in the 1992 movie version of *Mohicans.*

21. See, most recently, Peter Nabokov, ed., *Native American Testimony: A Chronicle of Indian-White Relations from Prophecy to the Present, 1492–1992* (New York: Penguin, 1991), and Roland Wright, *Stolen Continents: The Indian Story* (London: John Murray, 1992).

## 2. Cooper's Book

1. All page references to *The Last of the Mohicans* throughout this book will be to the Penguin edition, unless specifically noted otherwise.

2. Recommended biographies of Cooper are: George Dekker, *James Fenimore Cooper: The American Scott* (New York: Barnes and Noble, 1967) and Stephen Railton, *Fenimore Cooper: A Study of His Life and Imagination* (Princeton, N.J.: Princeton University Press, 1978).

3. Cooper wrote thirty novels in all. Perhaps the best known outside the Leatherstocking Tales was *The Spy* (1821), a tale of the American Revolution.

4. In the original books, the name is hyphenated ("Hawk-eye"), though modern audiences are much more familiar with the conflation "Hawkeye."

5. Ralph Waldo Emerson, *Gleanings in Europe* (Philadelphia, 1838), I, 35.

6. For an in-depth discussion of this creative clique, see James Beard, "Cooper and his Artistic Contemporaries," in *New York History* 35 (1954): 480–95.

7. Examples of "Indian stories" included *Yamoyden* (1820) and *Hobomok* (1824). Interestingly, many were written by women. For more on this subject, see Nina Baum, "How Men and Women Wrote Indian Stories," in Daniel Peck, ed., *New Essays on The Last of the Mohicans* (Cambridge: Cambridge University Press, 1992), 67–86.

8. There is evidence that Cooper had Indian companions and supported certain Indian land claims. See James Beard's introduction to the 1983 State University of New York Press edition of *Mohicans*, xv.

9. This characterization of the Indian is a contrast to that of the African in Edgar Rice Burrough's *Tarzan* novels, where the Africans are "childlike" by nature.

10. For an elucidation of this point about the "good Indian/bad Indian," see Richard Slotkin's introduction to the Penguin edition (1986) of *Mohicans*, esp. xxiv-xxv.

11. One wonders why a mixed marriage would be so feared. Perhaps it is because the merging of the two images produces an even more dangerous monster. As Roderick Nash says, the half-breed is feared as a "superior Indian" and a troublemaker, a "leader of rebellions." See Nash's *Wilderness and the American Mind* (New Haven, Conn.: Yale University Press, 1973), 279.

12. The seeming contradiction that a "racist" writer can produce a sympathetic portrayal of a race has not gone away in American literature. Most recently, a controversy was generated when Forrest Carter, the author of *The Outlaw Josey Wales*, a Western highly praised for its characterization of Sioux characters, was exposed as a Ku Klux Klan sympathizer.

13. See Virgil Bechman's 1982 song, "God, Guts and Guns."

14. Introduction to 1831 edition, reprinted in the 1986 Penguin edition of *Mohicans*, 7.

15. Occasionally, Cooper would not be so pedantic. Usually, he would insist that he wrote about "the truth," as in the Introduction to *Mohicans*.

But sometimes he admitted to taking artistic license. It depended on which audience he was playing to.

16. See Robert Lawson-Peebles, "The Lesson of the Massacre at Fort William Henry," in Daniel Peck, ed., *New Essays*, esp. 117–120.

17. Significantly, Cooper's family was dispossessed of land before the writing of *Mohicans*. See Daniel Peck's Introduction to *New Essays*, 4.

18. The word "frontier" has different connotations in America and in Britain. In the latter it is a border between two powers, to cross which means danger. In the former it has become an area which invites entrance and promises opportunity and riches. Slotkin also argues that it creates an inversion of normal social rank. Comparing the early and late parts of *Mohicans*, he points out: "In Part I, characters are subordinated according to rank and caste, irrespective of 'talent and virtue.' Munro commands Heyward; Heyward commands Hawkeye; Hawkeye in some sense commands the Mohicans. In Part II the structure is completely inverted. Even before their royal character is revealed, pragmatic considerations make the Mohicans leaders of the hunt, subject only to their deference to the skill of Hawkeye. Heyward follows Hawkeye, and is followed by Munro" (Introduction to the Penguin edition of *Mohicans*, xxi).

19. It is also worth noting ahead that some adaptations of *Mohicans*, as the real events receded, made play of reminding their audiences who had won, and which side key people (such as George Washington) were on. See chapter 6 below for examples.

20. Cooper's reputation never really recovered, and his decision to return to writing Leatherstocking stories in the 1840s was undoubtedly an attempt to revive it.

21. For a full account of the history of this criticism, see Daniel Peck, Introduction to *New Essays*, 1–24.

22. One source puts a figure of more than two million on sales of *The Last of the Mohicans* up to the 1940s, putting it among the all-time best-sellers historically. See Frank Luther Mott, *Golden Multitudes: The Story of Best-Sellers in the United States* (New York: R. R. Bowker, 1947), 74–76.

23. For the record, the first American novel is generally agreed to have been *The Power of Sympathy* by William Hill Brown (1789). Obviously, Cooper himself had also written novels before *Mohicans*.

24. Lora Romero, "Vanishing Americans: Gender, Empire and the New Historicism," *American Literature* 63.3 (1991): 385–404 (quoted at 386).

25. The reviewer was William Howard Gardiner, in the prestigious *North American Review*. This information is drawn from Louisa K. Barnett, *The Ignoble Savage: American Literary Racism, 1790–1890* (Westport, Conn.: Greenwood Press, 1975), 23.

26. Barnett, *The Ignoble Savage*, 26.

27. On this aspect of white representations of Indians, see in particular

Roy Harvey Pearce, *The Savages of America: A Study of the Indian and the Idea of Civilization* (New York: Johns Hopkins University Press, 1965). Pearce argues that the period up to the time when Cooper wrote was dominated not simply by images of savagery, but by a rising *need to know* about the lives, habits, practices and natures of native American societies. The link between the two is there in the figure of Thomas Jefferson. It was Jefferson who dismissed the arguments of Buffon that the Indians were "primitive peoples." Among his counters to Buffon was his acknowledgment of their rhetorical powers, which he calls a distinguishing mark of civilization, for it enables matters to be settled by persuasion, not force. It was the same Jefferson who, in 1803, sent the explorers Lewis and Clark on a westward expedition with a precise "shopping list" of kinds of information that were needed about native American life.

28. John Cawelti, *The Six-Gun Mystique* (Bowling Green, Ohio: Popular Press, 1970), 145.

29. "Appreciation of wilderness began in the cities," says Roderick Nash (*Wilderness and the American Mind*, 44). Interestingly, Nash shows that again and again those who celebrated wilderness as "sublime" and "rapture" ended their narratives by preferring tamed, farmed land—as though wilderness is good to think, but not to live in. What again distinguishes Cooper, and especially *Mohicans*, is that it does not end so.

30. In using this terminology of "coherence" and "commitment," we are making deliberately eccentric use of ideas wonderfully developed in John Berger's *Another Way of Telling* (London: Writers & Readers, 1982). Berger is discussing the nature of "expressive photography," that is, photographs that "make long quotations from appearance." By this he seems to mean that quality which enables some photographs to hold within them the real social and personal relations that typify a historical moment. His prime example is a photograph from Andre Kertesz of a Red Army soldier leaving his family. His point seems to us potentially an enormously productive one about the ways meanings can be condensed and contained. Our argument here is that Cooper himself contains a clear excess and contradictory potential of meaning, which needs the detailed working of other times and other media to produce different forms of coherence.

## 3. Becoming a Classic

1. Preface to the Abbey Classics edition of *Mohicans*, 1957.

2. Geoffrey Pearson, *Hooligan: A History Of Respectable Fears* (London: Macmillan, 1983) and "Falling Standards: Short, Sharp Lesson in Moral Decline," in Martin Barker, ed., *The Video Nasties: Freedom and Censorship in the Arts* (London: Pluto Press, 1984), 88–103.

3. "Nation fights to save boys and girls," London *Daily Mail*, 22 September 1954.

4. On the opposition between "fantasy" and "imagination," see the discussion in the final chapter of Martin Barker, *A Haunt of Fears: The Strange History of the British Horror Comics Campaign* (Jackson, Miss.: University Press of Mississippi, 1993).

5. Nicholas Garnham, *Capitalism and Communication: Global Culture and the Economy of Information* (London: Sage, 1992).

6. See, for instance, the British Penguin Books edition of *Mohicans*. In earlier times published with the Asher Durand painting on its cover, it was reissued with the 1992 film's poster image of Hawkeye lovingly hugging Cora! On the recent competition for the classics market, of which this was part, see Sarah Knibbs, "Classics UK—Enter the B Troop," *The Bookseller*, 17 June 1994.

7. For more about these concerns, see Martin Barker, *A Haunt of Fears*.

8. This blurb is taken from W. Foulsham's 1957 (London and New York) edition.

9. Promotional copy taken from the dust jacket of the Dean & Son (1976) edition. It is worth noting that this edition is identical to both the earlier Purnell and Bancroft Classics editions except in this dust jacket.

10. Philippe Aries, *Centuries of Childhood* (Harmondsworth, England: Penguin, 1960).

11. J.-J. Rousseau, *Emile* (1762; reprint, London: Dent, Everyman's Library, 1974), 30.

12. Peter Coveney, *The Image of Childhood: A Study of the Theme In English Literature* (Harmondsworth, England: Penguin, 1967), 31–32.

13. Matthew Davenport Hill, "Practical Suggestions to the Founders of Reformatory Schools," in J. C. Symons, *On the Reformation of Young Offenders* (London: Routledge, 1855), 2.

14. All these examples and other below are to be found in the unabridged Oxford English Dictionary.

15. On this period, see in particular Margaret Mathieson, *Preachers of Culture: A Study of English and Its Teachers* (London: George Allen & Unwin, 1975).

16. On George Sampson, see David Shayer, *The Teaching of English in Schools, 1900–1970* (London: Routledge, 1972). This quotation is from p. 78. Margaret Mathieson quotes a more melodramatic passage from Sampson: "Deny to working class children any common share in the immaterial, and presently they will grow into the men who demand with menaces a communism of the material" (Mathieson, *Preachers of Culture*, 74–75).

17. Much has been written about the Newbolt Committee, but see especially Brian Doyle, *English and Englishness* (London: Routledge, 1989). This quotation is from p. 67.

18. For those who do not know it, *fagging* was the system in British public schools whereby younger boys had to serve the older boys in everything from cooking to cleaning. The system was justified on the grounds that it would train the older boys to be officers who would also know how to take care of their charges, while the younger boys would learn obedience and a proper dependence—until their turn came. In practice, the system ranged from petty tyranny to sexual exploitation.

19. Henry Newbolt, *The Book of the Happy Warrior* (London: Longmans, Green, 1925), 274. The book was originally published around 1917.

20. One history of children's literature notes that by the 1840s Cooper is sitting alongside Walter Scott as a writer of adventures, and a source for play: in the 1840s "Sir Sidney Colvin, the friend of Robert Louis Stevenson, remembered playing Indian 'according to Cooper'" (Cornelia Meigs, Anne Thaxter Eaton, Elizabeth Nesbitt, and Ruth Hall Vigners, *A Critical History of Children's Literature* [London: Macmillan, 1969], 214) F. J. Harvey Darton, in *Children's Books in England* (Cambridge: Cambridge University Press, 1970), dates the first imports to the 1850s. However, we think Martin Green is right to place the date for mass circulation of Cooper's work considerably later. See his *Dreams of Adventure, Deeds of Empire* (London: Routledge, 1980).

21. Kirsten Drotner, *English Children and Their Magazines: 1751–1945* (New Haven, Conn.: Yale University Press, 1988).

22. Frank Kermode, *The Classic* (London: Faber & Faber, 1975), 86–87.

23. For more on Goodrich, see Caroline M. Hewins, "The History of Children's Books" (originally published 1888), in Virginia Haviland, ed., *Children and Literature: Views and Reviews* (Glenview, Ill.: Scott, Foresman, 1973).

24. Meigs, Eaton, Nesbitt, and Vigners, *A Critical History of Children's Literature*, xvii.

25. Green, *Dreams of Adventure, Deeds of Empire*.

26. See H. Wayne Morgan, *Unity and Culture: The United States, 1877–1900* (London: Allen Lane, 1971) for many details of this phenomenon.

27. Delacroix, quoted in Morgan, *Unity and Culture*, 88.

28. David B. Tyack, *The One Best System: A History of American Urban Education* (Cambridge: Harvard University Press, 1974).

29. Ellwood Cubberley, *Changing Conceptions of Education* (1909), quoted in Tyack, *The One Best System*, 188–89.

30. Many books recently have recovered this largely forgotten history. Worth seeing in particular are: Allan Chase, *The Legacy of Malthus: The Social Costs of the New Scientific Racism* (New York: Knopf, 1977), Leon Kamin, *The Science and Politics of IQ* (New York: Laurence Erlbaum, 1974), and Stephan Chorover, *From Genesis to Genocide: The Meaning of Human Nature and the Power of Behavior Control* (Boston: MIT Press, 1989).

31. It bears thinking that the American Social Darwinists may have so readily recognized compatriots in Germany, because of the shared language of "Manifest Destiny."

32. See John E. Sturm & John A. Palmer, *Democratic Legacy in Transition: Perspectives on American Education* (New York: Van Nostrand, 1971), 36.

33. All this information and the quotation from Kermit Vanderbilt, *American Literature and the Academy: The Roots, Growth and Maturity of a Profession* (Philadelphia: University of Pennsylvania Press, 1986). See also Russell Reising, *The Unusable Past: Theory and the Study of American Literature* (London: Methuen, 1986).

34. Herbert M. Kliebard, *The Struggle for the American Curriculum, 1893–1958* (London: Routledge, 1986).

35. On the history of the Book-of-the-Month Club, the following are useful: Joan Shelley Rubin, "Self, Culture, and Self-Culture in Modern America," *The Journal of American History* 71 (1985): 782–806, and Janice Radway, "Mail-Order Culture and Its Critics: The Book-of-the-Month Club, Commodification and Consumption, and the Problem of Cultural Authority," in Lawrence Grossberg et al., eds., *Cultural Studies* (London: Routledge, 1992), 512–27. A good standard history is Charles Lee, *The Hidden Public: The Story of the Book-of-the-Month Club* (New York: Doubleday, 1958).

On *Reader's Digest*, see Samuel A. Schreiner, *The Condensed World of the Reader's Digest* (New York: Stein & Day, 1977. For a critical examination, see Ariel Dorfman, "The Infantilisation of the Adult Reader," in his *The Empire's Old Clothes* (London: Pluto Press, 1983). On the controversy over these developments, see especially Christopher Bookeman, *American Culture and Society since the 1930s* (New York: Schocken, 1984), and James Gilbert, *A Cycle of Outrage* (New York: Oxford University Press, 1984).

36. *Twelve of the WORLD'S FAMOUS BOOKS condensed to about 20 minutes reading time each* (Keep-Worthy Books, 1945). Heralding itself as a product of the company that produced *Parents' Magazine*, and as complying strictly with war rationing rules, this edition also miniaturizes Thackeray's *Vanity Fair*, Dickens's *David Copperfield*, Hugo's *The Hunchback of Notre Dame*, Shakespeare's *Antony and Cleopatra*, Bunyan's *Pilgrim's Progress*, Dumas' *The Count of Monte Cristo*, Scott's *Kenilworth*, Kingsley's *Westward Ho!*, Hawthorne's *The House of Seven Gables*, Irving's *Rip Van Winkle*, and Poe's *The Gold Bug*. The prefatory remarks by Clara Savage Littledale, editor of *Parents' Magazine*, offer the volume as a way back in to a full reading of the classics for those who have forgotten how.

37. Kermode, *The Classic*, 114.

38. An interesting newspaper snippet: David Holloway ("True Confessions," London *Daily Telegraph*, June 1994) wrote of his long dislike for

*Mohicans.* In part, he found the book to be badly written, but that was not all. "I also blame my lack of interest on the edition that I was given. It was one of those cheap hardbacks that used to be sold in Woolworth's for 6d (2-1/2p), printed on appalling paper, with smudgy type and with spines that cracked from top to bottom when you opened them. Thank God for the Penguin revolution and real sixpenny books. Someone, one day, ought to write a thesis on the effect of the appearance of books on the reader."

39. Edward Blishen, "An insolent thing to do," London *School Bookshop News,* no. 8, Autumn 1977.

40. *The Last of the Mohicans,* abridged by J. B. Marshall, The A. L. Bright Story Readers (Leeds: E. J. Arnold, c. 1950), 96.

41. There are records of a play called *The Last of the Mohicans* having been performed at the Phoenix Theatre in London in 1866, but it is not clear if this was ours or another (lost) version. Our thanks to Christopher Robinson of the University of Bristol Theatre Collection for researching this point for us.

### 4. Movie Mohicans, 1909–1936

1. Frederick Monsen, "Picturing Indians with the Camera" (1910), cited in Paula Richardson Fleming and Judith Lynn Luskey, *The Shadow Catchers: Images of the American Indian* (London: Lawrence King, 1993), 12.

2. See Robert C. Allen, *Vaudeville and Film: A Study in Media Interaction* (Ph.D. diss., University of Iowa, 1977).

3. Thomas Bedding, "Vaudeville vitiates the picture," *Moving Picture World,* 11 June 1910, quoted in Allen, *Vaudeville and Film,* 238.

4. Useful studies of Griffith's career include: Karl Brown, *Adventures with D. W. Griffith* (London: Secker & Warburg, 1973); Scott Simmon, *The Films of D. W. Griffith* (Cambridge: Cambridge University Press, 1993); and Richard Schickel, *D. W. Griffith and the Birth of Film* (New York: Pavilion Books, 1984).

5. On the question of using literary adaptations to "legitimize" cinema, see W. Uricchio and R. Pearson, *Reframing Culture: The Case of the Vitagraph Quality Films* (Princeton, N.J.: Princeton University Press, 1993). Although the book is primarily concerned with Vitagraph's output, it is also relevant to Biograph: Vitagraph was indeed the main company to concentrate in this area, but Biograph adapted Poe, Shakespeare, Cooper, and others.

6. The only copy of the film that we have been able to consult came from the Library of Congress Paper Tape Collection. Unfortunately, it may be unreliable. Certainly the sequences were in the wrong order, and had to be re-edited. All caption frames are missing. There is, therefore, a possibility that some scenes have been lost.

7. That Henry Walthall played Hawkeye is an educated guess, based on the fact that he was the most well-known actor in the film and would therefore have been offered the lead role. Beyond this, it is impossible to put faces to names. (The cast list does not appear on the Library of Congress copy.)

8. That Linda Arvidson played Cora is similarly an educated guess.

9. In fact, there were odd exceptions to this rule. In the very early days of cinema, there were some native American actors and even one director, though they were not admitted to the film unions. On the subject of using white actors in "ethnic" roles, it is worth mentioning that *Birth of a Nation* featured white actors in blackface.

10. We can never know exactly how much control Griffith had over the making of *Leatherstocking*, but it is likely to have been substantial. Although the pace of filmmaking at Biograph was hectic, there is evidence that he paid more attention to literary adaptations, for the reasons described above.

11. For a fine history of these expeditions and reproductions of a good number of the surviving photographs, see Paula Richardson Fleming and Judith Lynn Luskey, *The Shadow Catchers*.

12. This quotation is from a December 1920 review of *The Last of the Mohicans* by Tourneur and Brown, republished in Stanley Hochman, ed., *From Quasimodo to Scarlett O'Hara: A National Board of Review Anthology 1920–1940* (New York: Frederick Ungar, 1982), 4. It is worth noting at this point that a number of film histories incorrectly give the date of 1922 for this film.

13. Brown, interviewed in Kevin Brownlow, *The Parade's Gone By* (New York: Knopf, 1968), 12.

14. This scene was gloriously filmed at Glacier Point in Yosemite Valley. The exact spot, with its jutting outcrop of rock, was already well known to many through photographs. Two good examples are reproduced in William H. Truettner, *The West as America: Reinterpreting Images of the Frontier, 1820–1920*, Washington, D.C.: Smithsonian Institution Press, 1991). See p. 239 and the closing illustration.

15. Jan-Christopher Horak, "Maurice Tourneur's Tragic Romance," in Gerald Peary and Roger Shatzkin, eds., *The Classic American Novel and the Movies* (New York: Frederick Ungar, 1977). See especially pp. 14–16.

16. Some original responses and reviews are reproduced in Gerald Mast, ed., *The Movies in Our Midst* (Chicago: University of Chicago Press, 1982).

17. Wagenknecht notes that this scene is in fact not present in Thomas Dixon's *The Clansmen* (1905), on which *Birth* was based. See Edward Wagenknecht, *The Movies in the Age of Innocence* (Norman: University of Oklahoma Press, 1962), 99.

18. Tourneur is reported to have said that his reason for going to America

was to learn from the master filmmaker Griffith. Another of Tourneur's films, *Women*, according to Wagenknecht, is also clearly influenced by Griffith's *Intolerance*. Kevin Brownlow in fact suggested that Griffith later tried to regain the ascendancy. Brownlow wrote: "I would have little doubt that *America* was made in part as a reply to *Last of the Mohicans*" (letter to the authors, 2 January 1993). *America*, Griffith's film of the War of Independence and including Paul Revere's famous ride to carry warning of the English approach, does indeed have some curious parallels, but with shifts and differences. Like both *Birth of a Nation* and the Tourneur/Brown *Mohicans*, it has a young woman's virtue threatened—but on this occasion it is the actions of a Mohawk chief that save her. Like *Mohicans* generally, it has to take a position on the question of Anglo-American relations, and indeed works hard to remove the possibilities of a conflict. Griffith in fact edited two versions of *America*, one for the home and the other for the British market.

19. In the version of the film we have been able to see, we do not in fact get to know what Uncas says to her. This may suggest an altered, perhaps incomplete, version—a not unlikely occurrence. Kevin Brownlow has informed us that most likely this copy was edited by the French, who were at this time notorious for mutilating films. If not that, then the absence of any actual words from Uncas suggests a conscious intent on the part of Brown and Tourneur to invoke a sense of mystery, perhaps because no real words could actually create such a feeling of "depth and imagination in a savage" without making us laugh at the results.

20. We must be careful, of course, about placing too much significance on the date of the film. This theme had been present before, and would return again. In 1913, the short film *The Squaw Man* touched on these themes. And in 1925, George B. Seitz's film *The Vanishing American* showed an Indian Chief attracted to a white schoolmarm. At the end the Chief dies, saving her from rape at the hands of the white villain, thus again avoiding miscegenation. This is significant, since Seitz was the maker of two versions of *Mohicans*: one (from 1924) now sadly lost; the other, the very important 1936 version. On these, see Raymond J. Merlock, *From Flintlock to Forty-Five: James Fenimore Cooper and the Popular Western Tradition in Fiction and Film* (Ph.D. diss., Ohio University, 1981).

21. The story of these influences has been brilliantly documented in a number of places, nowhere better than in Stephan Chorover's *From Genesis to Genocide*.

22. On this history, see in particular, Allan Chase, *The Legacy of Malthus*; Leon Kamin, *The Science and Politics of IQ*; Stephan Chorover, *From Genesis to Genocide*; and Jeffrey Blum, *Pseudoscience and Mental Ability* (New York: Monthly Review Press, 1978).

23. The London British Film Institute has a copy of this film, but again

their catalog contains virtually no information about it. The BFI copy, unfortunately, does not contain production information or a cast list. There is one question we wish to pose, though we cannot answer it. Is it accidental that the film's "hero" is called McTeague? In 1899 the American novelist Frank Norris wrote a novel with this title (*McTeague: A Story of San Francisco* [reprint, Harmondsworth, England: Penguin, 1985]). One of the early "realist" novels in America, this is a study of the life and downfall of a lower-middle-class dentist who, when his wife wins the lottery, develops pretensions above his station. But as he does so, San Francisco's class relations are hardening. He is debarred from dentistry because he learned as an apprentice rather than obtaining a professional diploma. Taking to drink, he becomes violent and eventually kills his wife and steals all their savings. At the end of the novel, he dies in Death Valley, reduced to prospecting for illusory gold. As far as we can see, there are no direct links between the book and the film, but there are suggestive parallels nonetheless. And certainly the book became notorious enough to have been stored in the popular memory, for use in 1926. Norris's McTeague, it is emphasized, is a huge man, more able with his fists than with his brain. The narration makes plain the author's mix of contempt for the "poor." As a literary man, he can pity but he cannot understand. The film almost reverses that scenario, giving McTeague the victory over his literati opponents. We wonder. . . .

24. Some of these serial films were wonderfully bad. Martin Barker has happy memories of watching, as a student at the Liverpool University Film Club, the weekly showings of episodes of *Zombies from the Stratosphere*. To great ironic cheers, the heroes would go through the identical takeoff and flight every week, the wires that held them only sometimes hidden by the inevitable swirling clouds.

25. Throughout every episode, any action is accompanied by the same snatch of music from Khatchaturian's *Spartacus* suite. This piece of music is best known to many British TV viewers as the theme music from *The Onedin Line*.

26. Here let us record our complete dissatisfaction with the very common move of seeing Cooper's work as somehow a preparation for the Western. As will become clear in our final chapter, we believe that Cooper's frontier represents something quite different. Hence, among other things, the strains when filmmakers sought to assimilate *Mohicans* to the Western mode.

27. For more information on Philip Dunne, see his autobiography *Take Two: A Life in Movies and Politics* (New York: McGraw-Hill, 1980).

28. Dunne, *Take Two*, 35.

29. It would be wrong to imagine that Hollywood remained unaffected by these wider political concerns. By 1936, there was a thriving Anti-Nazi League, while labor disputes on film sets had reached unprecedented levels.

In the same year, Chaplin's *Modern Times*, about a tragic assembly worker, was released.

30. For a useful history of the development of the studio system, see Nick Roddick, *A New Deal in Entertainment* (London: BFI Publishing, 1992).

31. On censorship and its effects in this period, see in particular Clayton R. Koppes and Gregory D. Black, *Hollywood Goes to War: How Politics, Profit and Propaganda Shaped World War II Movies* (London: I. B. Tauris, 1987); and Colin Shindler, *Hollywood Goes to War: Films and American Society, 1939–52* (London: Routledge, 1979).

32. This is one of several scenes that was "borrowed" for the title sequence of the Canadian TV version of *Mohicans*.

33. Entry on Randolph Scott in Edward Buscombe, ed., *The BFI Companion to the Western* (London: BFI Publishing, 1986), 75.

34. Dunne, *Take Two*, 35.

35. On attitudes to the British, Dunne's autobiography is again worth quoting: "We [Dunne and John Balderston] turned Colonel Munro's march into a miniature version of Braddock's defeat, with the British commander calling for his telescope while his men are being shot down by hidden enemies in the forest. 'Won't the British mind?' I asked. 'No, no,' said Anglophile John, 'make the British as stupid as you like, as long as you make them brave.'" *Take Two*, 35.

## 5. Movie Mohicans, 1947–1992

1. On this period, see Koppes and Black, *Hollywood Goes to War*, and Shindler, *Hollywood Goes to War*.

2. This shift in attitudes was reflected in Hollywood's output in a number of ways: there were movies presenting more sympathetic images of Jews and blacks, plus a few Westerns with Indians who were more than stereotypes.

3. Jim Hitt lists another movie as being loosely a version of *Mohicans*. This is the 1950 United Artists movie *The Iroquois Trail*. Of it Hitt says: "While Hawkeye (George Montgomery) is present, other characters related to *The Last of the Mohicans* are conspicuously absent, although Hawkeye does have an Indian stooge called Sagamore. A few characters seem familiar—the lovely daughter of the fort commander, her aristocratic officer fiancé, the stubborn, stiff-necked general, scoundrelly settlers, a Huron renegade. Once again, love finds Hawkeye, but the main thrust is action, and the film moves along without much pause for characterization or sweeping pageantry. Still, it has its moments, including the climactic Indian attack on the fort, all done with a sense of excitement and verve." Jim Hitt, *The American West from Fiction (1823–1976) into Film (1909–1986)* (Jefferson, N.C.: McFarland, 1990), 12.

4. One of the significant effects of bringing filmic traditions to television was the development of the fast-action TV police series, which has so long worried British critics of TV. British productions for a while avoided the fast-action mode, but when *The Sweeney* began in 1969, it was the first to accommodate itself to American styles of production, using exterior filming, car chases, and confrontational story lines and styles of acting.

5. Ralph Nelson, who directed *Soldier Blue*, was a political activist. It is also clear that films such as his were using the Western to "rethink" Vietnam. The burning of the Indian village in the film was seen by many to parallel the burning of Vietnamese villages such as My Lai. This is hardly surprising, but it shows the extent to which, even in radical hands, the "Indian" serves to signify and symbolize others.

6. Dee Brown, *Bury My Heart at Wounded Knee: An Indian History of the American West* (New York: Holt, Rinehart & Winston, 1970).

7. Around this time, another unlikely company dabbled in film production. The *Reader's Digest* put its resources and name behind four films. Of most interest to us were the successful *Tom Sawyer* (1973) and the flop *Huckleberry Finn* (1974), both made in association with United Artists. It is not clear why such a company should venture into what was for it a risky field at just this time.

8. We should be clear what we mean by the phrase "politically correct." This has been a controversial term, even rousing considerable abuse. We mean simply that this film was produced from within a new awareness that there had been massive ill-treatment and distorted representations of native Americans in the past. How they are talked about now, therefore, is a matter of importance.

9. If there were space, it would be worth discussing the theme of scalping in this and other films. Scalping was widely seen as the ultimate proof of Indian barbarism. In the 1960s and '70s strenuous attempts were made to shift the blame for this barbarism to Europeans—a claim that this film continues. In fact, subsequent research has suggested strongly that the practice was present in America before the arrival of Europeans (who were not above using it for their own purposes, of course).

10. The name "John Winthrop" can hardly be accidental, for Winthrop was one of the early Puritan leaders. To use his name, but to recast him so drastically as a plain-speaking spokesman for the colonials, bespeaks an interesting knowingness.

11. In fact the women are presented quite differently in this film than in any preceding version. Cora is a strong, convincing character who defies her father when she perceives injustice. Even Alice, depicted as hardly beyond her teens, in the end faces death with a calm and terrifying acceptance. This is not incidental to the film. There is a way in which these two women's responses to the "whole world being on fire" sum up the film's meaning.

12. This quotation is from *Vox* (London), June 1993, reviewing the video release. See also David Hepworth's review in *Empire* (London), November 1992.

13. Henry Sheehan, *Sight and Sound* (London), November 1992.

14. Derek Malcolm, *The Guardian* (London), 5 November 1992. Much the same thing happens in a London *Times* report on a season of silent movies, which opened with the Tourneur/Brown adaptation: "Although not as swiftly involving as the Daniel Day-Lewis remake . . . , it possesses the very quality that version lacks: genuine pictorial grandeur" (Kevin Thomas, " 'Mohicans' launches silent movie festival today," *The Times*, 30 August 1993, 8). Treating pictorial grandeur as an independent quality is fine for the 1920 film where, as we have argued, wilderness is very much an "outside," a place beyond the audience's experience and nature. But that, we aim to show, is what Mann does not want.

15. Michael Mann, interview in *Sight and Sound* (London), November 1992, 14.

16. Upton Sinclair, *The Jungle* (1909; reprint, Harmondsworth, England: Penguin, 1974).

17. Owen Wister, *The Virginian* (1902; reprint, London: Macmillan, 1966); and Jack London, *The Call of the Wild* (1903; reprint, Harmondsworth, England: Penguin, 1981). On the connections between these works and Cooper, it is worth seeing Daniel Leverenz, "The Last Real Man in America: From Natty Bumppo to Batman," *American Literary History*, 3.4 (1991): 753–81.

18. Also see E. Annie Proulx, *The Shipping News* (London: Fourth Estate, 1993). Thanks to Martin Barker's colleagues Anne Beezer and Geoff Channon for pointing us to this idea.

19. In this vein, see W. M. Verhoeven, "Neutralizing the Land: The Myth of Authority, and the Authority of Myth in Fenimore Cooper's *The Spy*," in V. M. Verhoeven, ed., *James Fenimore Cooper: New Literary and Historical Contexts* (Atlanta: Rodopi, 1993), 71–87. Verhoeven argues that "neutral ground" plays an active ideological role in Cooper's writings, enabling him to offer "alternative reality concepts" (77–78).

## 6. The Television and Cartoon Versions

1. 4-Color Comics no. 884, "Hawkeye and the Last of the Mohicans," (Dell Comics, USA, 1956). We do not discuss this comic in our chapter on comic book versions, as it entirely derivative from the TV series. The comic contains two stories, "False Witness" and "Powder Keg," both of which (like so many film and TV Westerns of that time) are built around the actions of "bad whites" who mislead and corrupt dangerous but childlike Indians. Our thanks to Tom Inge for obtaining us a copy of this comic.

2. *Hawkeye and the Last of the Mohicans: From the Television Series*, adapted by John Paton (London: Publicity Products, 1957). Featuring large publicity stills of John Hart (Hawkeye) and Lon Chaney, Jr. (Chingachgook), this book contains a story bearing no similarity to Cooper's original. The pocketbook comics with the same title were published as part of a weekly series *TV Picture Stories*. Six *Mohicans* stories drawn from the TV episodes were published between June 1958 and May 1959.

3. We have not seen this wallpaper, but at a day course one of us led on the *Mohicans* tradition, a participant told us of his clear memory of having his bedroom decorated with it as a child.

4. There is a puzzle which we cannot resolve. At the start of the first episode on the re-released (1992 ITC video) series, Hawkeye and Chingachgook are friends and companions. Yet the copy on the back cover of the video begins: "Hawkeye and Chingachgook were once deadly enemies but now the fighting has ceased between the 'Palefaces' and the 'Redskins,' they have become close companions and champions of peace and order." Just what was gained by introducing this irrelevant note? One explanation offered to us is that this is simply awkwardly written. We suspect not. Here is another example of such "awkwardness." The casing of a recent audio version introduces the story as "the classic story of a disillusioned man of moral courage who severs all connections with a society whose values he can no longer accept. Despite his chosen exile, Hawkeye (Natty Bumppo), the frontier scout, risks his life to escort two sisters through hostile Indian country. On the dangerous journey he enlists the aid of the Mohican Chingachgook. As these two men encounter deception, brutality and the death of loved ones, their friendship deepens" (Redback Audiobooks version, 1995, read by Lou Diamond Phillips).

This bending of the story neatly aligns it with the tradition of road movies, with alienated buddies finding themselves and each other in the course of a necessary adventure. It is not *false* to the original; it is rather a particular *interpretation* of its meaning. We suspect the same, though more clumsily, is true of the cover information of this video version.

5. There are echoes also of the 1936 film, first in the clips borrowed as trailers to the title; also, more curiously, in the imprisoning of Hawkeye and Chingachgook—an alteration that recurs in the 1992 version.

6. We know that it was also shown more than once on American television, although we have not managed to determine exactly when, and via which network.

7. David Maloney, interview, 3 April 1993.

8. In between *Doctor Who* and *Blake's Seven*, Maloney was asked to do another Cooper novel, *The Pathfinder*, as a serial. It was a disaster, regarded by critics as possibly the worst classic serial the BBC ever attempted.

9. On this whole BBC tradition, see in particular Robert Giddings, Keith

Selby and Chris Wensley, *Screening the Novel: The Theory and Practice of Literary Dramatisation* (London: Macmillan, 1990).

10. Leland went on to make a major career for himself as a director, of such films as *Wish You Were Here*.

11. Given the proximity of dates, it is worth directly comparing this emphasis with the 1977 TV movie's discourses on scalping. Though we cannot prove it, there are enough small links to suggest that perhaps the 1977 version was directly influenced by this BBC serial, which we know to have been shown in America more than once.

12. Philip Madoc, who played Magua with some distinction, has told us in a letter that in earlier episodes this authenticity went as far as requiring him to learn the language of the Hurons. When he spoke to other Hurons, he spoke that language and was subtitled. It is interesting to think, then, that this version would have been shown on American TV not long before the Schick Sunn film was made. This is especially interesting, given Maloney telling us that the BBC version *also* placed scalping as a European import.

13. "We did an enormous amount of research. What you have to understand was that there seemed to be money about in those days to get things right—none of this modern cost-cutting. The scenery was right, and we built a fort especially. We had a special advisor on the Indians who made sure we had the different tribes depicted correctly . . . and we also made sure the British uniforms were right. All the gear was made by the BBC. Characters were as accurate as possible. . . . I can even remember going so far as to make sure that the tunes Gamut played on his pipe were historically true— church music, verified by the Rev. Pockney of Twickenham." David Maloney, interview, 3 April 1993.

14. And of course films like *Little Big Man* have been argued to be symbolic renditions of the Vietnam War, with native Americans standing in for the Vietnamese.

15. This episode, produced in 1986, was shown on British TV in October 1987.

16. We shouldn't have been surprised. Sky TV is using movie successes for a number of series, so far notably *The Terminator* and *Highlander*.

17. This episode was broadcast in Britain on 10 April 1995.

18. The production notes for the series make much of what each actor brings to the role from past performances: Lee Horsley (a "true outdoors man") brings "talent, warmth and rugged good looks" to his part; Lynda Carter (of *Wonder Woman* fame) has specialized in "strong independent women"; and Rodney Grant (who came to fame for his part in *Dances with Wolves*) is notable for traveling America "in support of ethnic pride and environmental issues."

19. This episode was broadcast in Britain on 24 April 1995.

## 7. Comic Books: The Hidden Tradition

1. David Kunzle, *The Early Comic Strip, 1450–1825*, vol. 1 of *History of the Comic Strip*, (Berkeley: University of California Press, 1973); idem, *The Nineteenth Century*, vol. 2 of *History of the Comic Strip* (Berkeley: University of California Press, 1990).

2. Roger Sabin, *Adult Comics: An Introduction* (London: Routledge, 1993).

3. On the association of "literature" with "nationhood," see in particular Brian Doyle, *English and Englishness*.

4. See the unpublished thesis of Ian Gordon, *Revisioning Consumer Culture: Comic Strips, Comic Books, and Advertising in America, 1890–1945* (Ph.D. diss., University of Rochester, New York, 1992), and Steven Heller, "When the Comics Sold Soap: Advertising from the '30s and '40s," *Print*, November/December 1988, 164–71.

5. These aspects are well explored in Les Daniels, *Comix: A History of Comic Books in America* (Colorado Springs, Colo.: Wildwood House, 1973).

6. On Superman, see in particular Thomas Andrae, "From Menace to Messiah: The History and Historicity of Superman," in Donald Lazere, ed., *American Media and Mass Culture: Left Perspectives* (Berkeley: University of California Press, 1987), 124–38.

7. On this, see the excellent essay by Matthew McAllister, "Cultural Argument and Organizational Constraint in the Comic Book Industry," *Journal of Communication* 40.1 (1990): 55–71.

8. The best sources of information on Kanter's line of comics are Dan Malan, *The Complete Guide to Classics Collectibles: Volume 1* (St Louis, Mo.: Malan Classical Enterprises, 1991); and Michael Sawyer, "Albert Kanter and the Classics," *Journal of Popular Culture* 20 (1987): 1–26.

9. Fredric Wertham, *Seduction of the Innocent* (London: Museum Press, 1955). It is worth noting that Kitchen Sink Press is due to issue a new critical edition of *Seduction* in late 1995.

10. Meyer Kaplan, cited in Malan, *The Complete Guide to Classics Collectibles: Vol. 1*, 28.

11. Joseph Witek, *Comic Books as History: The Narrative Art of Jack Jackson, Art Spiegelman, and Harvey Pekar* (Jackson: University Press of Mississippi, 1989). This is a first in demonstrating with total conviction what can be shown by a close formal analysis of the conventions of a comic book retelling of an event.

12. The missing version is a mystery. It is the King Classics version from 1977. No one has been able to find a copy of it, which raises the serious question as to whether it was ever actually released.

13. There has been an increase in interest in the formal characteristics of

the comic medium in recent years. See, for instance, Will Eisner, *Comics and Sequential Art* (Tamarac, Fla.: Poorhouse Press, 1985); Scott McCloud, *Understanding Comics* (New York: Tundra, 1992); and Joseph Witek, *Comic Books as History*.

14. Comic books by and large adhere to a convention of capitalizing both narration and dialogue. This is not the place to debate the meaning of this in full. In outline, we would argue that such capitalization is not a sign of linguistic inadequacy. Rather, it marks the important capacity of comic book writing to be *heard* as much as it is seen. We have retained capitalization wherever it appears in the originals.

15. It is perhaps a measure of this version that in later episodes they got the name wrong in a different way.

16. Matthew McAllister, "Cultural Argument and Organizational Constraint in the Comic Book Industry," citing Ted White's "The Spawn of M. C. Gaines," from Dick Lupoff and Don Thompson, *All in Color for a Dime* (New York: Arlington House, 1970).

17. John Dower, *War without Mercy: Race and Power in the Pacific War* (London: Faber & Faber, 1986).

18. "Have you ever watched a well-trained monkey at a zoo? Have you seen how carefully he imitates his trainer? The monkey goes through so many human movements so well that actually seems to be human. But under his fur, he's still a savage little beast. Now, consider the imitative little Japanese who for seventy-five years has built himself up into something so closely resembling a human being that he actually believes he is just that." This example, taken from a 1942 US radio broadcast ("A Lesson in Japanese"), is cited in J. Fred MacDonald, *Television and the Red Menace: The Video Road to Vietnam* (New York: Praeger, 1985), 8.

19. For a useful general history of Marvel Comics, see Les Daniels, *Marvel: Five Fabulous Decades of the World's Greatest Comics* (London: Virgin Books, 1991). Unfortunately, Daniels does not deal directly with the Classics series, and we have been unable to get further details on this line.

20. It might be replied that there is warrant for this editorial approach in the original book, since Cooper himself talks of the tale surviving among the Delawares. This is true, but it misses the point. With so much else deleted, the tale surviving as an *Indian* tale takes on a redoubled significance.

21. See, for instance, Dorothy Nelkin, *The Creation Controversy: Science or Scripture in the School* (New York: Norton, 1982).

22. See, for instance, Manning Marable, *Race, Reform, and Rebellion: The Second Reconstruction of Black America, 1945–1982*, Jackson: University Press of Mississippi, 1991).

23. On Jackson generally, see the excellent chapter in Joseph Witek's *Comic Books as History*.

## 8. In the Matter of the Mohicans

1. Paul Coates, *Film at the Intersection of High and Mass Culture* (Cambridge: Cambridge University Press, 1994), 133.

2. For a good example, see Joseph Witek's discussion of the significance of the "first shot at Fort Sumter" in retellings of the American Civil War, in his *Comic Books as History* (see chapter 1).

3. Robert Spiller, *James Fenimore Cooper: Critic of Our Times* (New York: Minton Balch, 1931), quoted at 93–94.

4. See Fleming and Luskey, *The Shadow Catchers*, for a wonderful and evocative collection of such photographs. See also Ralph W. Andrews, *Curtis' Western Indians* (New York: Bonanza Books, 1962). This book, written by an uncritical enthusiast, recounts Curtis's life as a photographer of native Americans. Without meaning to, it reveals the extent to which Curtis fashioned his photographs according to his overriding belief that the "Indians" were a "vanishing race." Only photography could store up a record, like scientific specimens, before they went. Among those who were enthusiastic about Curtis's work were Theodore Roosevelt and the railway magnate E. H. Harriman, whose widow would fund the Eugenics Record Office a few years later. The projects—the photographic record and a new "science of races"—were closely related.

5. On Wyeth's life and work, see Kate F. Jennings, *N. C. Wyeth* (Lincoln, Nebr.: Bison Books, 1992).

6. An understanding of this phenomenon came to us very late. It seems to us to make an important difference to materials we learned from when we were researching and first thinking about *Mohicans*. For example, one essay from which we derived much precisely stops at noticing differences. See Lauren R. Tucker and Hemant Shah, "Race and the Transformation of Culture: The Making of the Television Miniseries *Roots*," *Critical Studies in Mass Communication* 9 (1992): 325–66. This fine essay explores the transformation of Alex Haley's book *Roots* to television, during which much of the politics of the original are shown to have been softened in order to make the work acceptable to white audiences. It seems to us that the argument could nonetheless be expanded by considering the ways in which this adaptation to white audiences (the moment of adaptation) is *authorized* and made more effective by being presented as "the novel of Alex Haley" (the moment of continuity).

7. One of the earliest films shot was a single-reeler by Thomas Edison designed to show off Glacier Point. See Peter J. Schmitt, *Back to Nature: The Arcadian Myth in Urban America* (New York: Oxford University Press, 1969) for information on this period.

8. We are walking the edge here of a large set of debates in cultural and literary theory about "intertextuality." Work around this subject ranges

from close textual analyses of the ways one novel, poem, film, or whatever makes explicit and implicit references to other texts, to wide-ranging theorizing of how meaning is generated by and between texts. There is not the space here to situate what we are saying in relation to these multifarious positions.

9. Jay Leyda, *Films Beget Films: Compilation Films from Propaganda to Drama* (London: George Allen & Unwin, 1964).

10. This quotation is cited in Alexander Saxton, *The Rise and Fall of the White Republic: Class Politics and Mass Culture in Nineteenth-Century America* (London: Verso, 1990), 153.

11. George Decker and Larry Johnston, introduction to J. F. Cooper, *The American Democrat* (Harmondsworth, England: Penguin, 1969), 36.

12. Cooper, *The American Democrat*, 11.

13. One example: introducing one of his characters, an "intelligent mechanic," who will make a speech embodying Cooper's views, the narrator informs us: "The speaker commenced with great moderation, both of manner and tone, and, indeed, he preserved them throughout. His utterance, accent and language, of course, were all tinctured by his habits and associations; but his good sense and his good principles were equally gifts from above. More of the 'true image of his Maker' was to be found in that one individual than existed in fifty common men." *The Redskins, Or, Indian and Injun* (1846; reprint, New York: Cooperative Publication Society, n.d.), 280.

14. Cooper, *The Redskins*, 30.

15. Cited in Stephen Railton, *Fenimore Cooper*, 44.

16. In the argument we are making, the precise date of publication really does not matter. The most pessimistic of the five novels, *The Prairie*, in which Hawkeye finally dies alone, was published in 1827. The most optimistic, *The Deerslayer*, was written at the peak of Cooper's disenchantment with "democracy" in 1841. It is as if the figure of Hawkeye, living on another plane, can continue to operate above the petty concerns of living politics—and that, of course, is exactly how myths must work.

17. See Frazier's remarkable book, *The Mohicans of Stockbridge* (Lincoln: The University of Nebraska Press, 1992).

18. For an argument closely paralleling our own but using Cooper's *Pioneers* as its main source, see Susan Scheckel, "In the Land of his Fathers: Cooper, Land Rights, and the Legitimation of American National Identity," in V. M. Verhoeven, ed., *James Fenimore Cooper: New Historical and Literary Contexts*, 125–50.

19. We have taken most of our information on the dime novels from Daryl Jones's study, *The Dime Novel Western* (Bowling Green, Ohio: Popular Press, 1978). These figures appear on p. 8. As will become clear, perhaps,

we do not fully accept Jones's conceptualization of their cultural significance.

20. On the use of children in the debate about the conditions of the working class, see Mark I. West, *Children, Culture, and Controversy* (Hamden, Conn.: Archon Books, 1988). We have argued elsewhere how frequently concerns about radical and working-class subversion are expressed as fears about "childhood"—a paternalism that deserves wider recognition and closer study than it has had so far.

21. Richard Slotkin, "Theodore Roosevelt's Frontier Hypothesis," in Bob Kroes, ed., *The American West as Seen by Europeans and Americans* (Amsterdam: Free University Press, 1989), 44–71. This brilliant essay unfortunately came to our attention late.

22. Roosevelt's private home was known as "Sagamore Hill."

23. David Brower, ed., *Wilderness: America's Living Heritage* (San Francisco: Sierra Club, 1961), iii.

24. Brower's book is particularly redolent with examples of this attitude. The book is mainly the proceedings of the 1961 Conference of the Sierra Club. In a discussion after all the main presentations, when the panel turns to issues of practical politics, an interesting distinction is drawn: between those who want (need?) wilderness and those who don't. This distinction is acknowledged to the point that they begin to talk of "intercept zones" and the engineering of distance. Then, in the words of Sen. Fred Farr: "If we plan for an adequate number of state parks, if we plan for our recreation areas so people will not have to penetrate the wilderness, we will be able to protect it" (133).

25. Saxton, *The Rise and Fall of the White Republic*. See also David Roediger, *The Wages of Whiteness: Race and the Making of the American Working Class* (London: Verso, 1991).

26. Roediger, *The Wages of Whiteness*, 53.

# BIBLIOGRAPHY

Allen, Robert C. *Vaudeville and Film: A Study in Media Interaction.* Ph.D. diss., University of Iowa, 1977.

Andrae, Thomas. "From Menace to Messiah: The History and Historicity of Superman." In Donald Lazere, ed., *American Media and Mass Culture: Left Perspectives,* 124–38. Berkeley: University of California Press, 1987.

Andrews, Ralph W. *Curtis' Western Indians.* New York: Bonanza Books, 1962.

Aries, Philippe. *Centuries of Childhood.* Harmondsworth, England: Penguin, 1960.

Barker, Martin. *A Haunt of Fears: The Strange History of the British Horror Comics Campaign.* Jackson: University Press of Mississippi, 1993.

———. *Comics: Ideology, Power and the Critics.* Manchester, England: Manchester University Press, 1989.

Barnett, Louisa K. *The Ignoble Savage: American Literary Racism, 1790–1890.* Westport, Conn.: Greenwood Press, 1975.

Beard, James. "Cooper and His Artistic Contemporaries." *New York History* 35 (1954): 480–95.

Berger, John. *Another Way of Telling.* London: Writers & Readers, 1982.

Billington, Ray Allen, ed. *Frontier and Section: Selected Essays of Frederick Jackson Turner.* Englewood, N.J.: Prentice-Hall, 1961.

Blishen, Edward. "An Insolent Thing to Do." *School Bookshop News* 8 (1987).

Blum, Jeffrey. *Pseudoscience and Mental Ability.* New York: Monthly Review Press, 1978.

Bookeman, Christopher. *American Culture and Society Since the 1930s.* New York: Schocken, 1984.

Bordwell, David, Janet Staiger, and Kristin Thompson. *The Classical Holly-*

wood Cinema: Film Style and Mode of Production to 1960. London: Routledge, 1985.

Brower, David, ed. *Wilderness: America's Living Heritage*. San Francisco: Sierra Club, 1961.

Brown, Dee. *Bury My Heart at Wounded Knee: An Indian History of the American West*. New York: Holt, Rinehart & Winston, 1970.

Brown, Karl. *Adventures with D. W. Griffith*. London: Secker & Warburg, 1973.

Brownlow, Kevin. *The Parade's Gone By*. New York: Knopf, 1968.

Buscombe, Edward, ed. *The BFI Companion to the Western*. London: BFI Publishing, 1986.

Cawelti, John. *The Six-Gun Mystique*. Bowling Green, Ohio: Popular Press, 1970.

Chase, Allan. *The Legacy of Malthus: The Social Costs of the New Scientific Racism*. New York: Knopf, 1977.

Chorover, Stephan. *From Genesis to Genocide: The Meaning of Human Nature and the Power of Behavior Control*. Boston: MIT Press, 1989.

Coates, Paul. *Film at the Intersection of High and Low Culture*. Cambridge: Cambridge University Press, 1994.

Cooper, James Fenimore. *The American Democrat*. Edited and introduced by George Decker and Larry Johnston. Harmondsworth, England: Penguin, 1969.

──────. *The Redskins, Or, Indian and Injun*. 1846. Reprint. New York: Cooperative Publication Society, n.d.

Coveney, Peter. *The Image of Childhood: A Study of the Theme in English Literature*. Harmondsworth, England: Penguin, 1967.

Daniels, Les. *Comix: A History of Comic Books in America*. Colorado Springs, Colo.: Wildwood House, 1973.

──────. *Marvel: Five Fabulous Decades of the World's Greatest Comics*. London: Virgin Books, 1991.

Darton, F. J. Harvey. *Children's Books in England*, Cambridge: Cambridge University Press, 1970.

Decker, George. *James Fenimore Cooper: The American Scott*. New York: Barnes & Noble, 1967.

Dorfman, Ariel. "The Infantilisation of the Adult Reader." In *The Empire's Old Clothes*. London: Pluto Press, 1983.

Dower, John. *War without Mercy: Race and Power in the Pacific War*. London: Faber & Faber, 1986.

Doyle, Brian. *English and Englishness*. London: Routledge, 1989.

Drotner, Kirsten. *English Children and Their Magazines, 1751–1945*. New Haven, Conn.: Yale University Press, 1988.

Dunne, Philip. *Take Two: A Life in Movies and Politics*. New York: McGraw-Hill, 1980.

Eisner, Will. *Comics and Sequential Art.* Tamarac, Fla.: Poorhouse Press, 1985.

Elley, Derek. *The Epic Film: Myth and History.* London: Routledge, 1984.

Emerson, Ralph Waldo. *Gleanings in Europe.* Philadelphia, 1838.

Fleming, Paula Richardson, and Judith Lynn Luskey. *The Shadow Catchers: Images of the American Indian.* London: Lawrence King Publishing, 1993.

Fossum, R. H., and J. K. Roth. *The American Dream.* London: British Association for American Studies, 1991.

Francis, Daniel. *The Imaginary Indian.* Vancouver, B.C.: Arsenal Pulp Press, 1992.

Frazier, Patrick. *The Mohicans of Stockbridge.* Lincoln: University of Nebraska Press, 1992.

Garnham, Nicholas. *Capitalism and Communication: Global Culture and the Economy of Information.* London: Sage, 1992.

Giddings, Robert, Keith Selby, and Chris Wensley. *Screening the Novel: The Theory and Practice of Literary Dramatisation.* London: Macmillan, 1990.

Gifford, Denis. *Books and Plays into Film, 1896–1915.* Jefferson, N.C.: McFarland, 1991.

Gilbert, James. *A Cycle of Outrage.* New York: Oxford University Press, 1984.

Gordon, Ian. *Revisioning Consumer Culture: Comic Strips, Comic Books, and Advertising in America, 1890–1945.* Ph.D. diss., University of Rochester (New York), 1992.

Green, Martin. *Dreams of Adventure, Deeds of Empire.* London: Routledge, 1980.

Hebdige, Dick. *Hiding in the Light.* London: Comedia, 1988.

Heller, Steven. "When the Comics Sold Soap: Advertising from the '30s and '40s." *Print,* November/December 1988, 164–71.

Hewins, Caroline. "The History of Children's Books." 1888. Reprinted in Virginia Haviland, ed., *Children and Literature: Views and Reviews.* Glenview, Ill.: Scott, Foresman, 1973.

Hill, Matthew Davenport. "Practical Suggestions to the Founders of Reformatory Schools." In J. C. Symons, ed., *On the Reformation of Young Offenders.* London: Routledge, 1855.

Hitt, Jim. *The American West from Fiction (1823–1976) into Film (1909–1986).* Jefferson, N.C.: McFarland, 1990.

Hochman, Stanley, ed. *From Quasimodo to Scarlett O'Hara: A National Board of Review Anthology, 1920–1940.* New York: Frederick Ungar, 1982.

Jennings, Kate F. *N. C. Wyeth.* Lincoln, Nebr.: Bison Books, 1992.

Jones, Daryl. *The Dime Novel Western.* Bowling Green, Ohio: Popular Press, 1978.

Kamin, Leon. *The Science and Politics of IQ*. Potomac, Md.: Lawrence Erlbaum, 1974.

Kermode, Frank. *The Classic*. London: Faber & Faber, 1975.

Kliebard, Herbert M. *The Struggle For the American Curriculum, 1893–1958*. London: Routledge, 1986.

Knibbs, Sarah. "Classics UK—Enter the B Troop." *The Bookseller* (London), 17 June 1994.

Koppes, Clayton R., and Gregory D. Black. *Hollywood Goes to War: How Politics, Profit and Propaganda Shaped World War II Movies*. London: I. B. Tauris, 1987.

Kunzle, David. *The Early Comic Strip, 1450–1825*. Vol. 1 of *History of the Comic Strip*. Berkeley: University of California Press, 1973.

————. *The Nineteenth Century*. Vol. 2 of *History of the Comic Strip*. Berkeley: University of California Press, 1990.

Lee, Charles. *The Hidden Public: The Story of the Book-of-the-Month Club*. New York: Doubleday, 1958.

Leverenz, Daniel. "The Last Real Man in America: From Natty Bumppo to Batman." *American Literary History* 3.4 (1991): 753–81.

Leyda, Jay. *Films Beget Films: Compilation Films from Propaganda to Drama*. London: George Allen & Unwin, 1964.

London, Jack. *The Call of the Wild*. 1903. Reprint. Harmondsworth, England: Penguin 1981.

McAllister, Matthew. "Cultural Argument and Organizational Constraint in the Comic Book Industry." *Journal of Communication* 40.1 (1990): 55–71.

McCloud, Scott. *Understanding Comics*. New York: Tundra, 1992.

MacDonald, J. Fred. *Television and the Red Menace: The Video Road to Vietnam*. New York: Praeger, 1985.

Malan, Dan. *The Complete Guide to Classics Collectibles: Volume 1*. St. Louis, Mo.: Malan Classical Enterprises, 1991.

Marable, Manning. *Race, Reform and Rebellion: The Second Reconstruction of Black America, 1945–82*. Jackson: University Press of Mississippi, 1991.

Mast, Gerald, ed. *The Movies in Our Midst*. Chicago: University of Chicago Press, 1982.

Mathieson, Margaret. *Preachers of Culture: A Study of English and Its Teachers*. London: George Allen & Unwin, 1975.

Meigs, Cornelia, Anne Thaxter Eaton, Elizabeth Nesbitt, and Ruth Hill Vigners. *A Critical History of Children's Literature*. London: Macmillan, 1969.

Merlock, Raymond J. *From Flintlock to Forty-Five: James Fenimore Cooper and the Popular Western Tradition in Fiction and Film*. Ph.D. diss., Ohio University, 1981.

Morgan, H. Wayne. *Unity and Culture: The United States, 1877–1900.* London: Allen Lane, 1971.

Mott, Frank Luther. *Golden Multitudes: The Story of Best-Sellers in the United States.* New York: R. R. Bowker, 1947.

Nabokov, Peter, ed. *Native American Testimony: A Chronicle of Indian-White Relations from Prophecy to the Present, 1492–1992.* New York: Penguin, 1991.

Nash, Roderick. *Wilderness and the American Mind.* New Haven, Conn.: Yale University Press, 1973.

Nelkin, Dorothy. *The Creation Controversy: Science or Literature in the School.* New York: Norton, 1982.

Newbolt, Henry. *The Book of the Happy Warrior.* London: Longmans, Green, 1925.

Norris, Frank. *McTeague: A Story of San Francisco.* 1899. Reprint. Harmondsworth, England: Penguin, 1985.

Nowlan, Robert A., and Gwendolyn Wright Nowlan. *Cinema Sequels and Remakes, 1903–87.* Jefferson, N.C.: McFarland, 1989.

Pearce, Roy Harvey. *The Savages of America: A Study of the Indian and the Idea of Civilization.* Baltimore: Johns Hopkins University Press, 1965.

Pearson, Geoffrey. *Hooligan: A History of Respectable Fears.* London: Macmillan, 1983.

————. "Falling Standards: A Short Sharp Lesson in Moral Decline." In Martin Barker, ed., *The Video Nasties: Freedom and Censorship in the Arts,* 88–103. London: Pluto Press, 1984.

Peary, Gerald, and Roger Shatzkin, eds. *The Classic American Novel and the Movies.* New York: Frederick Ungar, 1977.

Peck, Daniel, ed. *New Essays on the Last of the Mohicans.* Cambridge: Cambridge University Press, 1992.

Proulx, E. Annie. *The Shipping News.* London: Fourth Estate, 1993.

Radway, Janice. "Mail Order Culture and Its Critics: The Book-of-the-Month Club, Commodification and Consumption, and the Problem of Cultural Authority." In Lawrence Grossberg, ed., *Cultural Studies,* 512–27. London: Routledge, 1992.

Railton, Stephen. *Fenimore Cooper: A Study of His Life and Imagination.* Princeton, N.J.: Princeton University Press, 1978.

Reising, Russell. *The Unusable Past: Theory and the Study of American Literature.* London: Methuen, 1986.

Roddick, Nick. *A New Deal in Entertainment.* London: BFI Publishing, 1992.

Roediger, David. *The Wages of Whiteness: Race and the Making of the American Working Class.* London: Verso, 1991.

Romero, Lora. "Vanishing Americans: Gender, Empire and the New Historicism." *American Literature* 63.3 (1991): 385–404.

Rousseau, Jean-Jacques. *Emile*. 1762. Reprint. New York: Everyman's Library, 1974.

Rubin, Joan Shelley. "Self, Culture, and Self-Culture in Modern America." *Journal of American History* 71 (1985): 782–806.

Sabin, Roger. *Adult Comics: An Introduction*. London: Routledge, 1993.

Samuel, Raphael, ed. *Patriotism: The Making and Unmaking of British National Identity*, Vols. 1–3. London: Routledge, 1989.

Sawyer, Michael. "Albert Kanter and the Classics." *Journal of Popular Culture* 20 (1987): 1–26.

Saxton, Alexander. *The Rise and Fall of the White Republic: Class Politics and Mass Culture in the Nineteenth Century*. London: Verso, 1990.

Schickel, Richard. *D. W. Griffith and the Birth of Film*. New York: Pavilion Books, 1984.

Schmitt, Peter J. *Back to Nature: The Arcadian Myth in Urban America*. New York: Oxford University Press, 1969.

Schreiner, Samuel A. *The Condensed World of the Reader's Digest*. New York: Stein & Day, 1977.

Shayer, David. *The Teaching of English in Schools, 1900–1970*. London: Routledge, 1972.

Shindler, Colin. *Hollywood Goes to War: Films and American Society, 1939–52*. London: Routledge, 1979.

Simmon, Scott. *The Films of D. W. Griffith*. Cambridge: Cambridge University Press, 1993.

Sinclair, Upton. *The Jungle*. 1909. Reprint. Harmondsworth, England: Penguin, 1974.

Slotkin, Richard. "Theodore Roosevelt's Frontier Hypothesis." In Bob Kroes, ed., *The American West as Seen by Europeans and Americans*, 44–71. Amsterdam: Free University Press, 1989.

Spiller, Robert. *James Fenimore Cooper: Critic of Our Times*. New York: Minton, Balch, 1931.

Street, Brian. *The Savage in Literature: Representations of "Primitive" Society in English Fiction, 1825–1920*. London: Routledge, 1975.

Strinati, Dominic. "The Taste of America: Americanisation and Popular Culture in Britain." In Dominic Strinati and Stephen Wagg, eds., *Come on Down? Popular Media Culture in Post War Britain*. London: Routledge, 1992.

Sturm, John E., and John A. Palmer. *Democratic Legacy in Transition: Perspectives on American Education*, New York: Van Nostrand 1971.

Truettner, William H. *The West as America: Reinterpreting Images of the Frontier, 1820–1920*. Washington, D.C.: Smithsonian Institution Press, 1991.

Tucker, Lauren R., and Hemant Shah. "Race and the Transformation of

Culture: The Making of the Television Miniseries *Roots.*" *Critical Studies in Mass Communication* 9 (1992): 325–66.

Tyack, David. *The One Best System: A History of American Urban Education.* Cambridge: Harvard University Press, 1974.

Uricchio, William, and Roberta Pearson. *Reframing Culture: The Case of the Vitagraph Quality Films.* Princeton, N.J.: Princeton University Press, 1993.

Vanderbilt, Kermit. *American Literature and the Academy: The Roots, Growth and Maturity of a Profession.* Philadelphia: University of Pennsylvania Press, 1986.

Verhoeven, V. M., ed. *James Fenimore Cooper: New Literary and Historical Contexts:* Atlanta: Rodopi, 1993.

Wagenknecht, Edward. *The Movies in the Age of Innocence.* Norman: University of Oklahoma Press, 1962.

Wagner, Geoffrey. *The Novel and the Cinema.* Cranbury, N.J.: Fairleigh Dickinson University Press, 1975.

Washburn, W. *The Indian and the White Man.* New York: Doubleday, 1964.

Webster, Duncan. *Looka Yonder: The Imaginary America of Popular Culture.* London: Routledge, 1988.

West, Mark I. *Children, Culture and Controversy.* Hamden, Conn.: Archon Books, 1988.

Wiebe, Robert H. *Businessmen and Reform: A Study of the Progressive Movement.* Chicago: Quadrangle Books, 1962.

Wister, Owen. *The Virginian.* 1902. Reprint. London: Macmillan, 1966.

Witek, Joseph. *Comic Books as History: The Narrative Art of Jack Jackson, Art Spiegelman and Harvey Pekar.* Jackson: University Press of Mississippi, 1989.

Wright, Roland. *Stolen Continents: The Indian Story.* London: John Murray, 1992.

Zipes, Jack. *The Trials and Tribulations of Little Red Riding Hood.* London: Heinemann, 1983.

# INDEX

*Note:* page numbers in italics indicate an illustration.